STREET-LEVEL BUREAUCRACY IN WEAK STATE INSTITUTIONS

Edited by
Rik Peeters, Gabriela Lotta, and
Fernando Nieto-Morales

First published in Great Britain in 2025 by

Policy Press, an imprint of
Bristol University Press
University of Bristol
1-9 Old Park Hill
Bristol
BS2 8BB
UK
t: +44 (0)117 374 6645
e: bup-info@bristol.ac.uk

Details of international sales and distribution partners are available at
policy.bristoluniversitypress.co.uk

© Bristol University Press 2025

British Library Cataloguing in Publication Data
A catalogue record for this book is available from the British Library

ISBN 978-1-4473-6874-8 hardcover
ISBN 978-1-4473-6875-5 paperback
ISBN 978-1-4473-6876-2 ePub
ISBN 978-1-4473-6877-9 ePdf

The right of Rik Peeters, Gabriela Lotta, and Fernando Nieto- Morales to be identified as editors of this work has been asserted by them in accordance with the Copyright, Designs and Patents Act 1988.

All rights reserved: no part of this publication may be reproduced, stored in a retrieval system, or transmitted in any form or by any means, electronic, mechanical, photocopying, recording, or otherwise without the prior permission of Bristol University Press.

Every reasonable effort has been made to obtain permission to reproduce copyrighted material. If, however, anyone knows of an oversight, please contact the publisher.

The statements and opinions contained within this publication are solely those of the editors and contributors and not of the University of Bristol or Bristol University Press. The University of Bristol and Bristol University Press disclaim responsibility for any injury to persons or property resulting from any material published in this publication.

Bristol University Press and Policy Press work to counter discrimination on grounds of gender, race, disability, age and sexuality.

Cover design: Robin Hawes
Front cover image: iStock/ AsianDream

Contents

List of figures and tables		v
Notes on contributors		vi
1	Street-level bureaucracy in weak state institutions: an introduction *Gabriela Lotta, Fernando Nieto-Morales, and Rik Peeters*	1
PART I	**Coping with institutional weakness**	
2	Weak but not broken: resilience by repair in the times of COVID-19 *Ayesha Masood*	25
3	Paternalist street-level bureaucrats and virtuous recipients: the consequences of institutional weakness in a pensions programme in Uganda *Ronan Jacquin*	43
4	Street-level bureaucrats in environments of systemic corruption: sources of influence *Oliver Meza, Elizabeth Pérez-Chiqués, and Anat Gofen*	61
PART II	**Exploring institutional contexts**	
5	Weak institutions and dangerous working conditions: coping by the wiremen of public electricity distribution utility in India *Sneha Swami and Subodh Wagle*	79
6	Underserving the disadvantaged: institutional failures and their consequences for frontline workers and vulnerable publics *Roberto Pires, Maria Paula Santos, Beatriz Brandão, and Luiza Rosa*	104
7	Frontline implementation conditions of the Families programme: labour precarity and territorial gaps as aspects of weak state institutions in Chile *Taly Reininger, Gianinna Muñoz Arce, Cristóbal Villalobos, and Mitzi Duboy Luengo*	120
8	Regime transitions and institutional weakness: the case of police reform in Poland in the early 1990s *Barbara Maria Piotrowska, Izabela Szkurłat, and Magdalena Szydłowska*	137
PART III	**Bureaucratic encounters**	
9	Coping with violence and precarious working conditions: law enforcement through the eyes of municipal police officers in Morelia, Mexico *Paulina Yunuén Guzmán Linares and Rik Peeters*	159

10	'You can tell they are just villagers when you look at them': a phenomenological study of street-level bureaucrats' differential treatment of clients in a Ghanaian rural hospital *Abdul-Rahim Mohammed*	178
11	When frontline work functions as an enclave: insights from Turkey *Elise Massicard*	195
12	Citizen agency in street-level interactions: navigating uncertainty and unpredictability *Sergio A. Campos*	213
13	Frontline work in weak institutions: implementing inequities *Fernando Nieto-Morales, Gabriela Lotta, and Rik Peeters*	230

Index   245

List of figures and tables

Figures
5.1	Vines and vegetation thickets surrounding a distribution transformer during monsoon	85
5.2	Rubber gloves used by wiremen	86
5.3	Ladder purchased by staff of a section office to climb on a smooth pole	87
5.4	Swing-like contraption used by wiremen	88
8.1	Evaluation of the police in the early 1990s (annual average)	145
8.2	Survey evaluation of the police on a longer time scale	145
8.3	Positive evaluation of the police among those who were and were not members of Solidarność	146
9.1	Precarious working conditions perceived by police officers (percentage of participants)	167

Tables
2.1	Characteristics of the participant street-level bureaucrats	32
2.2	Strategies for public service gap repairing	33
4.1	Sources of influence	65
6.1	Comparisons within and across cities	110
9.1	Initial codes for violent environment and institutional deficiencies	164
9.2	Definitive codes for violent environment and institutional deficiencies	164
9.3	Initial codes for coping mechanisms	164
9.4	Definitive codes for coping mechanisms	165

Notes on contributors

Beatriz Brandão holds a PhD in Social Sciences from PUC-RIO and a Master's in Social Sciences from the State University of Rio de Janeiro (UERJ). She was a postdoc in Sociology at the University of São Paulo (USP). She is a faculty member of the Professional Master's Degree in Science Teaching (PPGEC) at Unigranrio. She was a research fellow at the Institute for Applied Economic Research (IPEA) in the project on care methodologies for problematic drug users. Her research centres on themes related to institutional trajectories, with emphasis on therapeutic communities and mental health services for drug users.

Sergio A. Campos is Visiting Professor of public administration at the Center for Research and Teaching in Economics (CIDE) in Aguascalientes, Mexico. His main research interests are street-level bureaucracy, citizen–state interactions, and citizen agency during bureaucratic encounters. In recent publications, he has analysed citizens' capacity to ease administrative burdens, street-level bureaucracy in weak state institutions, and street-level bureaucracy during the COVID-19 pandemic.

Mitzi Duboy Luengo holds a PhD in Social Work. Her research interests are social intervention, knowledge production, and social work. She is professor at the Alberto Hurtado University, where she teaches courses in the area of social intervention. Additionally, she trains state professionals on issues related to Violence Against Women from a gender perspective. Her recent publications include 'Putting (us) in common: Knowledge production and narratives in/from social work' (*Critical Proposals in Social Work*) and 'Decolonial feminism and practices of resistance to sustain life: Experiences of women social workers implementing mental health programmes in Chile' (*Affilia*).

Anat Gofen is Associate Professor at the Federmann School of Public Policy and Governance, Hebrew University of Jerusalem. Her research focuses on the role of outliers in the evolution, formation, and implications of public policy, with emphasis on the interrelationships between citizens and government during implementation. Her research demonstrates mechanisms, influences, and contributions of outliers to public life in various policy domains, including education, health, and welfare, through concepts such as family capital (*FAMREL*), entrepreneurial exit (*PADM*, *PMR*), street-level divergence (*JPART*), street-level management (*JPART*), negotiated compliance (*PADM*), and policy dissonance (*POLSC*). Gofen received her BSc in Computer Science and PhD in Public Policy from Hebrew University.

She serves as co-editor of *JCPA* and as a co-chair of the Public Policy study group of the European Group of Public Administration.

Paulina Yunuén Guzmán Linares was born in Morelia, Michoacán (Mexico). She holds a Master's degree in Administration and Public Policy from CIDE and a bachelor's degree in Humanities and Social Sciences from the Monterrey Institute of Technology and Higher Education (ITESM). She has done complementary studies in Political Science, citizen security, violence prevention, governance, geopolitics, and organisational capacity development. She currently works as a consultant and researcher on security and development issues.

Ronan Jacquin is a PhD candidate at the Centre for International Studies (CERI) at Sciences Po (Paris). He is interested in public policies and policy feedback, domination and political intermediation, and the government of populations. His dissertation explores the evolution of social policies and the government of poverty in Africa, through the study of cash transfer programmes in Uganda and Namibia.

Gabriela Lotta is Associate Professor of Public Administration at Fundação Getulio Vargas (FGV) in São Paulo (Brazil). She was a Visiting Professor at the University of Oxford in 2021. She coordinates the Bureaucracy Studies Center (NEB). She is a Professor at the National School of Public Administration, ENAP, a researcher at the Center for Metropolitan Studies (CEM), and a researcher in Brazil.Lab from Princeton University. She was a Visiting Professor at the University of Aalborg (Denmark) in 2019. Lotta received her BSc in Public Administration and PhD in Political Science at the University of São Paulo.

Ayesha Masood is Assistant Professor in the Suleman Dawood School of Business in Lahore University of Management Sciences (Pakistan). She is interested in innovation and creativity at the frontline, especially in health services. One of her main research agenda is administrative burden and the way people respond to inequity in state services. She has been working and collaborating with frontline workers and policy makers in the healthcare sector in Punjab, Pakistan, to understand the challenges of healthcare delivery in developing countries.

Elise Massicard is a permanent Senior Research Fellow at the French National Center for Scientific Research/Centre d'Etudes Internationales, Paris. From 2010 to 2014, she was a Research Fellow at the French Institute of Anatolian Studies in Istanbul, where she acted as the director of the Observatoire de la Politique Turque. She was a visiting Fellow at the

University of California at Berkeley (2009) and at Northwestern University (2019). Her research focuses on the political sociology of contemporary Turkey, especially state-society relations, policy studies, and informal politics. She has authored *Street-level Governing: Negotiating the State in Urban Turkey* (Stanford University Press, 2022). She has co-edited with Marc Aymes and Benjamin Gourisse, *Order and Compromise: Government Practices in Turkey from the Late Ottoman Empire to the Early 21st Century* (Brill, 2015). She has published extensively in academic journals.

Oliver Meza is a Research Professor at CIDE´s Division of Public Administration. He is mostly interested in local government's policy agendas, local governance, and corruption. Recently he has developed work around public officials' non-compliance (*IPMJ*), citizen dissatisfaction (*PADM*), corruption consolidation (*PADM*), institutional logics and implementation (*Governance*), and frontline workers policy tactics (*IJPA*). In 2020, he received an award for his research by the Mexican Science Academy.

Abdul-Rahim Mohammed is a senior lecturer in the Department of Development Management and Policy Studies, University for Development Studies (Ghana). Broadly, his research interests include exploring the notion of children's agency in the Global South, child labour, social policies in the Global South, policy implementation gaps, and qualitative inquiries into food insecurity. Abdul's recent research focuses on qualitatively exploring the policy implementation gaps of Ghana's School Feeding Programme.

Gianinna Muñoz Arce holds a PhD in Social Work from Bristol University (UK). She is Associate Professor at the Department of Social Work, University of Chile. Her research interests are critical theory, social intervention, and social work. She teaches Social Work Theoretical Approaches in several PhD programmes in Social Work (La Plata University, Argentina, and Alberto Hurtado University, Chile). Her recent publications include 'Decolonising community social work: Contributions of frontline professional resistances from a Mapuche perspective' (*Critical and Radical Social Work*) and 'Decolonial feminism and practices of resistance to sustain life: Experiences of women social workers implementing mental health programmes in Chile' (*Affilia*).

Fernando Nieto-Morales is Associate Professor of Public Administration at El Colegio de México in Mexico City. His main research interests include petty corruption, organisational change in the government, and bureaucratic pathologies. He is Chairman of the scientific board of the Interdisciplinary Program of Data Science of El Colegio de México and member of the National Institute of Public Administration of Mexico. He holds a PhD from the University of Groningen, the Netherlands.

Rik Peeters is Associate Professor of Public Administration at CIDE in Mexico City. His main research interests are street-level bureaucracy, citizen–state interactions, and digital government. In recent publications, he has analysed street-level interactions in social programmes, the distributive effects of administrative burdens, and the digitalisation of citizen–state interactions.

Elizabeth Pérez-Chiqués is a Research Professor at CIDE´s Division of Public Administration and is a Fellow at the Rockefeller Institute of Government in New York. Her research agenda focuses on government corruption, public personnel management, and policy implementation. Recently, she has developed work on corruption consolidation, local corruption networks, informal personnel practices, and street-level work in environments of systemic corruption.

Barbara Maria Piotrowska is a Leverhulme Early Career Fellow at the Department of Political Economy at King's College London. Her research concentrates on the motivation of civil servants and street-level bureaucrats (SLBs) under different political regimes. Barbara's new project 'Bureaucracy in the transition to democracy: Testing a theoretical assumption' assesses how ideology and opportunism shape the motivation of SLBs during regime transitions.

Roberto Pires is a Researcher at the Institute for Applied Economic Research (IPEA) in Brazil. He is also Professor in the Master and Doctoral Programs offered at the National School of Public Administration (ENAP) and at IPEA. His main research interests are policy implementation, state capacity, and the interfaces of street-level bureaucracy and social inequalities (reproduction and mitigation). In recent publications, he discusses the need to recontextualise street-level bureaucracy theory to the developing world, how social inequality has been treated in street-level bureaucracy research, and proposes mechanisms for understanding the reproduction of social inequalities in policy implementation.

Taly Reininger earned her PhD in Social Work and Social Welfare from Fordham University in New York. She is currently an Assistant Professor at the Department of Social Work, University of Chile. Her research interests include social policy, programme implementation, and poverty and inequality. She has recently published on the impacts of the COVID-19 pandemic on social programme implementation, frontline professional resistance, as well as the implementation of Chile's Conditional Cash Transfer Program.

Luiza Rosa is Research Fellow at the Institute for Applied Economic Research (IPEA), in Brasília, Brazil. She holds a bachelor's degree in Public

Policy Management from the University of Brasília and is currently a Master's degree student in Social Anthropology at the same university. Her main research interests are the implementation of public policies and the population's relationship with basic health services and drug policy in Brazil. In her current research, she intends to understand the meanings of good care for problematic users of psychoactive substances and the construction of a treatment itinerary based on the biopsychosocial needs of this group.

Maria Paula Santos is Researcher at the Institute for Applied Economic Research (IPEA), in Brasília, Brazil. She holds a PhD in Political Science from Instituto Universitário de Pesquisas do Rio de Janeiro (IUPERJ) and a Master's in Public Policy and Administration from the Institute of Social Sciences (ISS – Netherlands). In recent years, she has been working on drug policies and public security analyses.

Sneha Swami is a research scholar at the Centre for Policy Studies, the Indian Institute of Technology Bombay, India. Her doctoral research involves investigation into last-mile delivery of services in the electricity distribution sector, using the theoretical lenses of street-level bureaucracy and public service outsourcing. Her prior research experience includes studying women's self-help groups working for metering and billing activities of electricity services in Indian villages as well as conducting survey research in tribal communities for their energy needs. She is skilled in survey design, survey research, semi-structured interviews, conversational interviews, non-participant observation, and qualitative research methodologies.

Izabela Szkurłat holds a PhD in Political Science, with a specialisation in security policy. She is Assistant Professor at the Department of National Security of the Institute of Security and Management at the Pomeranian University in Słupsk, Poland. She is the author and co-author of articles related to, among others, terrorism and border defence. Her areas of interest are international security, local security, conflicts and international terrorism, and migration.

Magdalena Szydłowska holds a Master's in National Security with a specialisation in security management of business entities. In 2022, she started her dissertation research on 'The role of national identity in building the social potential of the national security system of the Republic of Poland' at the Pomeranian University in Słupsk, Poland. Research interests include personal security, the national security system, national identity, and the social potential of national security. She is the author of national and international scientific articles.

Cristóbal Villalobos is a sociologist and social worker from the Pontifical Catholic University of Chile, Chile. He holds a Master's in Economics Applied to Public Policies (Alberto Hurtado University, Chile) and a PhD in Social Sciences (University of Chile, Chile). Currently, he is Assistant Professor and Deputy Director of the Center for the Study of Policies and Practices in Education (CEPPE UC), both at the Pontifical Catholic University of Chile. His lines of research include educational inequality, social intervention, citizen education, social movements in education, and higher education, with an emphasis on Chile and Latin America.

Subodh Wagle is Professor at Centre for Technology Alternatives for Rural Areas (CTARA) and Associate Faculty at Centre for Policy Studies, Indian Institute of Technology (IIT) Bombay, India. Prior to this, he served as Founding Dean, School of Habitat Studies, Tata Institute of Social Sciences (TISS), Mumbai, India. For the past 30 years, Prof. Wagle has been working on policy and regulatory analysis, especially in the electricity, water, environment, and development sectors. After spending an initial ten years with a policy analysis and advocacy organisation called PRAYAS (Pune), Prof. Wagle has been involved in academics at TISS, IIT Bombay, and University of Delaware (USA). He has taught courses on Public Policy Theory, History and Theory of Regulatory Governance, Water Sector Policy and Governance, Energy and Environmental Policy, Research Methodology and Design, and Qualitative Research Methods. In recent years, his research has focused on the last-mile issues pertaining to policy delivery in different sectors, including electricity, education, nutrition, COVID-19 response, and urban services.

1

Street-level bureaucracy in weak state institutions: an introduction

Gabriela Lotta, Fernando Nieto-Morales, and Rik Peeters

Introduction

What laws formally guarantee, politicians promise, and public policies aim to achieve needs to be materialised in our daily interactions with public organisations. There, we often encounter street-level bureaucrats (SLBs), low-ranking public servants, or frontline workers who process our applications for a social benefit, provide access to public services such as healthcare or education, and enforce traffic and safety regulations. The academic literature has established a common ground in understanding these civil servants. It is well documented, for instance, that SLBs, or frontline workers, shape policies and public services rather than merely implement them (Lipsky, 1980; Maynard-Moody and Musheno, 2003). They do not simply apply formal rules to individual cases. Instead, a hospital's emergency staff decides which patients to attend to first, police officers on the street decide whom to pull over and how to treat each specific case, and social workers negotiate with their clients about treatment plans. Although the specific organisational and work context matters, SLBs always have some form of discretion in the way they interpret, apply, or bend the rules and deal with citizens (Hupe and Hill, 2007; Evans, 2011).

Evidence shows that most SLBs do not think of their work merely as formal rule application, but, instead, they act upon routines, organisational expectations, client experiences and judgments, and professional convictions, values, and norms (Maynard-Moody and Musheno, 2000). The nature of their work requires 'human judgement that cannot be programmed and for which machines cannot substitute' (Lipsky, 1980, 161). At the same time, they are part of a society and hence act in a broader context in which they are the face of the state, influencing access to public goods and services but also shaping identities and the experience of citizenship (Dubois, 1999; Zacka, 2017). Their inherent discretion, their relative autonomy from organisational authority, their role as ultimate policy makers, and their direct interactions with citizens at the frontlines of law enforcement, service provision, and policy implementation are the defining characteristics of SLBs (Maynard-Moody and Portillo, 2010). Scholars have explored how personal convictions and values shape their decision-making (Jilke and Tummers, 2018), how they cope with tensions and contradictory demands in their work (Evans, 2011; Tummers et al, 2015), and how they balance what is expected from them with the resources they have at hand (Hupe and Buffat, 2014; Thomann, 2015).

What happens in street-level bureaucracies, however, when basic resources are not provided or are simply non-existent? Or when adverse working conditions limit the extent to which job expectations and client demands can be met? For example, in many places, nurses and medics face a lack of basic materials to provide healthcare. Police officers are expected to enforce rules in violent urban contexts or remote rural areas. Desk clerks have to make decisions in the absence of clear formal guidelines. And many social workers lack the means to attend to the problems of highly marginalised communities. This book is about those SLBs and how structurally adverse working conditions affect their decisions and behaviour. Rather than understanding street-level bureaucratic behaviour and decision-making as a 'collection of isolated individual actions' (Gofen, 2014, 485), we tap into a strand of research that highlights the way organisational contexts (May and Winter, 2009; Brodkin, 2012), societal expectations (Sandfort, 2000; Møller and Stensøta, 2019), formal rule systems and accountability regimes (Hupe and Hill, 2007), and professional networks and deliberation (Møller, 2021) shape frontline work. We agree with the idea that street-level work is highly sensitive to context (Lotta et al, 2023) and, therefore, we build upon studies that draw attention to contexts where SLBs commonly face adverse social and working conditions, such as precarity, instability, and endemic violence or corruption (Peeters and Campos, 2022). Most research on street-level bureaucracy – in fact, most public administration research in general – has historically been conducted in countries characterised by high levels of administrative capacity, professional bureaucracies, stable rules of law, and in industrialised and often democratic societies (Bertelli et al, 2020). However, most of the world's SLBs work under very different institutional conditions. Politicised bureaucracies, low social trust in government, systemic corruption, precarious labour conditions, and limited state capacities are common traits of bureaucracies in developing countries and post-authoritarian regimes (Lotta et al, 2022).

To be clear, the analysis of how such conditions influence frontline work and citizens' experience of the state is neither apologetic nor exotic in relation to the established literature. First, there is little exotic or 'deviant from the norm' in presenting studies from contexts representative of how most of the world's population experiences its interactions with

SLBs – something that is insufficiently represented in studies from the Global North. This book aims to make sense of citizens' seemingly contradictory experiences of street-level bureaucracy in such settings. On the one hand, we may encounter corrupt or poorly trained officials, slow and inefficient bureaucratic procedures, and unreliable or patchy public services. On the other hand, we also see teachers and medical staff working miracles with the limited resources they have at hand, facing extreme social conditions, and still acting to guarantee people's well-being and rights. How do we explain this variety? Why do institutional contexts generate such diverse and unequal outcomes? Second, the analyses brought together here are not apologetic in the sense that we condone the multiple problems raised. However, we do argue that we need context-sensitive analyses to understand where issues such as unequal policy implementation and street-level corruption originate from. Accordingly, we do not assume that the characteristics of street-level bureaucracy in the Global North are necessarily applicable or realistic in other parts of the world. In the concluding section of this book we, for instance, highlight the importance of brokerage functions of street-level bureaucracy in contexts of large distances between vulnerable populations and a distant formal bureaucracy. Finally, understanding how variation in working conditions shapes street-level bureaucracy is relevant for scholars anywhere in the world interested in institutional analyses of frontline work. It helps to identify the institutional preconditions under which street-level bureaucracy can function as a source of social trust in government and as a provider of equal and reliable access to public services and benefits.

In the remainder of this introductory chapter, we first discuss the concept of weak institutions (Brinks et al, 2020), which we use to identify factors that influence street-level bureaucracy in developing contexts. Proposed by comparative political scientists, it was initially intended to provide a political – rather than the more common state capacity-based – explanation for the existence of enforcement gaps and implementation gaps in Latin America. In this book, we apply the concept beyond its original geographical context. Moreover, we do not focus on one specific explanation but identify organisational, political, social, and professional factors that may relate to institutional weakness. Second, we apply our discussion of weak institutions to street-level bureaucracy. Using well-documented concepts from the literature on street-level bureaucracy, we propose a framework for analysing how institutional factors may shape the behaviour of SLBs. This framework serves as a basis for the development of the chapters of this book, in which the different contributors delve into specific concepts and develop approaches based on or dialoguing with them. Third, we end this introductory chapter with an outline of the remainder of this book and discuss its contributions and limitations.

Understanding weak institutions

Since the foundational works of Wilson (1887) and Weber (1922), there is broad theoretical consensus among public administration scholars that the implementation of policies, the provision of public services, and the enforcement of rules depend on actions by government organisations and public servants (Hill and Hupe, 2022). Public bureaucracies translate legal mandates and policy objectives into courses of action that purportedly reduce arbitrary decision-making, rent-seeking, and political interference (Galligan, 1990). This is important because the ability of public administrations to organise impartial and predictable decision-making is closely associated with the trust in and quality of government (Dahl, 1982; Rothstein, 2013; Dahlberg and Holmberg, 2014). This also explains, however, the complicated relationship that street-level bureaucracies have with a rules system and organisational structure that is designed to reduce uncertainty and increase the predictability of bureaucratic behaviour (Gajduschek, 2003). Managerial directives, performance indicators, professional norms, and client demands complement formal rules as mechanisms through which SLBs' inherent discretion and relative autonomy are aligned with public values and interests (Hupe and Hill, 2007; Evans, 2011).

To a certain extent, all public administrations fall short in aligning formal rules and policy goals with bureaucratic behaviour. This may, for instance, be traced back to the nature of street-level bureaucracy or to inherently ambiguous policy objectives. However, a public administration's capacity to organise impartial and predictable decision-making, service provision, and policy implementation can also be hampered by institutional factors. Institutions are important because they produce solutions to cooperation and coordination in social dilemmas (Rawls, 1971). The concept of 'institutional weakness' (Brinks et al, 2020) is a useful analytical device for explaining the institutional origins of enforcement and implementation gaps that are common for places where citizens face patchy public service provision (McDonnell, 2017) and selective rule enforcement (O'Brien and Li, 1999). Following Elinor Ostrom's (2005) notion of institutions as formal prescriptions, Brinks, Levitsky, and Murillo define a weak institution as a rule or prescription that fails to significantly redistribute or refract power, authority, or social expectations (2020, 8). Institutional weakness can be observed when the material consequences of a rule cannot be practically predicted by social actors. For instance, high levels of impunity despite the existence of penal law are a sign of institutional weakness. Similarly, limited access to a social programme or public service despite rules that guarantee universality suggests institutional weakness. More generally, whereas strong institutions often quietly structure social interactions given their stability and legitimacy, weak institutions tend to be unstable and unpredictable in their material consequences.

Four things should be stressed for a proper understanding of the concept of weak institutions. First, the concept of 'weak institutions' uses the narrow understanding of institutions as formal and informal rules or prescriptions that structure human behaviour. Therefore, institutions are not limited to formal rules, but social or cultural norms and technological design are also examples of mechanisms that shape the way social expectations or power relations are structured (Siddiki et al, 2011). We acknowledge that those and other mechanisms play an important part in street-level bureaucracy as well. We refer to Scott's integrative definition of institutions as 'comprised of regulative, normative and cultural-cognitive elements that, together with associated activities and resources, provide stability and meaning' (2008, 48).

Second, it is important to point out that strong institutions do not necessarily seek to alter power relations and social expectations visibly or explicitly. In fact, many strong institutions appear to us as conservative in the sense that they aim to preserve a certain status quo and consolidate existing power relations, for instance by creating rule enforcing organisations. Following Brinks et al (2020), whether an institution is strong or weak should be assessed by comparing it to a (hypothetical) situation in which such an institution does not exist – in other words, whether a significant gap exists between the ambition expressed in a rule or prescription and the extent to which it is enforced or realised in practice. For instance, an effective law enforcement is considered a strong institution, even though it seeks to consolidate existing formal rules, because its absence would lead to a very different social outcome. Conversely, an institution can be considered weak if it fails to consolidate a status quo or fails to uphold existing rules.

Third, whether an institution can be classified as 'weak' or 'strong' is not dichotomous nor stable. Even the strongest institutions are not without their gaps between formal rules and daily practice (Goffman, 1961). Consequently, institutional weakness is not limited to developing countries but may also occur in places where institutions are predominantly strong. Likewise, institutional weakness in developing countries does not imply a complete lack of governance, implementation, or enforcement. The difference between strong and weak institutions is gradual. Hence, the variation among and within weak institutional environments is considerable. When the contributions in this book talk about weak institutions, they reflect varying degrees of weakness.

Fourth, our primary interest here is not the content of institutions – the precise goals they seek to realise – but, instead, the way they structure the working conditions and behaviour of SLBs and shape people's everyday experience of the state in many places worldwide. Our main argument is that a lack of impartial, equal, and predictable decision-making and rule enforcement at the street level can be explained by factors associated with institutional weakness. Following Peeters and Campos (2022), we identify four distinct institutional factors that influence the nature of street-level bureaucracy.

a) Organisational/administrative capacities

The well-established literature on state capacity argues that enforcement and implementation gaps result from limitations in a country's practical abilities to guarantee rights and services (Mann, 1984; Soifer, 2015; Amengual and Dargent, 2020). At the level of individual organisations, administrative capacities affect the ability to control bureaucratic behaviour and structure policy implementation (North, 1990; Nieto et al, 2014), standardise working procedures (Kelly, 2017), and provide sufficient resources for service delivery (Gibson, 2004). At the same time, limited organisational capacities may lead to heightened demands for formalism and more mistrust within bureaucrat-citizen interactions or increased opportunities for corruption, arbitrariness, and lack of transparency (Justesen and Bjørnskov, 2014). Organisational challenges may be further aggravated by urban and rural geographies and contexts that pose additional or particular limitations (Lameck and Hulst, 2020). For example, they can affect SLBs by forcing them to make difficult rationing decisions when attending to clients (Meza et al, 2021) or use personal resources to complement insufficient, formally provided work materials (Lavee, 2021).

b) Political influence

Weak public institutions are often characterised by low bureaucratic autonomy (Dasandi and Esteve, 2017), which increases the opportunities for politicians to influence bureaucratic decision-making directly or indirectly for their benefit (Cornell and Lapuente, 2014; Grindle, 2012; Nichter, 2008). At the street level, political influence can take the form of hiring frontline workers for the specific purpose of implementing part of a political programme (Perelmiter, 2016), pressuring bureaucrats to adopt clientelist working practices (Hassan, 2020), and instructing workers (backed up by hiring and firing power) to refrain from rule enforcement (Holland, 2017). Political polarisation may also affect SLBs, generating counterbalance, collaboration, and resistance during policy implementation (Eiró, 2022).

c) Social trust and inequality

Social resistance – either active (Nisar, 2018), implicit through social conventions and institutions (Masood and Nisar, 2020), or based on a lack of trust in government as a reliable service provider (Peeters and Dussauge Laguna, 2021) – against formal rule enforcement or policy implementation may contribute to institutional weakness (and partly explain politically motivated non-enforcement) (Brinks et al, 2020). Furthermore, social conflict, violence, and disorder (Ballvé, 2012; Lotta et al, 2022; Davidovitz and Cohen, 2022), as well as social inequality and marginalisation (Lotta and Pires, 2019), can further aggravate problems and exert pressure on state capacity. At the street level, this social context is associated with potentially dangerous working conditions (Sundström, 2016), complex service delivery to marginalised population groups (Bhavnani and Lee, 2018), and citizens more likely to display avoidance (Chudnovsky and Peeters, 2021), resistance (Nisar, 2018), or attempts to game bureaucratic encounters (Peeters et al, 2020). At the same time, in contexts like this, SLBs have even more critical roles in defining identities and citizenship status (Dubois, 1999; Auyero, 2011), as they may be the only gateway to an absent or capricious state (Peake and Forsythe, 2022).

d) Professionalisation and labour conditions

Countries with weak institutions are often characterised by limited professionalisation of their civil services. Street-level professionalisation through, for instance, training, professional communities, and career opportunities has been recognised as an important element in the development of professional norms, operating procedures, and normative decision-making (Evans, 2011). Limitations therein may result in a patchy composition of the workforce, a lack of meritocratic systems and norms, and public management practices that lead to arbitrariness and inconsistencies (Nieto Morales and Rios, 2022). For instance, systemic corruption in local police forces (Justesen and Bjørnskov, 2014) may exist side-by-side with highly motivated primary school teachers (Mangla, 2015), just as highly educated medical professionals may exist side-by-side with poorly trained desk clerks (Chudnovsky and Peeters, 2022). To be sure, not all forms of street-level bureaucracies are characterised by a strong need for the development of professional training and norms. Moving beyond professionalisation, the resources and conditions SLBs require to perform their job can also be hampered by a lack of training and resources, precarious labour conditions, low salaries, and limited job security (Cerna et al, 2017; Lima and D'Asenzi, 2017; Lotta et al, 2023), or poorly equipped offices and facilities (Walker and Gilson, 2004).

Street-level bureaucracy in adverse working conditions

The contributions in this book explore how the circumstances associated with institutional weakness presented previously affect street-level bureaucracies. Such an approach does not negate the agency of SLBs. It assumes that social and working conditions shape the incentives and constraints – or 'action possibilities' (Norman, 2013) – for the agency of SLBs. For instance, they provide rules that guide and legitimise their work or bring people together to negotiate specific outcomes. Here, we consider that SLBs 'inhabit' the institutions (Maynard-Moody and Musheno, 2012). This means that their agency is shaped by the institutional context but that their agency, in turn, also shapes public service provision, rule enforcement, and policy implementation. Encounters between frontline workers and citizens constitute an action situation that is influenced by both the actors' agency and factors such as the location of their interaction (on the street or in a government office), the frontline workers' task (service delivery or rule enforcement), the resources at hand (time, skills), interests and capacities of the citizen, and the formal bureaucratic rules that guide decision-making.

In short, we assume that the behaviour and role of SLBs critically relate to the type of institutional environments in which they work and that, at the same time, their actions also shape how these settings function. Weak institutions, in all their variety, present a specific set of challenges for frontline workers across the globe. For example, it makes a difference whether nurses need to attend to more patients than the medicine supplies allow for or whether police officers work in cities where violent gangs make daily work dangerous. Similarly, in many contexts, social workers have to enrol beneficiaries in social programmes without clear eligibility criteria, and health inspectors are routinely exposed to bribery. Such challenges often require SLBs to develop certain forms of agency to comply with their personal and professional standards. Alternatively, such contexts may entice them to seek personal benefit from their work or stifle their discretion because of managerial directives, overly complex rules, and resource shortages. Conversely, the agency of SLBs may also affect how institutions exist in actuality. For example, frontline workers' interpretation of the rules, arbitrary demands, or changes in the way public services are provided feed back into the citizen experience of the state.

Peeters and Campos (2022) identify three ideal-typical agency patterns specific for SLBs in developing countries. Although a wide range of strategies and coping mechanisms exist – and many of those are not dissimilar from what is documented in the 'mainstream' literature on street-level bureaucracy – these patterns provide an analytical tool to identify types of agency more common in weak institutional settings and find associations between them and specific institutional incentives and constraints. First, SLBs are sometimes known to develop forms of 'informal privatisation' (Blundo, 2006), or the application of personal norms and pursuit of personal interests in frontline work – including corrupt behaviour by demanding material or immaterial rewards from citizens (Khan et al, 2016; Hausken et al, 2018) or applying personal and subjective criteria to decide on client eligibility and access to services or benefits (Aitken, 1994; Schmoll, 2021). Second, and contrary to the first pattern, SLBs may try to repair gaps and limitations in service delivery and policy implementation (Masood and Nisar, 2022), for instance by seeking local embeddedness in line with communities' interests and dynamics (Bhavnani and Lee, 2018; Hrynick et al, 2019), by using personal resources to complement a lack of formally provided resources (Lavee, 2021) or by developing professional values, norms, and procedures to fit the demands of their environment (Aberese-Ako et al, 2014; Nzinga et al, 2019). Whereas patterns of informal privatisation are likely to aggravate institutional weakness, selective enforcement, patchy policy implementation, and unreliable and untrustworthy service delivery, forms of policy repair are associated with mitigating and partially compensating institutional weakness. Third, SLBs are also known to display 'alienative commitment' (Usman et al, 2021) and focus on mere job survival and self-preservation. They may emotionally detach from their clients and exhibit minimal compliance with job requirements (Aberese-Ako et al, 2018; Chesoli et al, 2018) or ration services as a response to overdemand (Atinga et al, 2018; Ramani et al, 2020).

This orderly analytical distinction between agency patterns often becomes blurred in daily practice. For instance, studies on how medical staff cope with resource scarcity in Africa (Jitta et al, 2003; Agyepong and Nagai, 2011; Diarra and Ousseini, 2015) show that wealthier clients are sometimes informally charged for services in order to generate additional income to care for other clients. Other studies demonstrate that frontline workers may facilitate political vote-buying because they fear losing their job or being transferred (Brierley, 2020). Studies also show that bureaucrats may take bribes to protect themselves from criminal gangs (Sundström, 2016). Similarly, a study on obstetric violence in Mexican public hospitals (Smith-Oka, 2013) describes how mistreatment can often be traced back to service overdemand and subsequent stress and rationing behaviour by the medical staff. And if SLBs use locally salient norms in the face of absent formal guidelines, they may inadvertently disadvantage certain groups from accessing social benefits (Ehrhardt, 2017). According to Brodkin, street-level discretion is 'the wild card of policy delivery' (2008, 326). Perhaps more than anywhere, this is true for contexts of institutional weakness where significant gaps appear in the alignment between street-level bureaucracy on the one hand and formal rules, guidelines, and policy designs on the other hand. Institutional deficiencies are often left unresolved and subsequently pushed towards the street level, where public servants must deal with them in diverse ways. Thus, citizens are as likely to encounter transit police officers seeking a bribe as they are to find primary school teachers investing their time and money to provide the best education possible under challenging conditions.

Outline of the book

The following chapters analyse how contexts with different forms of weak institutions shape street-level bureaucracy and, by extension, the everyday citizen experience of rule enforcement, public service delivery, and policy implementation. This book makes three general contributions to the study of street-level bureaucracy. First, it sheds light on the varied and specific nature of street-level bureaucracy and citizen–state interactions in weak institutional settings, common in developing and post-authoritarian countries but also increasingly existent among developed countries. Rather than being deviant from the norm, these practices represent how most of the world's population experiences the state. Second, and thanks to its global focus, this book contributes to more mainstream street-level bureaucracy literature by analysing how variations in working conditions shape street-level bureaucracy. Such an institutional analysis also helps to identify the institutional preconditions under which street-level bureaucracy can contribute to equal, trustworthy, and reliable access to public services. A third contribution of this book is more practical in nature. Consistent with the idea that '[t]he face of politics for most citizens ... is a bureaucrat' (Pepinsky et al, 2017, 250), the studies presented here emphasise the importance of complementing the dominant focus on policy design in developing countries with more attention to implementation, frontline work, and citizens' bureaucratic encounters. Without attending to the institutional preconditions and resources, gaps between goals and the reality of street-level interactions are likely to remain significant. As studies on state-citizen interactions consistently demonstrate, this aggravates the selective (O'Brien and Li, 1999), patchy (McDonnell, 2017), and, ultimately, distributive (Peeters and Nieto Morales, 2020) nature of service delivery and rule enforcement and, more broadly, the experience of citizenship and trust in government (Rothstein, 2013).

In line with our ambition to develop a representative argument for street-level bureaucracy in weak institutional contexts, we have aimed for maximum variation in our author and topic selection. Geographically, the book includes studies from the Middle East, Asia, Latin America, sub-Saharan Africa, and Eastern Europe. Furthermore, the chapters cover a broad range of SLBs, such as municipal employees, social workers, health workers, electricity company staff, police officers, and local community leaders. The contributing authors also come from varied institutional and geographical backgrounds – most of them working in the countries they study – and include senior and early career scholars. Finally, the authors apply different disciplinary approaches to street-level bureaucracy, including sociology, political science, anthropology, and public administration – thereby affirming the relevance of including frontline worker agency in understanding topics such as bureaucratic performance and citizen experiences of the state and democracy. However, the inevitability of having to select countries, authors, and bureaucratic practices also limits the scope and ambition of this book. This book is primarily explorative and not necessarily representative of all the varied shapes street-level bureaucracy takes on in weak institutional settings. We hope future studies will do justice to the high levels of diversity in the field by attending to more country – or region-specific, as well as sector-specific characteristics, including more comparative studies.

The book is organised into three sections. The first part focuses on examples of the frontline agency patterns discussed in this introduction. In her chapter on policy repair, Ayesha Masood (Lahore University of Management Sciences, India) explores how health workers in Punjab, Pakistan, create organisational resilience through emergent, creative, and adaptive responses to policy breakdown during crisis situations. Using ethnographic data, she analyses health workers' strategies such as the repurposing of equipment, the collective development of ad hoc procedures, taking on new roles and tasks, and providing emotional support for each other. In doing so, they are partially able to overcome more structural shortcomings in their working environment.

Next, Ronan Jacquin (Sciences Po, France) analyses the role of SLBs in the implementation of a pension programme in Uganda, which relies heavily on local political and administrative leaders in the absence of professional frontline workers. In practice, this leads to interactions between frontline workers and beneficiaries characterised by high levels of proximity, paternalism, and authoritarian control practices. Moreover, this leads beneficiaries to see the social benefit as a favour rather than as something they are formally entitled to. This contribution, thereby, shows how mechanisms of paternalism and clientelism can emerge and persist at the street-level in countries characterised by weak institutions.

Finally, Oliver Meza (CIDE, Mexico), Elizabeth Pérez-Chiqués (CIDE, Mexico), and Anat Gofen (Hebrew University of Jerusalem, Israel) present an analytical framework for understanding predatory and other corrupt behaviours by SLBs. Drawing from quantitative and qualitative data on municipal governments in Mexico, they argue that what can be observed as predatory behaviour by SLBs might rather reflect the role they play in a broader context of corrupted politics, management, and peers, in which SLBs are tools for pursuing private interests. Rather than analysing street-level corruption as petty or isolated forms of corruption, they reinterpret them as part of wider patterns of systemic corruption.

In the second part of the book, we take a closer look at institutional factors that shape street-level bureaucracy. First, Sneha Swami and Subodh Wagle (Indian Institute of Technology) provide a case study of precarious frontline working conditions in the Indian electricity distribution sector. Fieldwork from the state of Maharashtra shows how 'wiremen' cope both emotionally and behaviourally with a variety of dangers in their everyday job, ranging from electric shocks and physical injuries to snake bites and violence by customers. Even though 'wiremen' tend to receive a large part of the public's blame for the unreliability of electricity services, the authors trace the roots of the challenges in their work to a lack of adequate human resources, training, tools, and materials provided by the public distribution utilities. Furthermore, the chapter shows how the concept of street-level bureaucracy can be context-dependent. Workers not commonly identified as SLBs may qualify as such in institutional settings that force them to have (informal) client interactions and prioritise certain tasks given resource scarcities that, in turn, have direct consequences for the quality and equity of basic service provision to citizens. By stretching the concept of street-level bureaucracy, this chapter invites the reader to reflect on the diverse nature of public service provision and how institutional settings compromise its proper implementation at the frontline.

Next, Roberto Pires, Maria Paula Santos, Beatriz Brandão, and Luiza Rosa (Institute of Applied Economic Research, Brazil) analyse the social consequences of implementation gaps for vulnerable target groups. Fieldwork from care services for people experiencing drug-related problems in Brazil highlights the micro-level processes of the institutional production of disadvantages as well as their broader implications in terms of reinforcing existing social inequalities. By building on insights from organisational theories and policy implementation studies, the chapter provides a critical perspective on implementation gaps for the access to and quality of public services.

In the third contribution, Taly Reininger, Gianinna Muñoz Arce, Cristóbal Villalobos, and Mitzi Duboy Luengo (University of Chile) describe how neoliberal outsourcing contracts lead to precarious working conditions of social workers in one of Chile's central social protection programmes – including not having a contract covering basic health and security rights, not being sure of pay dates, and lacking basic work materials for the programme's adequate implementation. Furthermore, a highly centralised policy design in combination with limited municipal resources cause territorial differences in the programme's implementation. Taken together, these conditions create both adverse policy outcomes and take their toll on the physical and emotional well-being of frontline professionals.

In the last contribution of this section, Barbara Maria Piotrowska (King's College, United Kingdom), Izabela Szkurłat, and Magdalena Szydłowska (Pomeranian University, Poland) analyse historical longitudinal survey data from the late 1980s and 1990s in Poland to track developments in citizens' trust in the police. They focus on three specific challenges: transforming the police from an institution of oppression to one that serves the public; reforms in the personnel dimension of the police force; and effectiveness of the police force in dealing with an increase of crime following the opening of a formerly strictly controlled society. The chapter does not directly focus on street-level interactions but, rather, uses historical analysis to trace institutional developments and, thereby, provide valuable lessons for building trust in weak institutional settings elsewhere.

The third and final part of the book focuses on the interactions between SLBs and citizens. In their study of the municipal police of the Mexican city of Morelia, Paulina Yunuén Guzmán Linares and Rik Peeters (CIDE, Mexico) analyse how police officers cope behaviourally and emotionally with highly precarious working conditions and a violent social context. On a daily basis, they face possibly life-threatening situations, high levels of crime, and distrusting citizens while simultaneously being insufficiently trained, equipped, and psychologically supported by their organisation to fulfil those tasks. In response, they may back down from intervening in situations involving organised crime or, conversely, adopt strict and aggressive approaches to individual citizens. Thereby, police officers shape the nature and experience of law enforcement for the citizens of Morelia and convey messages about what citizens may expect from their municipal police. Moreover, the chapter stresses the importance of taking into account cognitive and emotional coping mechanisms and job attitudes in high-stress working environments.

Next, Abdul-Rahim Mohammed (University for Development Studies, Ghana) explores the gatekeeping and categorising practices by SLBs in the implementation of Ghana's National Health Insurance Scheme. Based on participant observation and interview data from a rural hospital, he finds differential treatments based on frontline workers' subjective views of their clients' socio-economic status. Formally dressed patients are more often recognised as clients that genuinely need care, whereas informally dressed patients are categorised as difficult, villagers, or time wasters. Against a background of high caseloads and scarce human resources, frontline staff has a significant impact on policy implementation by prioritising certain clients over others.

Elise Massicard (Sciences Po, France) sheds light on street-level intermediary functionaries between formal bureaucracy and local communities, common for countries and regions with weak state institutions and marginalised communities. 'Muhtars' are the lowest elected political position in Turkey but function as public officials at street-level. They usually come from the communities they serve, have little job security, no training, and almost no financial resources. In daily practice, they facilitate people's access to the state by providing information and using personal relations. However, this personalisation of state–citizen interactions also opens up a space for informality that risks bypassing the institutional order. Furthermore, this chapter invites the reader to understand street-level bureaucracy beyond its common definitional boundaries and understand the varied ways in which state-citizens interactions may be organised in weak institutional settings.

Shifting attention even further to the citizen experience of street-level bureaucracy in weak institutions, Sergio A. Campos (CIDE, Mexico) analyses the way citizens use their agency to navigate bureaucratic uncertainty and unpredictability. A case study of the street-level interactions in a Mexican conditional cash transfer shows the way weak institutions may generate administrative burdens for beneficiaries as well as spaces for informal interactions. Paradoxically, these informal practices can impose access barriers and simultaneously give beneficiaries opportunities to manipulate or negotiate compliance criteria. Thereby, this last chapter problematises citizen agency and argues that it can significantly alter policy implementation and the nature of state-citizen interactions.

We end this book with a concluding chapter in which we formulate several critical lessons and findings from the sum of chapters. We also outline the book's main contributions. Finally, we pose several concluding remarks on the crucial role of SLBs in advancing the functioning of public administrations in weak institutional settings and on how reflecting on the characteristics of weak institutions can improve our understanding of public administration in general. A general conclusion that emerges from the contributions in this book is *the inevitability of implementing inequities* in service delivery, treatment of citizen–clients, and law enforcement as the defining characteristic of street-level bureaucracy in weak institutional settings – primarily because SLBs lack the institutional resources to do otherwise.

References

Aberese-Ako, M., Agyepong, I.A., and van Dijk, H. (2018). Leadership styles in two Ghanaian hospitals in a challenging environment. *Health Policy and Planning*, 33(2), 16–26. https://doi.org/10.1093/heapol/czy038

Aberese-Ako, M., van Dijk, H., Gerrits, T., Arhinful, D.K., and Agyepong, I.A. (2014). 'Your health our concern, our health whose concern?': Perceptions of injustice in organizational relationships and processes and frontline health worker motivation in Ghana. *Health Policy and Planning*, 29(2), 15–28. https://doi.org/10.1093/heapol/czu068

Agyepong, I.A., and Nagai, R.A. (2011). 'We charge them; otherwise we cannot run the hospital': Front line workers, clients and health financing policy implementation gaps in Ghana. *Health Policy*, 99(3), 226–33.

Aitken, J.-M. (1994). Voices from the inside: Managing district health services in Nepal. *International Journal of Health Planning and Management*, 9(4), 309–40. https://doi.org/10.1002/hpm.4740090405

Amengual, M., and Dargent, E. (2020). The social determinants of enforcement: Integrating politics with limited state capacity. In D.M. Brinks, S. Levitsky and M.V. Murillo (eds), *The Politics of Institutional Weakness in Latin America*. Cambridge: Cambridge University Press, pp 161–82.

Atinga, R.A., Agyepong, I.A., and Esena, R.K. (2018). Ghana's community-based primary health care: Why women and children are 'disadvantaged' by its implementation. *Social Science & Medicine*, 201, 27–34. https://doi.org/10.1016/j.socscimed.2018.02.001

Auyero, J. (2011). Patients of the state: An ethnographic account of poor people's waiting. *Latin American Research Review*, 46(1), 5–29.

Ballvé, T. (2012). Everyday state formation: Territory, decentralization, and the narco landgrab in Colombia. *Environment and Planning D: Society and Space*, 30(4), 603–22.

Bertelli, A.M., Hassan, M., Honig, D., Rogger, D., and Williams, M.J. (2020). An agenda for the study of public administration in developing countries. *Governance*, 33(4), 735–48.

Bhavnani, R.R., and Lee, A. (2018). Local embeddedness and bureaucratic performance: Evidence from India. *The Journal of Politics*, 80(1), 71–87.

Blundo, G. (2006). Dealing with the local state: The informal privatization of street-level bureaucracies in Senegal. *Development and Change*, 37(4), 799–819.

Brierley S. (2020). Unprincipled principals: Co-opted bureaucrats and corruption in Ghana. *American Journal of Political Science*, 64(2), 209–22.

Brinks, D.M., Levitsky, S., and Murillo, M.V. (eds) (2020). *The Politics of Institutional Weakness in Latin America*. Cambridge: Cambridge University Press.

Brodkin, E.Z. (2008). Accountability in street-level organizations. *International Journal of Public Administration*, 31(3), 317–36.

Brodkin, E.Z. (2012). Reflections on street-level bureaucracy: Past, present, and future. *Public Administration Review*, 72(6), 940–9.

Cerna, D., García, L., Puémape, F., Sosa, P., Rentería, M., and Rozas, L. (2017). *Acá no hay ventanillas: La burocracia de la calle en los programas sociales*. Lima, Peru: Instituto de Estudios Peruanos.

Chesoli, R.N., Schuster, R.C., Okelo, S., and Omotayo, M.O. (2018). Strengthening care delivery in primary care facilities: Perspectives of facility managers on the immunization program in Kenya. *International Journal of Health Policy and Management*, 7(12), 1130–7. https://doi.org/10.15171/ijhpm.2018.83

Chudnovsky, M., and Peeters, R. (2021). The unequal distribution of administrative burden: A framework and an illustrative case study for understanding variation in people's experience of burdens. *Social Policy & Administration*, 55(4), 527–42. https://doi.org/10.1111/spol.12639

Chudnovsky, M., and Peeters, R. (2022). A cascade of exclusion: Administrative burdens and access to citizenship in the case of Argentina's national identity document. *International Review of Administrative Sciences*, 88(4), 1068–85. https://doi.org/10.1177/0020852320984541

Cornell, A., and Lapuente, V. (2014). Meritocratic administration and democratic stability. *Democratization*, 21(7), 1286–304.

Dahl, R.A. (1982). Dilemmas of pluralist democracy: Autonomy vs control. *Ethics*, 94(4), 701–10.

Dahlberg, S., and Holmberg, S. (2014). Democracy and bureaucracy: How their quality matters for popular satisfaction. *West European Politics*, 37(3), 515–37.

Dasandi, N., and Esteve, M. (2017). The politics–bureaucracy interface in developing countries. *Public Administration and Development*, 37(4), 231–45.

Davidovitz, M., and Cohen, N. (2022). Frontline social service as a battlefield: Insights from street-level bureaucrats' interactions with violent clients. *Social Policy & Administration*, 56(1), 73–86.

Diarra, A., and Ousseini, A. (2015). The coping strategies of frontline health workers in the context of user fee exemptions in Niger. *BMC Health Services Research*, 15(S3), S1.

Dubois, V. (1999). *La Vie au Guichet: Relation Administrative et Traitement de la Misère*. Paris: Economica.

Ehrhardt, D. (2017). Indigeneship, bureaucratic discretion, and institutional change in Northern Nigeria. *African Affairs*, 116(464), 462–83. https://doi.org/10.1093/afraf/adx016

Eiró, F. (2022). Translating politics into policy implementation: Welfare frontline workers in polarized Brazil. *International Journal of Law in Context*, 18(3), 303–16.

Evans, T. (2011). Professionals, managers and discretion: Critiquing street-level bureaucracy. *British Journal of Social Work*, 41(2), 368–86.

Gajduschek, G. (2003). Bureaucracy: Is it efficient? Is it not? Is that the question?: Uncertainty reduction: An ignored element of bureaucratic rationality. *Administration & Society*, 34(6), 700–23.

Galligan, D.J. (1990). *Discretionary Powers: A Legal Study of Official Discretion*. Oxford: Clarendon Press.

Gibson, D. (2004). The gaps in the gaze in South African hospitals. *Social Science & Medicine*, 59(10), 2013–24.

Gofen, A. (2014). Mind the gap: Dimensions and influence of street-level divergence. *Journal of Public Administration Research and Theory*, 24(2), 473–93.

Goffman, E. (1961). *Asylums: Essays on the Social Situation of Mental Patients and Other Inmates*. New York: Anchor Books.

Grindle, M.S. (2012). *Jobs for the Boys: Patronage and the State in Comparative Perspective*. Cambridge, MA: Harvard University Press.

Hallett, T., and Ventresca, M.J. (2006). Inhabited institutions: social interactions and organizational forms in Gouldner's 'Patterns of Industrial Bureaucracy'. *Theory and Society*, 35(2), 213–36.

Hassan, M. (2020). *Regime Threats and State Solutions: Bureaucratic Loyalty and Embeddedness in Kenya*. Cambridge: Cambridge University Press.

Hausken, K., and Ncube, M. (2018). Service delivery versus moonlighting: Using data from Kenya, Uganda, Tanzania and Senegal. *African Development Review-Revue Africaine de Developpement*, 30(2), 219–32. https://doi.org/10.1111/1467-8268.12327

Hill, M., and Hupe, P. (2022). *Implementing Public Policy*. New York: Sage.

Holland, A.C. (2017). *Forbearance as Redistribution: The Politics of Informal Welfare in Latin America*. Cambridge: Cambridge University Press.

Hrynick, T.A., Barasa, V., Benschop, J., Cleaveland, S., Crump, J.A., Davis, M. et al (2019). Street-level diplomacy and local enforcement for meat safety in northern Tanzania: Knowledge, pragmatism and trust. *BMC Public Health*, 19(1), 863. https://doi.org/10.1186/s12889-019-7067-8

Hupe, P., and Buffat, A. (2014). A public service gap: Capturing contexts in a comparative approach of street-level bureaucracy. *Public Management Review*, 16(4), 548–69.

Hupe, P., and Hill, M. (2007). Street-level bureaucracy and public accountability. *Public Administration*, 85(2), 279–99.

Jilke, S. and Tummers, L. (2018). Which clients are deserving of help? A theoretical model and experimental test. *Journal of Public Administration Research and Theory*, 28(2), 226–38.

Jitta, J., Whyte, S., and Nshakira, N. (2003). The availability of drugs: What does it mean in Ugandan primary care. *Health Policy*, 65(2), 167–79.

Justesen, M.K., and Bjørnskov, C. (2014). Exploiting the poor: Bureaucratic corruption and poverty in Africa. *World Development*, 58, 106–15.

Kelly, G. (2017). Patient agency and contested notions of disability in social assistance applications in South Africa. *Social Science & Medicine*, 175, 109–16.

Khan, A.Q., Khwaja, A.I., and Olken, B.A. (2016). Tax farming redux: Experimental evidence on performance pay for tax collectors. *The Quarterly Journal of Economics*, 131(1), 219–71. https://doi.org/10.1093/qje/qjv042

Lameck, W., and Hulst, R. (2020). Explaining coping strategies of agricultural extension officers in Tanzania: The role of the wider institutional context. *International Review of Administrative Sciences*, 86(4), 749–64.

Lavee, E. (2021). Who is in charge? The provision of informal personal resources at the street level. *Journal of Public Administration Research and Theory*, 31(1), 4–20. https://doi.org/10.1093/jopart/muaa025

Lima, L.L. and D'Ascenzi, L. (2017). O papel da burocracia de nível de rua na implementação e (re)formulação da Política Nacional de Humanização dos serviços de saúde de Porto Alegre (RS). *Revista de Administração Pública*, 51(1), 46–63.

Lipsky, M. (1980 [2010]). *Street-Level Bureaucracy: Dilemmas of the Individual in Public Services [30th Anniversary Expanded Edition]*. New York: Russell Sage Foundation.

Lotta, G., Krieger, M.G.M., Cohen, N., and Kirschbaum, C. (2023). Not separate, but certainly unequal: The burdens and coping strategies of low-status street-level bureaucrats. *Governance*, 1–20. https://doi.org/10.1111/gove.12815

Lotta, G., Lima-Silva, F., and Favareto, A. (2022). Dealing with violence: Varied reactions from frontline workers acting in highly vulnerable territories. *Environment and Planning C: Politics and Space*, 40(2), 502–19.

Lotta, G., and Pires, R. (2019). Street-level bureaucracy research and social inequality. In P. Hupe (ed), *Research Handbook on Street-Level Bureaucracy*. Cheltenham: Edward Elgar Publishing, pp 86–101.

Mangla, A. (2015). Bureaucratic norms and state capacity in India: Implementing primary education in the Himalayan region. *Asian Survey*, 55(5), 882–908.

Mann, M. (1984). The autonomous power of the state: Its origins, mechanisms and results. *European Journal of Sociology*, 25(2), 185–213.

Masood, A., and Nisar, M.A. (2020). Crushed between two stones: Competing institutional logics in the implementation of maternity leave policies in Pakistan. *Gender, Work & Organization*, 27(6), 1103–26.

Masood, A., and Nisar, M.A. (2022). Repairing the state: Policy repair in the frontline bureaucracy. *Public Administration Review*, 82(2), 256–68. https://doi.org/10.1111/puar.13414

May, P., and Winter, S. (2009). Politicians, managers, and street-level bureaucrats: Influences on policy implementation. *Journal of Public Administration Research and Theory*, 19(3), 453–76.

Maynard-Moody, S., and Musheno, M. (2000). State agent or citizen agent: Two narratives of discretion. *Journal of Public Administration Research and Theory*, 10(2), 329–58. doi.org/10.1093/oxfordjournals.jpart.a024272

Maynard-Moody, S.W., and Musheno, M.C. (2003). *Cops, Teachers, Counselors: Stories from the Front Lines of Public Service*. Ann Arbor: University of Michigan Press.

Maynard-Moody, S., and Musheno, M. (2012), Social equities and inequities in practice: Street-level workers as agents and pragmatists. *Public Administration Review*, 72: S16–23.

Maynard-Moody, S., and Portillo, S. (2010). Street-level bureaucracy theory. In R.F. Durant (ed), *The Oxford Handbook of American Bureaucracy*. Oxford: Oxford University Press, pp 252–77.

McDonnell, E. (2017). Patchwork leviathan: How pockets of bureaucratic governance flourish within institutionally diverse developing states. *American Sociological Review*, 82(3), 476–510.

Meza, O., Perez-Chiques, E., Campos, S.A., and Varela Castro, S. (2021). Against the COVID-19 pandemic: Analyzing role changes of healthcare street-level bureaucrats in Mexico. *Journal of Comparative Policy Analysis*, 23(1), 109–19.

Møller, A.M. (2021). Deliberation and deliberative organizational routines in frontline decision-making. *Journal of Public Administration Research and Theory*, 31(3), 471–88.

Møller, M.Ø., and Stensöta, H.O. (2019). Welfare state regimes and caseworkers' problem explanation. *Administration & Society*, 51(9), 1425–54.

Nichter, S. (2008). Vote buying or turnout buying? Machine politics and the secret ballot. *American Political Science Review*, 102(1), 19–31.

Nieto Morales, F., Heyse, L., Pardo, M.C., and Wittek, R. (2014). Building enforcement capacity: Evidence from the Mexican civil service reform. *Public Administration and Development*, 34, 389–405.

Nieto Morales, F., and Ríos, V. (2022). Human resource management as a tool to control corruption: Evidence from Mexican municipal governments. *Public Administration*, 100(4), 1019–36.

Nisar, M.A. (2018). Overcoming resistance to resistance in public administration: Resistance strategies of marginalized publics in citizen–state interactions. *Public Administration and Development*, 38(1), 15–25.

Norman, D. (2013). *The Design of Everyday Things: Revised and Expanded Edition*. New York: Basic Books.

North, D.C. (1990). *Institutions, Institutional Change and Economic Performance*. Cambridge: Cambridge University Press.

Nzinga, J., McGivern, G., and English, M. (2019). Hybrid clinical-managers in Kenyan hospitals: Navigating between professional, official and practical norms. *Journal of Health Organization and Management*, 33(2), 173–87. https://doi.org/10.1108/JHOM-08-2017-0203

O'Brien, K.J., and Li, L. (1999). Selective policy implementation in rural China. *Comparative Politics*, 31(2), 167–86.

Ostrom, E. (2005). *Understanding Institutional Diversity*. Princeton, NJ: Princeton University Press.

Peake, G., and Forsyth, M. (2022). Street-level bureaucrats in a relational state: The case of Bougainville. *Public Administration and Development*, 42(1), 12–21. https://doi.org/10.1002/pad.1911

Peeters, R., and Campos, S.A. (2022). Street-level bureaucracy in weak state institutions: A systematic review of the literature. *International Review of Administrative Sciences*. https://doi.org/10.1177/00208523221103196

Peeters, R., and Dussauge Laguna, M.I. (2021). Acting out or playing along: A typology of citizens' low trust responses to public organizations. *Governance*, 34(4), 965–81. https://doi.org/10.1111/gove.12631

Peeters, R., and Nieto Morales, F. (eds) (2020). *La máquina de la desigualdad: Una exploración de los costos y las causas de las burocracias de baja confianza*. Ciudad de México: CIDE & Colegio de México.

Peeters, R., Gofen, A., and Meza, O. (2020). Gaming the system: Responses to dissatisfaction with public services beyond exit and voice. *Public Administration*, 98(4), 824–39.

Pepinsky, T.B., Pierskalla, J.H., and Sacks, A. (2017). Bureaucracy and service delivery. *Annual Review of Political Science,* 20, 249–68.

Perelmiter, L. (2016). *Burocracia plebeya: la trastienda de la asistencia social en el Estado argentino.* Buenos Aires, Argentina: UNSAM.

Ramani, S., Gilson, L., Sivakami, M., and Gawde, N. (2020). Sometimes resigned, sometimes conflicted, and mostly risk averse: Primary care doctors in India as street level bureaucrats. *International Journal of Health Policy and Management,* 1. https://doi.org/10.34172/ijhpm.2020.206

Rawls, J. (1971). *A Theory of Justice.* Cambridge: Harvard University Press.

Rothstein, B. (2013). Corruption and social trust: Why the fish rots from the head down. *Social Research: An International Quarterly,* 80, 1009–32.

Sandfort, J.R. (2000). Moving beyond discretion and outcomes: Examining public management from the front lines of the welfare system. *Journal of Public Administration Research and Theory,* 10(4), 729–56.

Schmoll, M. (2021). Weak street-level enforcement of tax laws: The role of tax collectors' persistent but broken public service expectations. *The Journal of Development Studies,* 57(2), 209–25. https://doi.org/10.1080/00220388.2020.1779928

Scott, W.R. (2008). *Institutions and Organizations. Ideas and Interests.* Thousand Oaks: Sage.

Siddiki, S., Weible, C.M., Basurto, X., and Calanni, J. (2011). Dissecting policy designs: An application of the institutional grammar tool. *Policy Studies Journal,* 39(1), 79–103.

Smith-Oka, V. (2013). Managing labor and delivery among impoverished populations in Mexico: Cervical examinations as bureaucratic practice. *American Anthropologist,* 115(4), 595–607. https://doi.org/10.1111/aman.12046

Soifer, H.D. (2015). *State Building in Latin America.* Cambridge: Cambridge University Press.

Sundström, A. (2016). Violence and the costs of honesty: Rethinking bureaucrats' choices to take bribes. *Public Administration,* 94(3), 593–608.

Thomann, E. (2015). Is output performance all about the resources? A fuzzy-set qualitative comparative analysis of street-level bureaucrats in Switzerland. *Public Administration,* 93(1), 177–94.

Tummers, L.L., Bekkers, V., Vink, E., and Musheno, M. (2015). Coping during public service delivery: A Conceptualization and systematic review of the literature. *Journal of Public Administration Research and Theory,* 25(4), 1099–126.

Usman, M., Ali, M., Mughal, F., and Agyemang-Mintah, P. (2021). Policy alienation and street-level bureaucrats' psychological wellbeing: The mediating role of alienative commitment. *Journal of Public Administration Research and Theory,* 31(2), 278–94.

Walker, L., and Gilson, L. (2004). 'We are bitter but we are satisfied': Nurses as street-level bureaucrats in South Africa. *Social Science & Medicine*, 59(6), 1251–61.

Weber, M. (1922). *Economy and Society*. Berkeley: University of California Press.

Wilson, W. (1887). The study of administration. *Political Science Quarterly*, 2(2), 197–222.

Zacka, B. (2017). *When the State Meets the Street: Public Service and Moral Agency*. Cambridge, MA: Belknap Press.

PART I

Coping with institutional weakness

2

Weak but not broken: resilience by repair in the times of COVID-19

Ayesha Masood

Introduction

In the past few decades, multiple global crises and disasters, both manmade and natural, have exposed the fragility of public delivery systems. Researchers have pointed to the role of excessive administrative burden, long-term scarcity of resources, and efficiency focused reforms in public management in creating a lack of slack in public service delivery systems (Radnor and Osborne, 2013; Masou, 2017). Similarly, challenges in recovery after crisis, and returning services to pre-crisis status, has increased the interest in resilience: the ability of public services to withstand, adapt, and transform in response to crisis situations (Linnenluecke and Griffiths, 2010).

The concept of resilience helps academics and practitioners understand and design public management systems for complex, unpredictable, and volatile situations. Unlike traditional values of efficiency and effectiveness, resilience foregrounds adaptability and robustness in public delivery systems (Boin and Lodge, 2016). More importantly, instead of a classical Weberian bureaucracy with hierarchical structure and strict role definitions, research on resilience highlights collaborative cross-linkages, where iterative trial and error policy experiments result in local and experiential bodies of knowledge and social learning within a policy system (Nicholls and Murdock, 2011). Incorporating resilience thinking in Public Administration research has been especially helpful in understanding how governance systems are able to bounce back from crises (Meek and Marshall, 2018), improving disaster and crisis management (Boin and Lodge 2016; Kapucu and Hu 2016), and conservation of common pool resources like climate and fisheries (Toonen, 2010; Mansbridge, 2014; Carlisle and Gruby, 2019).

However, there are still important gaps in the conceptualisation of resilience in the PA literature. First, most previous research conceptualises resilience as a top-down phenomenon, analysing it at the organisational or governance level (Duit, 2016). Most research, therefore, focuses on how resilient policies, organisations, or institutions can be designed (Boin and Lodge, 2016), how public service delivery can be maintained to improve social resilience through proper disaster management (Bourgon, 2009), or on the work of high reliability organisations (Boin and Van Eaten, 2013). However, the actual work of crisis management – recognising an event as an impending crisis, making sense of resources and expectations, and adoption to mitigate its effects – takes place at the street level (Brodkin, 2021). Despite this, emergence of resilience at the local level through the everyday, microlevel processes of understanding, adapting, and creativity in response to ongoing crises is relatively understudied. As a result, we have limited understanding of the role of individual bureaucrats in managing crises as they make sense of and deal with the uncertainty and scarcity in their day-to-day work. Similarly, how organisations become resilient through these micro-level practices, is relatively less examined.

Second, due to this top-down approach, crisis management is often considered as separate from the everyday work of public service providers. Especially significant in this regard is the role of SLBs who not only modify and translate policies to fit different contexts but also respond to crisis situations by influencing policies as street level policy entrepreneurs (Lipsky, 2010; Brodkin, 2021; Gofen and Lotta, 2021). However, the role of street level bureaucracy in creating resilience through their discretion, entrepreneurship, and innovation is not fully understood.

Finally, and perhaps most importantly in the context of this book, most research on resilience comes from countries where institutions and societies are often resource rich and developed. Consequently, a crisis or disaster is usually operationalised as a fast-moving, usually unprecedented process or event that overwhelms an organisation or institution's operational capacity. However, I suggest that this conceptualisation disregards what I call 'slow-moving' disasters: a situation where breakdown of processes and lack of adequate resources is not a one-off or sudden event, but an everyday occurrence and accepted norm in everyday work. I further argue that capacities and knowledge required to deal with crises develop differently in countries with weak institutional systems. However, we have limited understanding of how countries with weak institutions that are often struggling with political instability, institutional fragility, and prolonged austerity, respond to slow- and fast-moving disasters.

To understand the emergence of resilience at the micro level, I draw on the theory of repair and maintenance to build a typology of creative and innovative activities by SLBs to overcome scarcity and breakdown to maintain public service delivery during crisis situations. Based on the ethnographic data of frontline healthcare professionals in Punjab, Pakistan, my research suggests that SLBs develop creative capacities, pathways, and knowledge in their everyday work that allows them to understand the resource limitations and slack in the service delivery system. During the time of the COVID-19 epidemic, they used these capacities to create resilience by repairing policies in different ways. Through policy repair, SLBs lead the recovery and adaptation of public service delivery to the rapidly changing demands during times of crises, even before the formal policy processes are able to respond. SLBs also build collaborative and emergent networks across and within professional groups and with the citizens to respond to various aspects of policy breakdown. This research underscores the importance of SLBs' work in the emergence of resilience especially in resource scarce economies and weak institutional systems.

Street-level bureaucracy and resilience

Since Wildavsky's (1988) and Hood's (1991) pioneering works, the idea of resilience has captured the imagination of public administration and policy researchers. Broadly defined as the ability of a system to handle and bounce back after external shocks (Boin and van Eaten, 2013), resilience seems the ideal policy strategy in an increasingly volatile and unstable world marred by fiscal austerity, political fragmentation, institutional instability, and ever-present threat of ecological collapse. Despite its increasing relevance, there are important limitations in how resilience thinking can be applied in public administration praxis. First and foremost, most of this research takes a macro level, complex adaptive systems-based perspective to resilience. With few exceptions, resilience is conceptualised as a property of large-scale governance systems, where the unit of analysis is the whole system (Duit, 2016) or the whole organisation (Brodkin, 2021). While this has been useful in highlighting adaptation and recovery especially in the context of crisis and disaster management studies (Comfort et al, 2010; Drennan et al 2014; Saja et al, 2019), we have limited understanding of how resilience looks like at the micro level, how resilience emerges as a property of sociotechnical systems through the activities of individual actors, and how these individual practices of adapting and transforming in response to crises affect organisational and societal resilience.

An important aspect of resilience in public bureaucracies, which has not been fully explored in previous research, is through the activities of SLBs – 'public service workers who interact directly with citizens in the course of their jobs, and who have substantial discretion in ... their work' (Lipsky, 2010, 3). There are multiple reasons why understanding the work of street-level bureaucracy is important for theorising resilience of public organisations. First, formal policy designs, including those for resilience, cannot account for the complexity of human conditions and infinite variations in implementation contexts. One of the defining features of SLBs, therefore, is their discretion to interpret and translate vague or conflicting policy directives to fit real-life situations. Because of this discretion, SLBs are often considered de facto policy makers (Lipsky, 2010). Importantly,

SLBs already use their discretion to cope with their routine stressful work conditions (Tummers and Rocco, 2015). They also deal with resource constraints, uncertain work demands and high workloads (Lipsky, 2010). They can bend, subvert or even outright thwart policy directives if a strict reliance on rules is seen to be harmful for the interests of clients and/or co-workers (Evans, 2016). As this research suggests, understanding the creative and improvisational aspect of SLBs' work can be an important lens to understand emergent responses to crisis situations.

Research on COVID-19 has highlighted the role of SLBs in crisis management especially through innovation, adaptation, and entrepreneurship during implementation. Importantly, research indicates the importance of situational knowledge of SLBs in fast moving policy cycles during crises where rapid exchange of information between SLBs and policy makers improved how service delivery systems coped with ever-changing situations (Gofen and Lotta, 2021).

Perhaps the most important omission in the research on the role of SLBs in resilience is that with few exceptions, it primarily focuses on crisis response in developed economies with well-developed and strong institutional systems. These countries usually have pre-defined processes and organisational capacities that it can trigger in response to an external or internal shock. These processes allow disaster relief organisations and frontline public service organisations to mount a coordinated response to crisis situations. Only when the uncertainty and resource scarcity increased to an unprecedented level, for example during COVID-19, SLBs had to engage in improvisation (Gofen et al, 2021). Even in these cases, the degree of improvisation and entrepreneurship (compared to resistance by quitting or voicing dissent) was determined by loyalty, organisational support, and available resources. Thus, street-level entrepreneurship during crisis situations in strong institutional systems was triggered and delimited by the contours of the crisis and the state response.

This situation is a sharp contrast to weak institutional systems, common in developing economies of the Global South (Jessop, 2012). Research suggests that people living in areas with weak institutional systems are often living in informal urban morphologies without adequate infrastructure support (Quesada-Román, 2022). It means that they are more likely to experience natural and man-made disasters. More importantly, in weak institutional systems, the mismatch between supply and demand is not just a feature of disasters and crises, it is a *common everyday occurrence*. Breakdowns resulting from inadequate or untrained personnel, shortage of material resources and breakdown of infrastructure is so common that frontline workers often develop alternate processes and role expectations that are attuned to the operational realities of ever-present resource scarcity. Indeed, I suggest that everyday reality of public management in such systems can be considered a slow-moving disaster, where the effects unfold in complex pathways over long periods of time. Unlike crises and disasters that have a sudden onset, in weak institutional systems, practitioners have already developed organisational capacities, collaborative networks, and informal processes, which accounts for breakdown and contingencies, precisely because they are already and always dealing with a slow-moving disaster. I suggest that because of this particular set of circumstances, public service delivery systems in weak institutional economies develop a special type of everyday resilience mediated primarily through the repair and maintenance capabilities of street-level bureaucracy.

Research suggests that, in the absence of a formal institutionalised response to crises, communities in weak institutional systems develop their own localised bodies of knowledge, processes, and informal organisations to recognise and respond to crisis situations (Carmin et al, 2012). However, usually in cases of large-scale disasters, external donor agencies and policy makers tend to ignore the knowledge and capacities of the local communities and practitioners (Jessop, 2012). Again, this is in sharp contrast to street-level entrepreneurship in the bureaucracies of strong institutional systems, where SLBs often participate in the rapidly updating policies during crisis response (Gofen et al, 2021). In weak institutional states, however, the innovative and improvisational capacity is premised on a fundamentally different relationship with state. Here SLBs engage in improvisation not because they expect such innovations to be part of formal policies but because they know that the state will not be able to respond in time or support them. SLBs in strong states improvise because they are participants and agents of the state; SLBs in weak states improvise because they are alienated. Significantly, this knowledge of SLB–state relationship comes from the experience of long-term neglect and institutional fragility in such states. Resilience during crisis management in weak institutional states is thus primarily through the innovative, improvisation, and jugaad ('hack') capacities of SLBs.

Repair and maintenance

To understand this type of bottom-up micro level resilience through street level bureaucracy, I build on the theory of maintenance and repair. Repair highlights the role of routine activities in maintaining and repairing order in sociotechnical systems (Graham and Thrift, 2007; Henke, 2019). A fundamental assumption of this research is 'the broken world thinking': unlike classical crisis management perspectives, research on repair assumes that entropy, erosion, and breakdown are inherent parts of social systems, not one-off events (Jackson, 2014). Importantly, breakdowns and crises have world-revealing properties: they reveal the organisation and hidden logics of the system. Research on repair often takes disruptions and breakdowns as its starting point, instead of innovation and growth (Vinsel and Russell, 2016). Moreover, repair seeks to draw attention to the resilience, creativity, and the amount of work that goes on in continuously maintaining and restoring social systems in a dynamic equilibrium against the forces of decay (Graham and Thrift, 2007). This research has been especially useful in highlighting the often-invisible work that goes on in maintaining the social and technical infrastructure of society. In urban studies, a focus on repair has highlighted how cities bounce back from crisis and are able to thrive despite the pervasive misanthropy and decay. It has further highlighted how divestment from repair and maintenance, often due to policies geared towards efficiency or austerity, has contributed to brittleness in social systems (Vinsel and Russell, 2016).

Research points to three fundamental dimensions of repair (Graham and Thrift, 2007; Hall and Smith, 2015): first, repair is improvised. Repair work is similar to bricolage, working creatively with the available materials to solve immediate problems. However, unlike bricolage (which is often geared towards innovation), repair uses creativity to restore the status quo. Similarly, repair can precede breakdowns: those involved in repair are not just dealing with the immediate aftermath of emergent problems, they can also anticipate how and when systems in which they operate can malfunction. Due to their position, they find it imperative to do something, often without formal procedural changes and without adequate resources. Second, repair requires craft (technè): a tacit and practical knowledge of how systems work. Those involved in repair often have access to localised knowledge, learned and acquired through repetitive interaction and continuous tinkering with the system and often not encoded in formal organisational memory. Finally, perhaps the most important dimension of repair is that it is motivated by care and kindness. Those involved in repair often feel an ethical and moral responsibility to safeguard people against the decay of their present and future capabilities.

Methods and data collection

Research context

The data presented here was collected through an ongoing research project on the experiences of SLBs in the healthcare sector of Pakistan, focusing on the recent changes in health management in Punjab. Specifically, I want to understand how SLBs cope with the institutional fragility, resource scarcity, and changing work arrangements resulting from austerity based and efficiency driven policies. However, during the course of research, the COVID-19 crisis struck Pakistan in February 2020, and this provided me with a perfect opportunity to understand how frontline bureaucracies, especially those which are closely involved with crisis response (like healthcare in the case of COVID-19), deal with the emergent and rapidly changing crisis situations.

Even before the pandemic struck, Punjab's health sector was facing all the systemic strains characteristic of weak state institutions. For the past four decades, Punjab had invested less than 10 per cent of its annual budget for health. This lack of investment was exacerbated by the austerity-based policies adopted by the federal and provincial governments since June 2019 as a requirement for the bailout deal with the International Monetary Fund (IMF). As part of these austerity-based and efficiency-driven policies, the Punjab government had also implemented a policy of re-organisation of public health institutions as autonomous businesses. This act (called the Medical Institutions Act or MTI for short) effectively deprived all healthcare professionals working in public sector tertiary care hospitals of their job security, healthcare benefits, and housing allowances. Additionally, since 2010, healthcare professionals, especially young physicians, have started a political movement, Young Doctors Association (YDA), for better working conditions and against the policy reforms in the health sector. Due to multiple strikes, protests, and violent standoffs between health workers and police, working relations between the top tiers of bureaucracy and the frontline workers were already strained. This macro-level environment of austerity and political instability allowed us to understand how public organisations are able to respond to crisis situations despite their fragility.

Data collection and analysis

During this research, I interviewed 58 frontline healthcare professionals working in 10 different public healthcare facilities in Lahore, Punjab. Details of all the participants are given in Table 2.1. The participants were selected based on purposive sampling to include SLBs from different tiers of healthcare (doctors, nurses, and paramedical staff), different levels of organisations (primary, secondary, and tertiary care), and different types of medical care (emergent and routine, indoor and outdoor). It is important to note here how SLBs in healthcare compare with other SLBs. I had already conducted detailed face-to-face interviews with these participants before the COVID-19 crisis started. However, after February 2020, I conducted interviews through different online mediums to respect the social distancing guidelines. In these interviews, I asked the participants how they were dealing with various aspects of the COVID-19 pandemic at their workplace, how their work routines were changing, and how they were coping with the shortages of resources essential for their work. The interviews lasted an average of 45 minutes and one or two follow-up interviews were conducted with all participants. Apart from the interviews, I also participated in different online communities and support groups for healthcare professionals to understand how SLBs collaborate and cooperate in response to emergent crises. Names have been changed to protect the privacy of participants.

Table 2.1: Characteristics of the participant street-level bureaucrats

Gender	
Male	21
Female	37
Profession	
Doctors	22
Nursing staff	21
Paramedical Staff	15
Healthcare organisation	
Primary care	14
Secondary care	12
Tertiary and specialised care	32

The data from interviews and online participation were analysed iteratively through thematic analysis. I read all the texts to identify patterns and typologies of responses to the COVID-19 crisis. These thematic codes were then compared and contrasted across and within different interviews to build a typology of repair that informs the discussion in the next section.

Policy repair in crisis situations

Drawing on the theory of repair and maintenance, I suggest that SLBs deal with breakdown and crisis situations by doing policy repair. Most, if not all, crisis situations manifest at the frontlines through policy breakdown. Policy breakdown happens in situations where there is a public service gap: there is a shortage of resources required by the frontline workers to maintain public service delivery. It also happens when there is a policy vacuum. Frontline workers are dealing with an unprecedented situation where little or no formal guidelines or policies exist. In both conditions SLBs must find ways to keep the bureaucratic system running and to maintain the public service delivery by making do with existing resources or by creating improvised processes and rules. The following section details the interconnected and overlapping strategies used by SLBs to repair gaps in public service delivery in their organisations (summarised in Table 2.2).

Material repair

Perhaps the most important and immediate problem faced by Pakistani doctors was a shortage of necessary equipment, which ranged from limited supply of infrared thermometers and test kits for screening, shortage of beds

Table 2.2: Strategies for public service gap repairing

Types	Definition	Exemplars
Material repair	Repair, reconstruction, reuse, and repurposing of material resources	Local stockpiles of equipment Off label and less than optimal reuse of medical supplies
Process repair	Creation of new protocols Changing and tweaking old processes to fix organisational context	Changing admission process to accommodate isolation guidelines New protocols for patients in intensive care unit or in allied medical and surgical wards
Personnel repair	Acquisition of new roles and professional capabilities	Taking over work demand from absent colleagues Learning new skills for unprecedented situations
Social repair	Maintenance of relations through kindness	Caring for and about colleagues and patients Providing emotional support

and hospital space for isolation, various medical equipment like ventilators and oxygen required for serious patients, and protective equipment and masks for healthcare workers. During my research, before the COVID-19 pandemic started, I had noticed that public sector hospitals in Pakistan are routinely short of any protective equipment required by the doctors; many doctors reported buying gloves and masks used in routine consultations and medical procedures on their own. During the pandemic, the frontline workers often used the same capabilities to respond to this novel situation.

It is interesting to note that health workers, especially doctors, started to respond to the impending COVID-19 crisis very early, some even before it officially reached Pakistan. Many of the participants noted that they had stockpiled some protective equipment like masks for collective use in their departments. Immediately after the first few COVID-19 cases were reported in Pakistan, most of the protective equipment either became extremely expensive or went out of stock in the market. However, many doctors had come up with some interesting ways to work around it. Zahid, a medical officer in a large tertiary care hospital, noted that all doctors in his department had pooled their money to buy some face masks and gloves, which they would not have been able to afford individually. The existing supplies were then rationed and reused to make them last longer. Amir, working in a surgical department, similarly explained the reasoning behind this proactive action:

'We knew that it would take very long for the government to respond, if at all. And it was the right decision in hindsight, even months after the pandemic started we still don't have any masks or PPE [provided by the government], and the only triage centre with temperature scanners is at the hospital entrance.'

These narratives indicate that the doctors often relied on their instincts developed by working in constant scarcity and breakdown to anticipate the extent of the crisis. These examples also indicate that, because of experiential knowledge of working in weak institutional systems, SLBs realised that the formal response to this crisis by the state will take some time, and therefore they needed to step in early to prevent escalation of the crisis.

Examples of using this contextual and implicit craft of repair (technè) to supplant material shortages were commonplace. Nurses often collected used protective clothing and sterilised them for reuse. Similarly, they repurposed plastic raincoats and large garbage bags for personal protective equipments (PPEs). Nearly all doctors that I interviewed reported wearing ordinary cloth masks (sometimes sewn by themselves or their family members) over the N95 masks to prevent contamination and to make them last longer. It should be noted here that these artisanal and homemade masks did not provide the protection needed by the frontline staff, but in crowded hospitals where there was little to no protection or screening available, these little fixes went a long way. This improvisation was already such an important part of the routine work of SLBs that they had specific words to describe such activities. Many doctors referred to this work as jugaad (frugal and transient solutions to local problems), guzara (to make do), kam chalao (keep it working), and time pass (transient). Similarly, another commonly used phrase, idhar udhar se (from here and there), emphasised that the materials used in this improvisation were often junk lying around which was used in ingenious ways by the frontline staff.

Working around material shortages also required SLBs to build on their ties with the community and other related professional groups. For example, healthcare workers not only donated money themselves but also actively sought donations from their family and friends to cover for the equipment shortages. One doctor, using personal connections on social media, collected donations from friends and family, found a supplier in China to buy protective gear, and organised volunteers to distribute them across various hospitals. This emergent and collaborative organising of SLBs and citizens was a common feature of this repair activity.

Process repair

Another important dimension of repair was the need to change or create new procedures within hospitals to implement various guidelines set by the state. In the initial stages of pandemic, the Punjab government adopted a policy of 'test, track, quarantine' instead of imposing a complete lockdown, which presented multiple implementation challenges for SLBs. Public hospitals had limited physical infrastructure to establish effective quarantine facilities. Many hospitals were housed in relatively old buildings, with large communal wards where such considerations were not possible given the building design. Public hospitals often did not have closed ventilation systems, dedicated quarantine wards, or decontamination facilities. It was, therefore, up to the SLBs to rearrange and repurpose available structures to create, if not ideal, some workable solutions to such constraints. In nearly all hospitals, this led to very different arrangements. In many departments, doctors reported creating makeshift barriers through plastic wrap or screens and repurposing meeting rooms and offices to create the required space. In one hospital, doctors repurposed a cardiology ward by putting up screens to make it an isolation unit.

Moreover, doctors immediately realised that within Pakistan's social arrangements, effective contact tracing will be a next to impossible task. Per standard procedure, doctors were expected to wait until a positive COVID-19 test to start isolation, contact tracing, and treatment. However, doctors realised that extensive community transmission of the virus had already started, even though the state was reluctant to admit it. Therefore, they tweaked official protocols to rely on clinical symptoms, history, and their clinical judgment. This was especially useful in the later stages of the pandemic when there was a shortage of testing kits. This capacity to foresee the breakdown allowed doctors to actually anticipate some of the problems with existing policies and forge alternative solutions. Doctors, for example, soon realised that public facilities were extremely limited to allow isolation, and hospitals would quickly run out of space. To work around this, they started educating their people to self-isolate and self-treat at home against government policy. Sidrah, an assistant professor, noted that she told the patients that "there is no point in coming to hospital if you are not very sick. Staying at home where you can at least have access to food and water is the best idea right now". My patients were worried that they were not getting tested. She told them that "testing is not going to add any new information. We already know they are sick because of their symptoms. So, they should just stay home".

To further facilitate this process of patient screening and education, SLBs often created their own alternate guidelines and treatment regimens, using guidelines from more developed countries. They educated patients to buy their own medical equipment and provided basic training on tracking and managing their symptoms at home. Notably, the Punjab government also changed its official policy in May to home-quarantine most COVID-19 cases instead of admitting them to hospitals. Hence, the local policy solution devised by many frontline health workers ended up informing formal changes in public policy.

Again, nearly all of these repairs in the policy process required extensive collaboration and sharing. In many cases such collaborative networks of SLBs existed across different countries, allowing SLBs to share information and policy learning across different institutional contexts. Many of my participants had friends and former co-workers who had emigrated to other countries, and they used this network for active policy transfer at a micro level. In many cases, this collaborative policy repair existed in spaces which were not the priority for the state, for example, doctors took the initiative to create and adopt treatment and isolation protocols for allied medical and surgical fields where COVID-19 was a secondary issue.

Personnel repair

Another important problem in Pakistan's healthcare system is chronic shortage of healthcare professionals, especially the nursing staff. During the COVID-19 pandemic, increasing infection rate among the healthcare professionals worsened this deficiency. Equally important was the lack of trained staff for critical and intensive care required for managing COVID-19 patients. The frontline healthcare workers had to find ways to make up for this personnel scarcity. Shams, a medical officer working in a small primary healthcare facility, arranged classes on personal safety for his staff including nurses, lady health workers, and polio vaccinators. In at least two public hospitals, doctors who had training in intensive care started classes for peers for this purpose. Some other participants enrolled in online courses hosted by the World Health Organization (WHO) for management of COVID-19 patients. It is important to note that in most cases this training was managed and organised by the frontline doctors themselves with no help from the bureaucratic leadership of the health department.

In some ways, this aspect of repair was close to what Weick (1993) described as belonging to a virtual role system where people have a shared vision of risk and responsibilities and fill in the roles of their absent colleagues. However, importantly, repairing for personnel shortages went beyond simply filling-in for others. It required actively acquiring and disseminating new skills that were required by the unprecedented nature and unpredictability of the COVID-19 crisis. It also involved dealing with the moral and ethical consequences of working or not working in potentially life-threatening situations and actively engaging in harm reduction, not just for themselves but for citizens as well. Perhaps most significant in this regard was the way healthcare professionals took up multiple roles outside their organisations. Many of them advised, monitored, and treated patients on social media platforms or in their homes after their regular duties which were already quite demanding. This care was mostly accorded to the patients who were either self-isolating at home or who were not COVID-19 patients but were unable to go to hospitals to receive regular care. This informal unpaid work was especially important in maintaining service delivery at an acceptable level in a healthcare system which was already overburdened.

Social repair

Perhaps the most important component of repair work by frontline workers of health which I observed in the context of the COVID-19 pandemic, was social repair (Hall and Smith, 2015): safeguarding human capabilities through kindness and care. All of the participants reported feeling various negative emotions like stress, apprehension, fear, and depression. Pandemic led to unforeseen and unexpected work life conflicts for all SLBs, especially female doctors and nurses. As the majority of doctors lived in extended families, sharing homes with elderly patients, small children, and other family members, they were apprehensive that they were risking their families by continuing to work. Many of the participants working in intensive care units described harrowing stories of patients collapsing and their desperation or inability to help. Although in many developed countries, support mechanisms emerged to prevent stress in frontline healthcare professionals, frontline healthcare professionals in Pakistan worked on their own to create emotional support systems to deal with stress and grief.

Especially important in this regard is the role of social media, which allowed SLBs to maintain relationships and provide emotional support to peers. Zehra, an anaesthesiologist, for example, mentioned that both she and her husband were working with COVID-19 patients. She shared how they had discussed the possibility of death with their children, made their wills, and talked about the ongoing projects that they would like to finish. Shahid, another medical resident, noted that he started a weekly Zoom call with his class fellows in Pakistan and abroad. These weekly meetings allowed them to compare notes on their work, share local solutions, and check on each other's well-being. Through these interactions, doctors, and nurses working on the frontlines of the pandemic response were able to emotionally cope (at least to an extent) with the ongoing crisis.

These conversations were especially important for the female participants, many of whom were living in multi-generational joint families and were finding it difficult to translate social distancing to culturally appropriate practices. More importantly, by sharing their stories of similar struggles, participants were able to not only come up with local culturally specific solutions but also empathise with each other. The most saddening aspect of this repair was providing end-of-life care. Many of the participants noted that the majority of the patients in Pakistan who required ventilation did not survive. Due to this, doctors often had to prepare and educate patients for the possibility of death. Many of the participants described how they arranged patients to meet their family members or talk to them on phone calls before they were taken to intensive care. Many doctors also described providing religious rites because patients felt it was important to them.

An important aspect of this social repair was undoing the damage done by misinformation and rumours spread through social media sites. Participants described patients who hid their symptoms and travel history, and refused treatment because they feared that the COVID-19 was a global conspiracy. Many participants described aggressive behaviour and physical assaults from the patients or their attendants. Because of this, it was often an uphill task for doctors to inform the patients about the urgency of the crisis, to dispel various rumours, and to educate them about following social distancing guidelines.

Conclusion

Based on these narratives of policy repair given earlier, I suggest that the creative and improvised responses of SLBs to unpredictable and emergent demands of crisis situations at the frontlines is critical in understanding how public organisations are able to maintain their service delivery in crisis situations.

This work has multiple theoretical and practical implications for our understanding of SLBs and resilience. First, the concept of repair provides a conceptual framework to integrate creative and dynamic responses by frontline workers to multiple types of scarcity experienced during crisis situations. Importantly, this conceptual framework focuses on the ordinary, day-to-day, and routine work practices at organisational frontlines, which are often ignored in policy designs focused on resilience. Understanding resilience as a bottom-up phenomenon through street level bureaucrats' policy repair can bridge the disconnect in resilience research between formal policy design and its implementation challenges. Second, this data further emphasises the unique importance of SLBs in dealing with crisis situations, especially in weak institutional states. As this research shows, SLBs' knowledge of local processes and their capacity to improvise in unexpected situations are the transformative capabilities that enable public organisations to maintain their service delivery during times of crisis. Importantly, SLBs are in a position where they are often dealing with the immediate effects of social problems on the citizens. Thus, they have a unique vantage point of crisis situations and are able to adopt the strategies that they think are most beneficial for the citizens, regardless of formal policies.

Third, this data also indicates how SLBs create new collaborative networks or use their friendship networks for directed, goal-oriented problem solving. Importantly, SLBs' position as the frontline workers allows them to mobilise support from citizens and other professional groups as well. In doing so, the SLBs mobilise geographical, cultural, political, and social solidarities to create the collective narrative of an imagined community organised to solve emergent problems. In this way, this research extends the research on emergent networks in emergency response (Kapucu and Hu, 2016) to include personnel networks of SLBs as well as creative use of social media applications to mobilise and build social capital.

Finally, an important question in this regard is why, in this particular case, SLBs responded by taking control of the crisis situation early on, instead of quitting, voice their grievances, or even using corrupt means to further their private interest as is common in other weak institutional contexts. The answer lies partly in the particular moment of Punjab's healthcare system at which the pandemic happened. The SLBs, especially junior doctors and nurses, were already locked in a long political struggle with the government. During this time, they had developed strong activist organisations and networks, which allowed them to mobilise and coordinate early. Significantly, as the data indicates, doctors had long-term, experiential, and institutional knowledge of managing the frontline without the help or support from the state. In this context, their professional loyalty was to the patients (and not the state). Thus, resistance to the state took the form of staying and working in hazardous conditions, rather than quitting. More importantly, informal privatisation of services in weak states occurs because of an extant market gap in the supply of bureaucratic knowledge or services. This did not happen in this case, because in Pakistan a private healthcare system was already present. This does not mean that artificial shortages of medical equipment and supplies due to statewide corruption did not occur; just that doctors at the frontline knew that it would happen and knew how to work around such shortages.

I would also like to acknowledge here that in strong institutional states, it would not be fair to compare healthcare professionals with other SLBs, as they enjoy a great degree of discretion due to their professional norms. However, I would argue that in weak states and in this context specifically, doctors and allied health staff of public hospitals were working in chronically resource scare conditions, which were stretched beyond limits during COVID-19. However, the impact of professionalisation, organisational norms, and ethics on the innovation of SLBs is an open question that should be explored further.

This work also offers valuable practical insights for policy makers and public managers. Too often, the policy decisions during crisis management are taken without involving the frontline workers entrusted with the task of implementing them. As I have mentioned throughout this chapter, frontline workers have first-hand knowledge of not only the local constraints faced by them but also quick, cost-effective, and context-specific solutions to such constraints. It is precisely the people with this knowledge of local solutions that are often not present in routine and/or emergency policy and planning meetings. Policy makers removed from the frontlines often end up looking at other policy contexts and end up choosing more expensive or seemingly attractive solutions which may or may not work in other contexts. Therefore, it is critical that adequate representation of frontline workers is ensured in such meetings. In addition to devising more agile and responsive policies, doing so will also result in greater ownership of policies at the frontlines, which will also translate into better service delivery and implementation.

References

Barber, S., and Murdock, A. (2017). Innovation in products and services. In A. Murdock (ed), *Private Action for Public Purpose: Examining the Growth of Falck, the World's Largest Rescue Company*. London: Palgrave Macmillan, pp 75–104.

Boin, A., and Lodge, M. (2016). Designing resilient institutions for transboundary crisis management: A time for public administration. *Public Administration*, 94(2), 289–98.

Boin, A., and Van Eeten, M.J. (2013). The resilient organization. *Public Management Review*, 15(3), 429–45.

Bourgon, J. (2009). New directions in public administration: Serving beyond the predictable. *Public Policy and Administration*, 24(3), 309–30.

Brodkin, E.Z. (2021). Street-level organizations at the front lines of crises. *Journal of Comparative Policy Analysis: Research and Practice*, 23(1), 16–29.

Carlisle, K., and Gruby, R.L. (2019). Polycentric systems of governance: A theoretical model for the commons. *Policy Studies Journal*, 47(4), 927–52.

Carmin, J., Anguelovski, I., and Roberts, D. (2012). Urban climate adaptation in the global south: Planning in an emerging policy domain. *Journal of Planning Education and Research*, 32(1), 18–32.

Comfort, L.K., Boin, A., and Demchak, C.C. (2010). Resilience revisited: An action agenda for managing extreme events. In L.K. Comfort, A. Boin and C.C. Demchak (eds), *Designing Resilience: Preparing for Extreme Events*. Pittsburgh: University of Pittsburgh Press, pp 272–84.

Drennan, L.T., McConnell, A., and Stark, A. (2014). *Risk and Crisis Management in the Public Sector*. London: Routledge.

Duit, A. (2016). Resilience thinking: Lessons for public administration. *Public Administration*, 94(2), 364–80.

Evans, T. (2016). *Professional Discretion in Welfare Services: Beyond Street-Level Bureaucracy*. London: Routledge.

Fischbacher-Smith, D., and Fischbacher-Smith, M. (2013). The vulnerability of public spaces: Challenges for UK hospitals under the 'new' terrorist threat. *Public Management Review*, 15(3), 330–43.

Gofen, A., and Lotta, G. (2021). Street-level bureaucrats at the forefront of pandemic response: A comparative perspective. *Journal of Comparative Policy Analysis: Research and Practice*, 23(1), 3–15.

Gofen, A., Lotta, G., and Marchesini da Costa, M. (2021). Working through the fog of a pandemic: Street-level policy entrepreneurship in times of crises. *Public Administration*, 99(3), 484–99.

Graham, S., and Thrift, N. (2007). Out of order: Understanding repair and maintenance. *Theory, Culture & Society*, 24(3), 1–25.

Hall, T., and Smith, R.J. (2015). Care and repair and the politics of urban kindness. *Sociology*, 49(1), 3–18.

Henke, C.R. (2019). Negotiating repair: The infrastructural contexts of practice and power. In I. Strebel, A. Bovit, and P. Sormani (eds), *Repair work ethnographies*. Singapore: Palgrave Macmillan, pp 255–82.

Hood, C. (1991). A public management for all seasons? *Public Administration*, 69(1), 3–19.

Jackson, S.J. (2014). Rethinking repair. In T. Gillespie, P.J. Boczkowski, and K.A. Foot (eds), *Media Technologies: Essays on Communication, Materiality, and Society*. Cambridge, MA: MIT Press, pp 221–39.

Jessop, B. (2012). Economic and ecological crises: Green new deals and no-growth economies. *Development*, 55(1), 17–24.

Kapucu, N., and Hu, Q. (2016). Understanding multiplexity of collaborative emergency management networks. *The American Review of Public Administration*, 46(4), 399–417.

Linnenluecke, M.K., and Griffiths, A. (2010). Corporate sustainability and organizational culture. *Journal of World Business*, 45(4), 357–66.

Lipsky, M. (2010). *Street-Level Bureaucracy: Dilemmas of the Individual in Public Service*. New York: Russell Sage Foundation.

Mansbridge, J. (2014). The role of the state in governing the commons. *Environmental Science & Policy*, 36, 8–10.

Masou, R. (2017). Behind managerial reforms: The French experience. *Public Money & Management*, 37(7), 485–90.

Meek, J.W., and Marshall, K.S. (2018). Cultivating resiliency through system shock: The Southern California metropolitan water management system as a complex adaptive system. *Public Management Review*, 20(7), 1088–1104.

Nicholls, A., and Murdock, A. (eds) (2011). *Social Innovation: Blurring Boundaries to Reconfigure Markets*. Basingstoke: Palgrave Macmillan.

Quesada-Román, A. (2022). Flood risk index development at the municipal level in Costa Rica: A methodological framework. *Environmental Science & Policy*, 133, 98–106.

Radnor, Z., and Osborne, S.P. (2013). Lean: A failed theory for public services?. *Public Management Review*, 15(2), 265–87.

Saja, A.A., Goonetilleke, A., Teo, M., and Ziyath, A.M. (2019). A critical review of social resilience assessment frameworks in disaster management. *International Journal of Disaster Risk Reduction*, 35, 101096.

Toonen, T. (2010). Resilience in public administration: The work of Elinor and Vincent Ostrom from a public administration perspective. *Public Administration Review*, 70(2), 193–202.

Tummers, L., and Rocco, P. (2015). Serving clients when the server crashes: How frontline workers cope with E-government challenges. *Public Administration Review*, 75(6), 817–27.

Vinsel, L., and Russell, A. (2016). *Hail the Maintainers: Capitalism Excels at Innovation but Is Failing at Maintenance, and for Most Lives It Is Maintenance That Matters More*. London: Aeon.

Weick, K.E. (1993) The collapse of sensemaking in organisations: The Mann Gulch disaster. *Administrative Science Quarterly*, 38(4), 628–52.

Wildavsky, A.B. (1988). *Searching for Safety*. Piscataway: Transaction Publishers.

3

Paternalist street-level bureaucrats and virtuous recipients: the consequences of institutional weakness in a pensions programme in Uganda

Ronan Jacquin

Introduction

Over the past 20 years, cash transfers have become a key instrument for development and poverty reduction. They are based on the simple idea of distributing money directly to poor people, assuming that they know best what is good for them, thus rendering 'the policing, paternalism, and surveillance of the traditional welfare state' (Ferguson, 2015, 156) unnecessary. However, street-level bureaucracies always maintain some degree of discretion and control over policy implementation and regulation practices (Lipsky, 1980). This chapter proposes insights on street-level bureaucracy in weak institutional settings and how it affects the 'two bodies' (Dubois, 2016) of SLBs, focusing on a cash transfer programme called SAGE (Social Assistance Grant for Empowerment) implemented in Uganda since 2010. Pensions were developed since the beginning of the 2000s, with support from international donors, as the flagship of a broader system of social protection in Uganda (Hickey and Bukenya, 2020). In 2022, over 330,000 elderly people received a pension of 25,000 Ugandan shillings (UGX) per month (around 6.5 US dollars) from the government.[1]

In the SAGE programme, SLBs in charge of registering, paying, and monitoring beneficiaries are less often professional agents hired by the programme itself than local civil servants and village chairpersons. They exert a paternalist supervision on recipients to push them towards locally defined norms of virtuous and productive uses of pensions, although the pension is presented as a right with no formal conditionalities. Beneficiaries consequently interpret the pension as a favour rather than a right. They feel bound by a moral debt, which encourages them to comply with paternalist injunctions, not only for fear of sanctions but also in search of material gains, social respectability, and moral affirmation of the self. This chapter explores why paternalism structures relationships between SLBs and recipients within the programme and how it regulates their interactions. Two hypotheses are proposed: first, low organisational and administrative capacities, as the SAGE programme has been progressively shaped as a 'weak institution' because of political reluctance, identification issues, and financial constraints. It did not rely on a professionalised, separate, and autonomous bureaucracy but on pre-existing, local political, and administrative authorities with almost no training. Second, the broader social and political context marked by the political hegemony of the NRM[2] regime. As a result of institutional weakness, the programme is deeply embedded within local norms and structures of leadership and government, where elites' dominance relies, besides patronage and authoritarianism (Tripp, 2010), on paternalism, developmentalism, and 'relationality' (Peake and Forsyth, 2022) with local citizens. Indeed, the Ugandan state is not weak in itself (Fisher, 2014) but rather 'patchy' with 'pockets of effectiveness' (McDonnell, 2017) unequally constructed and distributed (Hickey et al, 2021; Kjær et al, 2021). The policy makers who designed the SAGE programme conceptualised it as an unconditional benefit and a right for elderly citizens, but as a weak institution, it is unable to 'redistribute and refract' (Peeters and Campos, 2022) the usual relationships of power produced by otherwise strong local institutions. Although lopsided and authoritarian relationships based on moral judgements from SLBs towards recipients are usual in welfare programmes (Nisar and Masood, 2020), they are in this case deeply influenced by local social and political dynamics pervading the programme.

The chapter is based on a four months' fieldwork research conducted in 2018–19. Semi-structured interviews were conducted with bureaucrats and development professionals involved in the design of the programme in Kampala, and with local authorities and recipients in Kiboga District, a rural district in central Uganda where the programme has been implemented since its inception in 2010. I also carried out observations in recipients' houses and during payment days, as well as consultation of the archives of the programme's regional centre.

Political reluctance, financial constraints, and the challenge of identification: the making of a weak institution

In this section, I briefly expose the origins of the cash transfers programme in Uganda, showing its institutional weakness comes from low administrative and organisational capacities granted by political authorities resulting in a lack of an autonomous, professionalised bureaucracy. When the SAGE programme started in 2010, poverty reduction and social protection were new policy priorities in Uganda. During colonialism and even after independence in 1962, public authorities traditionally refused to develop specific social policies (Veit et al, 2017), rather focusing on development through commercial agriculture, commodification of land, and development of the labour force and policies like health and education (Ulriksen and Katusiimeh, 2014). Poor, destitute, and elderly people were supposed to be taken care of through 'traditional' solidarities within the extended family and local communities. No formal system of social protection or pensions existed, except for a minority of civil servants and private sector employees (Mubiru and Bukuluki, 2014). This developmentalist agenda and the denial of specific social issues that would require specific public policies was maintained quite consistently by the different governments after independence. Moreover, different political crises led to a decay of the administration which resulted in the 1980s in the impossibility of any meaningful state intervention. The seizing of power by Museveni's National Resistance Movement (NRM) in 1986, although self-presented as a complete disruption from past governments, also built on this agenda to support the objective of overcoming divisions and rebuilding the country after two decades of conflict and civil war. Only at the end of the 1990 did poverty reduction officially become a policy priority. In 1997, the Ugandan government published a Poverty Eradication Action Plan supported by international donors, which would now condition financial support on poverty reduction objectives. But real government priorities initially remained the same: 'education, rural roads, primary health care, water and sanitation as well as modernization of agriculture' (Ulriksen and Katusiimeh, 2014, 4). The Ugandan government lacked political will and was still focused on economic growth and structural transformation rather than poverty reduction (Hickey, 2013).

The government started moving on from the 2000s, under pressure from a coalition of donors such as the World Bank, the United Nations Children's Fund (UNICEF), and the Department for International Development of the United Kingdom (DfID), and representatives of the Ministry of Gender, Labor and Social Development, who advised on the development of social protection, particularly through the implementation of a cash transfers programme (Hickey and Bukenya, 2020). The coalition embarked on a decade-long advocacy campaign against reluctant senior bureaucrats (mainly from the Ministry of Finance) and politicians who saw cash transfers as handouts creating dependency and laziness, a political strategy for vote-buying or favoured infrastructure development over social protection.[3] The coalition reached its goal in June 2010 when the government announced the creation of the SAGE programme, which includes a monthly pension (the Senior Citizens Grant). Reluctances were overcome by focusing on older persons (who were considered as legitimate beneficiaries of public assistance), keeping a modest amount in order not to foster dependency and make recipients richer than the poorest non-recipients, and communicating on the benefits of social protection in terms of economic growth and development. Another key reason that convinced the government to finally start the programme was that it would, at least at the beginning, largely rely on donors' funds. Such a strategic choice enabled the coalition to obtain approval from the government, which, however, remained reluctant to provide funds for the programme at the expense of other budget priorities. Therefore, it relied heavily on international donors: DfID provided the biggest share of the budget (£51.5 million) for the first phase (2010–15), supplemented by Irish Aid (£7 million). The Ugandan government contributed only £1.4 million, through material and technical assistance (Expanding Social Protection, 2016). Government's lack of financial commitment is consistent in the programme: during the second phase (2015–20), donors expressed the will to gradually withdraw from the programme in favour of the government,[4] but against the government's reluctance, they still provided 70 per cent of the budget to ensure the programme's sustainability and adequate funding, the government providing only 30 per cent.[5] Moreover, the eligibility criteria were drastically reduced, from everyone above 65 years old to the hundred oldest persons in each sub-county (which would only represent about 10 per cent of older persons)[6] during the second phase, to every person above 80 years old from 2020 onward. Therefore, the SAGE programme is in a constant state of underfunding, which implies frequent, often extensive delays in the payment of pensions to recipients and prevented the establishment of an autonomous bureaucracy.

Another factor of institutional weakness is the lack of proper identification and information systems for the management of recipients. While the eligibility criterion was until 2015 quite simple (anyone over 65 years old), the administrative staff was confronted with administrative difficulties in the identification and registration of eligible people. SAGE leaders decided not to let people voluntarily register at an open desk but to directly 'target' (according to their own words) and register them, to ensure the rightful distribution of pensions to those who were supposed to receive them.[7] However, until 2015, Uganda lacked a national civil registration file as well as a national identity card. This created uncertainties about the identification of eligible individuals and verification of their age in each village. The SAGE administration therefore had to rely on the 'relational state', especially local authorities such as chairpersons of Local Councils (village chiefs) or Parish Chiefs (local civil servants). The strength of the relational state described by Peake and Forsyth (2022) relies on two factors, which we also encounter in the case of Uganda: first, a wide human infrastructure capable of reaching the population, in the absence of a real, efficient state bureaucracy. Local authorities in Uganda have a deep knowledge of the target population, as they often know residents personally and maintain regular relations with them. They were able to provide a list of eligible persons, identify them spatially (where such and such a person lives, how to get there), and often confirm their identity and age (or know who could testify) when they did not have valid identity papers (voter card, tax receipt, birth certificate, and so on).[8] Second, the moral authority carried by this human infrastructure (fostered by inter-knowledge and reciprocity), in the absence of administrative accountability. Indeed, using this method of interpersonal identification (locally described as 'community registration') was also seen as a solution against risks of fraud and cheating[9] in a contemporary context marked by greater mobility of individuals and a loss (perceived at least) of mutual knowledge and trust in rural areas (Brisset-Foucault, 2021a).

Such recurring budget constraints (fuelled by political reluctance) and identification issues explain the impossibility of building a separate, autonomous, and professional delivering administration and the centrality of local authorities in the implementation process. The SAGE programme was initially a pilot programme deployed in only 14 districts in 2010–15, with an office in each district, working in cooperation with local authorities, particularly through 'district SAGE committees', which included members of the local government as well as SAGE staff (Angucia and Katusiimeh, 2015, 12). After 2015, 40 new districts were included in the programme, and the SAGE administration moreover had to prepare the expansion of the programme to the entire country, initiated in 2020. Local offices were no longer located in each district, but at the level of regions, grouping from four to seven districts each. This change in scale also meant a greater involvement of lower local authorities, particularly chairpersons and Parish Chiefs.[10] Prior to 2015, the SAGE staff stationed in each district was more directly involved in implementation activities, while after 2015, they retreated to a more supervisory role and delegated them to local authorities. Local authorities thus function as SLBs for the programme and conduct a multitude of tasks (establishing lists of eligible people and verifying identities, registering applicants, organising payment sessions, and mobilising recipients, monitoring them, and writing reports, and so on), especially dealing with interactions with recipients. On the contrary, the SAGE staff (composed of operations officers, a monitoring and evaluation officer, an IT officer, an administrative officer) weakly supervises them and mainly takes care of the technical work. Thus, for recipients, the faces of the programme are not SAGE agents themselves but the local authorities they know and engage with on a regular basis, embedding pensions within the local political structures and social networks. As a result of institutional weakness, the delivery of pensions is not insulated from a social context marked by inequalities. Thus, paternalism became a key feature in the relations and interactions between recipients and SLBs in the programme.

Local authorities as street-level bureaucrats: sociological profiles, motives, and attitudes towards recipients

Institutional weakness also comes from a social context marked by inequalities, as paternalism has become a key feature in the relations and interactions between recipients and SLBs in the programme. Paternalism is defined as 'an active form of subordination', which seeks 'to replace the reasoning or will of a subordinate group of people with that of a dominant group ... justified with the claim that it lies in the best interests of the subordinate group' (Phillips, 2018, 1). Moral, political, and emotional judgements are usual in the work and decisions of SLBs (Zacka, 2017). However, in this case the strength of paternalism is not a specific feature of the programme but is consistent with the broader social and political context, historical government–citizens relationships, and leadership styles in Uganda. Since the colonial period, education and knowledge have become central to the legitimacy of political leaders. It implies a moral obligation for them to monitor, advise, and educate, a 'pedagogic mission to enlighten the masses' (Brisset-Foucault, 2022), especially peasants, thought to be backward and ignorant, in order to modernise the country (Kassimir, 1999). In rural areas, it is institutionally channelled through the Local Councils system, a pyramidal political–administrative structure dating back from the NRM guerrilla war and officially established since 1986 (Tidemand, 1994). It has been described as both a means of control (with education as a central condition for the selection and legitimacy of local political leaders) and a system of inclusion and representation, giving more voice and participation to citizens (especially in rural areas) within the state apparatus (Banégas, 1998). LC1 chairpersons and Parish Chiefs are at the grassroot level of this system. LC1 chairpersons draw their legitimacy from geographical proximity and long-term sociability with their constituents. They are regularly solicited as intermediaries, particularly in the mobilisation of villagers (for political activities, development projects, and so on), the circulation of information, and the issuing of various documents (Brisset-Foucault, 2021a). Parish Chiefs are territorial civil servants operating at the parish level (an administrative grouping of a few villages), through whom most local and national policies, whether regular public services or development programmes, are channelled (Jones, 2008, 64 and 67–81). In both cases, their direct knowledge of constituents explains their promotion as SLBs of the programme.

However, there is also a certain social distance between them and most village residents. Most LC1 chairpersons display micro-trajectories of notability, described as mostly 'policemen, tax collectors, field and plant inspectors, seminarists, and clerks' (Brisset-Foucault, 2021a, 260). The position of LC1 chairperson can be a symbolic compensation for frustrated career aspirations. As for Parish Chiefs, the position requires a college diploma and most of those I met during my fieldwork (like other local officials) did not live in the villages they administer but in Kiboga Town, the district capital. Although most of them are natives of the area, they often see their professional situation as transitory, with the hopes of obtaining a higher degree and applying for higher positions. On the contrary, recipients live in rural villages, often dropped out of school at an early age (very few speak English, many are illiterate) and live off subsistence agriculture (some have been able to engage in small-scale commercial farming of coffee or beans, however generating small and irregular incomes). Leaders thus share geographical proximity and sociability networks with beneficiaries, but they socially distance themselves from them through micro-trajectories of notability. Relying on this system has consequences for pensions. In many policies, formal guidelines are contradicted by local social dynamics and norms (or replace them in case of absence or unclarity) (Ehrhardt, 2017), especially when bureaucrats are permeable to them (Kelly, 2016). In the case of pensions in Uganda, there is a contradiction between the SAGE programme formally proclaiming pensions as an unconditional right bureaucratically delivered and its embeddedness in an institutional system based on social inequality, authoritarian leadership, and a developmentalist ideology.

Most local authorities try to make sure recipients use their money in a virtuous and productive manner. This social distance translates into patronising attitudes, including regarding pensions, as illustrated by one Parish Chief:

'In that area where we work, most of the old people, senior citizens, they're drunkards. In most cases, they want to use that money to buy alcohol, smoking, things of that kind, but we encourage them to use this money to invest in things which can benefit their life, like piggery, poultry.'[11]

Local and national authorities interviewed often fear that recipients will use their pension for what they consider as immoral expenses (mainly consuming alcohol, described as "drinking the money", but also smoking, buying airtime credit, or taking a second wife), although the practice seems to be marginal. But they also aim at favouring income-generating activities (animal rearing, petty trade, commercial farming, and so on, as well as payment of school fees for kids for example, considered as an investment in 'human capital') rather than 'mere consumption' of the pension in basic necessities (food, clothes, kitchen tools, and so on). One development officer was keen to stress that "they should not misuse or abuse the money, because this is meant for their development, improve your home, support your family, so why do you drink the money? It's about changing the mind, it's about mindset".[12] This testimony both stigmatises recipients while emphasising the duty of local authorities to help them. Although patronising attitudes are common between SLBs and recipients of welfare benefits, especially when they don't share the same social position (Eiró, 2019), the difference here is that local authorities share long-term familiarity with recipients, which legitimates a paternalistic attitude of supervision and advising, trying to reform and orient behaviours without explicitly constraining or excluding.

Paternalist control as a consequence of institutional weakness and social inequality

Because of institutional weakness, pensions are weakly bureaucratised: there is no open desk where recipients are supposed to go to handle paperwork and administrative matters with the administration, procedures are often planned and done on an ad hoc basis, with no regularity, and SLBs are familiar faces rather than impersonal figures. Although an operations manual has been published, working procedures are in fact weakly formalised. Key stages of the implementation process (registration of recipients, payment sessions, and monitoring and evaluation activities), far from being standardised and impersonal procedures, rely on a dense web of relationships of domination – or the 'relational state' as Peake and Forsyth (2022) would call it[13] – between local authorities and village residents. For example, as they target isolated rural populations, pensions are distributed through a private service provider[14] using mobile vans touring through rural areas to set up temporary counters. Recipients from neighbouring villages are informed a few days beforehand by local leaders, peers, or via the radio to go to the designated location, often a public building (the sub-county headquarters, a school, a church, and so on), at a specific date and time (although such time is rarely respected, often generating long hours of waiting). It is therefore a collective event highlighting the social and political hierarchies at the village level (in addition to local authorities and the SAGE and Post Bank staff involved in the distribution of pensions, important politicians are sometimes present, such as the district chairperson or MPs of the constituency). During interviews, many recipients described these payment sessions as special days that provide an opportunity to travel to a bigger town or rural centre, to dress nicely, and to greet friends and acquaintances. In other words, the SAGE programme (whether considering the staff, institutional architecture, delivery procedures, and so on) is deeply embedded within local political structures, social networks, and moral norms.

The supervision and control of recipients by local authorities in the programme is thus distinct from the (more) bureaucratic control that takes place in conditional cash transfer programmes, where recipients must explicitly comply to certain behaviours and are controlled by professional SLBs who have a formal mandate (Cookson, 2018). Here, it is more based on this paternalist concern to educate and local authorities, far from sticking to standardised and neutral distribution roles, usually build on the collective and exceptional character of implementation activities to foster their paternalist agenda. It usually begins during payment sessions with a 'pre-payment address' during which recipients are reminded of the main information: how the payment is going to take place, how much money they will receive and for which period, but also the need to use it wisely and sparingly so that it 'lasts' until the next payment. Examples of expenses are also suggested: purchase of food, basic household necessities or clothing, small animals (mainly chickens and goats, sometimes pigs or cows) to rear and resell later, payment of school fees or school materials for those who take care of grandchildren, and so on. These 'tips' are reexplained during each payment, constituting a series of non-coercive but recurring injunctions, calling for a parsimonious and virtuous use of pensions. Thus, relationships of domination are expressed in a particularly visible way, going beyond the sole question of pensions, as illustrated by these extracts from a speech by the Post Bank team leader to gathered recipients:

'The last time I was here, I brought you money for Christmas, you used that money very well. … This time, I have brought money for Easter. If you don't spend your money wisely, then that is your problem. … The last time I was here, I told you that you had been behaving in a very bad manner, you could push each other, and I asked you to keep order. And I was very happy that the last time you were very organized. Thank you for being organized and not causing any commotion. This time round, I also ask you kindly to be organized. We have brought all your money; everyone is going to get paid. Even the ones who didn't get paid because they were sick but today, they are going to get paid.'[15]

Such speeches and addresses illustrate the paternalist control of recipients by local authorities. Leaders and staff speak to recipients in a very childish tone, for example by asking them to remain disciplined. Moreover, speeches are not limited to the delivery of information but include injunctions and moral expectations, both about how recipients should behave at the counter and how they should use their money.

Local authorities also supervise recipients at home. Parish Chiefs regularly conduct visits of recipients' homes, which they record in official reports as part of the programme monitoring and evaluation policy.[16] The reports, produced for administrative purposes, usually contain a very normative and developmentalist dimension, with authors arbitrarily dividing beneficiaries' expenditures into 'success stories' or 'challenges'. One report, for example, emphasises the need for 'monitoring those that have managed to establish some businesses projects from SAGE funds to ensure the stability'.[17] Another warns about the presence of 'beneficiaries misusing the grant for non-productive purposes like drinking alcohol'.[18] However, without formal conditionalities, Parish Chiefs are not able to coerce or sanction recipients. But these evaluations, like payment sessions, provide them with an opportunity to exert pressure, albeit indirect, non-coercive, and supposedly benevolent, but nevertheless real:

> 'We just have to sit with that older person, and we advise him that [the pension] is meant, at least, to uplift their life and not for drinking, because drinking doesn't have a positive impact. We have weekly programmes of visiting their homes, at least to see the impact of the money. But if they misuse the money, you just have to sit with them.'[19]

For this Parish Chief, supervision means discussing with the 'faulty' recipients, suggesting more useful expenses and, through subtle pedagogy, convincing them to improve their behaviour. However, other leaders sometimes adopt a more coercive behaviour (which they perceive as legitimate), as illustrated by this LC1 chairperson:

> 'As a leader, you have to apply carrot and stick, you cannot be good all the time. ... We tell them that this is government money, and it has sent it to you purposely to help yourself. When they get this money, some of them take it home, because we know these people are using it profitably. But there are some people, we know that this one, when he gets the money, he just wastes it through drinking. ... We know that if we let them go, this money will not reach home, so we force them to buy soap, we insist you buy clothes. ... So, we try to force them, to make sure that those who are not using it profitably, we give them kind of threats and those who are using it well, we encourage them to do even better.'[20]

Thus, even without any formal constraint or conditionalities, local authorities can control and orient how recipients use their pension. Institutional weakness enables paternalistic relationships to spread through personal supervision and practices of control. However, the discretion enjoyed by local authorities does not translate into arbitrary practices either, as in other cases in developing countries where SLBs can move 'against' or 'away' from citizens (Peeters and Campos, 2022). But it also contrasts with other (often western) contexts where, regardless of SLBs' profiles and attitudes, stronger bureaucratic institutions provide a framework that structures and limits their interactions with clients (Rice, 2013; Dubois, 2016). Here, the regulation of interactions between SLBs and recipients is structured by collective moral norms, as is the case in other sectors like security (Brisset-Foucault, 2021b) in Uganda.

Undeserving but respectable: how recipients understand and use pensions

Institutional weakness (as the absence of a clear, separate, and autonomous bureaucracy) as well as paternalistic attitudes and control practices from local authorities have wider consequences on how people understand the SAGE programme, behave as recipients, and relate to the street-level bureaucracy (Soss, 1999; Campbell, 2003). The first major effect is that recipients understand the pension as a gift from the government, and specific leaders (such as President Museveni or their local MP) rather than a right or a bureaucratic scheme determined by clear rules. As pointed out by Titeca about western Uganda, 'service provision activities are perceived to be very personalised. Most services are perceived to be provided by a certain "big man" or its political camp, rather than by state institutions' (Titeca, 2006, 52). Beyond the hegemonic centrality of the NRM based on patronage (Vokes and Wilkins, 2016), it is linked to the fact that local authorities are the usual intermediaries in the programme. For example, recipients were usually registered through their LC1 chairperson, or Parish Chief, asking for their identity and age with only a vague explanation (for those who inquired about the reason) that they would soon receive money. Many concluded that 'old people's money' (*sente ze bakande* in Luganda) was a gift from President Museveni himself, on the grounds that he had fought in the region during the Bush war (1980–86) and wanted to thank the (now old) civilians. The supervisory role of local authorities also reinforces the belief that pensions are a personal favour. The division between legitimate and illegitimate expenses they insist on also conveys the idea that they are not a guaranteed right (implying they can be withdrawn if misused). Thus, pensions are understood by most recipients as part of a more general economy of patronage (Médard and Golaz, 2013) where generous political leaders distribute benefits 'for free' (since recipients have not worked for it). Surprisingly though, despite their embeddedness within local political structures, pensions are empirically not subject to clientelist diversions, contrary to many social policies in weak institutions (Ansell and Mitchell, 2011; Eiró and Koster, 2019).

The second effect is that paternalistic attitudes from SLBs create for recipients a moral obligation to use their pension in a decent and virtuous manner. Most of them will express gratitude and display attitudes of modesty, honesty, and decency in their use of pensions and towards those who distribute them. For example, despite frequent delays in payment, one of the recipients explained that they were 'not complaining so much because those who designed this programme ... know better why [the distribution of pensions] has [been] delayed',[21] strengthening a sense of arbitrariness, in a manner similar to the 'patients of the State' described by Auyero (2012) in Argentina. Such an attitude was particularly clear regarding the issue of the amount of the pension. Virtually all recipients think it is too low, but very few considered possible and desirable the possibility of complaining about it to local authorities, as expressed this man: 'If somebody is serving you food, and gives you a certain piece of meat, would you say, "you have given me too little"? You only become grateful for what that person has given you, and you only remain praying that this person increases on it.'[22]

This pattern is consistent with the wider institutional context. Like in Tanzania (Lameck and Hulst, 2020), state policies delivered in rural areas (other than health, education, and temporary development programmes) are rare (generating low expectations from the public) and thus considered as favours rather than rights (besides the fact that they are considered as part of wider patronage strategies).

The paternalist control of recipients by local authorities incites them to comply with the injunctions, where they are encouraged to go beyond daily life consumption expenses for what they would call 'productive', and income-generating uses or 'investment in human capital'. Although this might be interpreted as a typical attitude of 'loyalty' from policy clients, a more subtle exploration of individual rationales and practices suggest that it might as well be a way of 'gaming the system' (Peeters et al, 2020) for different reasons. Here, I argue that they follow the advice not only for fear of sanctions but also in search of material gains, social respectability, and moral affirmation of the self. One recipient explains:

Recipient:	When we were given money, they emphasized that we should use that money or invest it into something, but we should not eat it. So, I used the money to buy iron sheets and other materials, like bricks, cement, and other materials for building [a house]. I also use that little money I get to take care of grandchildren who lost their parents. ... I tried to invest it.
Researcher:	And what happens if you don't follow their advice?
Recipient:	It is very bad, because they normally tell us that it is for us to feel that guiltiness, that you have used the money in a bad way, and next time, when you go there, it would be hard for you to face those people once you misuse the money. ... It is good advice according to me, it is very good advice because it helps me relieve the stress, because after investing somewhere, I am expecting something at the end of it.[23]

This example illustrates the strength of paternalistic relationships, which go beyond mere coercion. Paternalist supervision towards virtuous and developmental use of the money is not always seen as a burden but sometimes as an opportunity. Some recipients were keen to see local authorities visit their home and witness the accomplishments they made with their pension, expecting in return an increase of their pension. Compliance with local authorities' injunctions and developmentalist strategies is not only a conscious strategy for material benefits or blame avoidance but also one of social respectability and moral reaffirmation of the self. Many recipients, for example, are prone to incriminate those who allegedly use their pension for drinking alcohol (although they often explain that they don't know anyone personally in this case), to highlight, by contrast, their own respectability. Thus, pensions distributed through the SAGE programme, and paternalist injunctions to development and productive investments that accompany them, can be re-appropriated (at least symbolically and rhetorically) by concerned recipients, desirous to present themselves as respectable citizens and 'legitimate interlocutors of the authorities' (Brisset-Foucault, 2022, 22).

Conclusion

This chapter analysed the consequences of institutional weakness in a pension programme in Uganda. I showed that the SAGE programme is a weak institution because of identification issues, political reluctance, and financial constraints, resulting in street-level bureaucracy embedded in local political structures, social networks, and moral norms. The first consequence is that local authorities in charge of implementation impose a paternalist supervision on recipients based on developmentalist norms. The second is that pensions are interpreted by recipients as an arbitrary favour rather than a bureaucratic right. Thus, most of them try to follow the development norms, in pursuit of blame avoidance but also social respectability and moral affirmation of the self. Of course, conflict and moral dilemmas sometimes arise, both from recipients claiming autonomy and refusing to be patronised, or local authorities interrogating themselves on the legitimacy of asking elder citizens to participate in development. But the embeddedness of pensions in local polities promotes a 'developmental citizenship', where the behaviour of recipients, how they use their pension, and by extension their value as individuals, are defined and measured according to moral norms and to their (perceived) contribution to local development and welfare. The apparent desire of recipients to comply with paternalist injunctions and benefit from the advice of local authorities can be understood as such. It allows them to affirm themselves as legitimate and virtuous citizens, even through the authoritarian politics of Museveni's Uganda.

Regarding the study of street-level bureaucracy, the chapter showed that weakness is not an obvious feature of the Ugandan state. On the contrary, it is the product of political choices, translating into low financial and administrative resources. The street-level bureaucracy is unable to 'refract' power and authority at the local level because it is embedded in, or even confused with them. In fact, pensions in Uganda do not create new forms of governance or structures of power, nor do the street-level bureaucracies delivering them produce specific practices or outcomes, but they reproduce historical forms of political domination characterised by paternalistic relationships, informal practices of control, and developmentalist injunctions. In this sense, the case of the SAGE programme enriches the study of street-level bureaucracy in weak institutions, showing how frontiers can be blurred between service delivery and everyday forms of governance and political domination, a process that constrains as much as it facilitates the delivery of pensions.

Notes

[1] Ugandan Media Centre, Statement to the media on the joint remedial of older persons with national identification and registration authority by Hon. Gidudu Mafwaabi Dominic, Minister of State for Elderly Affairs, Ministry of Gender, Labor and Social Development, Kampala, 17 February 2022.

[2] The National Resistance Movement has been the dominant political movement since it seized power through a guerrilla war in 1986. Its leader, Yoweri Museveni, has been president of Uganda since.

[3] Interviews with the Policy and Advocacy Advisor of ESP (Expanding Social Protection, the semi-autonomous agency administering the SAGE program), 7 February and 8 February 2018 and the Communication Advisor of ESP, 7 February 2018. For more details, see (Hickey & Bukenya, 2020).

[4] Interview with the Team Leader of ESP, Kampala, 6 February 2018.

[5] Around £30 million from the government, £57 million from the DfID and £13 million from Irish Aid.

[6] Interview with the Operations advisor of ESP, 6 February 2018.

[7] Both because of the need to make the program a 'success story' (and ensure its financial and political sustainability) and because they were aware of the obstacles that can prevent people from registering (lack of information, mistrust, physical or financial traveling difficulties, and so on).

[8] Interview with the Information Technology Officer of the program's regional office, Kiboga, 5 March 2018.

[9] Interview with the Operations Adviser of ESP, Kampala, 6 February 2018.

[10] Upper and middle-level district authorities (district and sub-county development officers, administrative officers, sub-county chiefs, and so on) are also supposed to participate in the implementation process, but according to my observations, they limit themselves to technical or supervisory functions and rarely interact directly with recipients.

[11] Interview with a Parish Chief, Kiboga, 21 March 2019.

[12] Interview with the District Community Development Officer of the district, Kiboga, 8 March 2018.

[13] Although contrary to the case they describe in Bougainville, state administrations are not intrinsically weak in Uganda. Institutional weakness is, as we saw it previously, a result

of explicit policy choices denying resources to the SAGE program for the construction of a solid, autonomous, and professionalized administration.
14. First MTN, a South African telecommunications company, leader of the market in Uganda with more than 50 per cent of the market share, Post Bank from 2015 to 2021, a government-owned commercial bank, and now Centenary Bank, a Ugandan commercial bank mostly owned by the Catholic church.
15. Personal observations (the speech was recorded and translated), Nakasongola, 18 March 2019.
16. Interview with the SAGE Community Development Officer of the regional office of ESP, Kiboga, 5 March 2018.
17. *Kiboga Town Council Sub-County SAGE report for November 2015*, p 4.
18. *SAGE Quarterly Report for the Month of October-December 2018*, p 7.
19. Interview with a Parish Chief, Kiboga, 8 March 2018.
20. Interview with a LC1 chairman, Kiboga, 13 March 2019.
21. Interview with a recipient, Kiboga district, 14 March 2019.
22. Interview with a recipient, Kiboga district, 16 March 2019.
23. Interview with a recipient, Kiboga district, 8 March 2019.

References

Angucia, M., and Katusiimeh, M.W. (2015). *The Politics of Promoting Social Protection in Uganda: A Case of the Cash Transfer Scheme for Elderly People* (Partnership for African Social and Governance Research Working Paper No. 009).

Ansell, A. and Mitchell, K. (2011). Models of clientelism and policy change: The Case of conditional cash transfer programmes in Mexico and Brazil. *Bulletin of Latin American Research*, 30(3), 298–312. https://doi.org/10.1111/j.1470-9856.2010.00497.x

Auyero, J. (2012). *Patients of the State: The Politics of Waiting in Argentina*. Durham, NC: Duke University Press.

Banégas, R. (1998). Entre guerre et démocratie: L'évolution des imaginaires politiques en Ouganda. In D.-C. Martin (ed), *Nouveaux langages du politique en Afrique orientale*. Karthala [u.a.], pp 187–262.

Brinks, D.M., Levitsky, S., and Murillo M.V. (eds) (2020). *The Politics of Institutional Weakness in Latin America*. Cambridge: Cambridge University Press.

Brisset-Foucault, F. (2021a). Bureaucratic interpersonal knowledge: Village identity papers and the production of moral homelands in Uganda. In S.A. Dalberto and R. Banégas (eds), *Identification and Citizenship in Africa: Biometrics, the Documentary State and Bureaucratic Writings of the Self* (1st edn). London: Routledge, pp 254–73.

Brisset-Foucault, F. (2021b). Démocratiser le fusil: L'imagination composite d'une citoyenneté coercitive en Ouganda. *Participations*, 29(1), 123–56.

Brisset-Foucault, F. (2022). The radio polity: Construction-site democracy, technocratic domination and bureaucratic patriotism in Uganda. *Les Cahiers d'Afrique de l'Est/The East African Review*, 57, Art. 57, 1–35. https://doi.org/10.4000/eastafrica.1655

Campbell, A.L. (2003). *How Policies Make Citizens: Senior Political Activism and the American Welfare State.* Princeton, NJ: Princeton University Press. www.jstor.org/stable/j.ctt7rtmp

Cookson, T.P. (2018). *Unjust Conditions: Women's Work and the Hidden Cost of Cash Transfer Programs.* Berkeley: University of California Press. https://doi.org/10.1525/luminos.49

Dubois, V. (2016). *The Bureaucrat and the Poor: Encounters in French Welfare Offices.* London: Routledge. https://doi.org/10.4324/9781315614205

Ehrhardt, D. (2017). Indigeneship, bureaucratic discretion, and institutional change in Northern Nigeria. *African Affairs*, 116(464), 462–83. https://doi.org/10.1093/afraf/adx016

Eiró, F. (2019). The vicious cycle in the Bolsa Família Program's implementation: Discretionality and the challenge of social rights consolidation in Brazil. *Qualitative Sociology*, 42(3), 385–409. https://doi.org/10.1007/s11133-019-09429-9

Eiró, F. and Koster, M. (2019). Facing bureaucratic uncertainty in the Bolsa Família Program: Clientelism beyond reciprocity and economic rationality. *Focaal*, 2019(85), 84–96. https://doi.org/10.3167/fcl.2019.850108

Expanding Social Protection. (2016). *Senior Citizens Grant (SCG) Operational Manual.* Kampala: Ministry of Gender, Labour and Social Development.

Ferguson, J. (2015). *Give a Man a Fish: Reflections on the New Politics of Distribution.* Durham, NC: Duke University Press.

Fisher, J. (2014). When it pays to be a 'fragile state': Uganda's use and abuse of a dubious concept. *Third World Quarterly*, 35(2), 316–32, https://doi.org/10.1080/01436597.2014.878493

Hickey, S. (2013). Beyond the poverty agenda? Insights from the new politics of development in Uganda. *World Development*, 43, 194–206. https://doi.org/10.1016/j.worlddev.2012.09.007

Hickey, S. and Bukenya, B. (2020). The politics of promoting social cash transfers in Uganda: The potential and pitfalls of 'thinking and working politically'. *Development Policy Review*, 20(1), 1–20. https://doi.org/10.1111/dpr.12474

Hickey, S., Bukenya, B., and Matsiko, H. (2021) *Pockets of Effectiveness, Political Settlements and Technopols in Uganda: From State-Building to Regime Survival? ESID Working Paper No. 172.* Manchester: The University of Manchester. www.effective-states.org

Jones, B. (2008). *Beyond the State in Rural Uganda.* Edinburgh: Edinburgh University Press.

Kassimir, R. (1999). Reading Museveni: Structure, agency and pedagogy in Ugandan politics. *Canadian Journal of African Studies/Revue Canadienne des Études Africaines*, 33(2/3), 649–73. https://doi.org/10.2307/486282

Kelly, G. (2016). *Hard and Soft Medicine: Doctors' Framing and Application of the Disability Category in Their Assessments of Grant Claimants' Fitness to Work in South Africa* [Working Paper]. University of Cape Town. https://open.uct.ac.za/handle/11427/21584

Lameck, W. and Hulst, R. (2020). Explaining coping strategies of agricultural extension officers in Tanzania: The role of the wider institutional context. *International Review of Administrative Sciences*, 86(4), 749–64. https://doi.org/10.1177/0020852318824398

Lipsky, M. (1980). *Street-Level Bureaucracy: Dilemmas of the Individual in Public Services*. New York: Russell Sage Foundation.

McDonnell, E.M. (2017). Patchwork leviathan: How pockets of bureaucratic governance flourish within institutionally diverse developing states. *American Sociological Review*, 82(3), 476–510. https://doi.org/10.1177/0003122417705874

Médard, C. and Golaz, V. (2013). Creating dependency: Land and gift-giving practices in Uganda. *Journal of Eastern African Studies*, 7(3), 549–68. https://doi.org/10.1080/17531055.2013.811027

Mubiru, J.-B. and Bukuluki, P. (2014). *The Status of Social Security Systems in Uganda: Challenges and Opportunities*. Kampala: Konrad-Adenauer-Stiftung. http://rgdoi.net/10.13140/RG.2.1.4225.7764

Nisar, M.A. and Masood, A. (2020). Dealing with disgust: Street-level bureaucrats as agents of Kafkaesque bureaucracy. *Organization*, 27(6), 882–99. https://doi.org/10.1177/1350508419883382

Peake, G. and Forsyth, M. (2022). Street-level bureaucrats in a relational state: The case of Bougainville. *Public Administration and Development*, 42(1), 12–21. https://doi.org/10.1002/pad.1911

Peeters, R. and Campos, S.A. (2022). Street-level bureaucracy in weak state institutions: A systematic review of the literature. *International Review of Administrative Sciences*. https://doi.org/10.1177/00208523221103196. https://doi.org/10.1177/00208523221103196

Peeters, R., Gofen, A., and Meza, O. (2020). Gaming the system: Responses to dissatisfaction with public services beyond exit and voice. *Public Administration*, 98(4), 824–39. https://doi.org/10.1111/padm.12680

Phillips, K.D. (2018). Paternalism. In *The International Encyclopedia of Anthropology*. New York: John Wiley & Sons, Ltd, pp 1–2. https://doi.org/10.1002/9781118924396.wbiea1478

Rice, D. (2013). Street-level bureaucrats and the welfare state: Toward a micro-institutionalist theory of policy implementation. *Administration & Society*, 45(9), 1038–62. https://doi.org/10.1177/0095399712451895

Soss, J. (1999). Lessons of welfare: Policy design, political learning, and political action. *The American Political Science Review*, 93(2), 363–80. https://doi.org/10.2307/2585401

Tidemand, P. (1994). *The Resistance Councils in Uganda: A Study of Rural Politics and Popular Democracy in Africa* [PhD in International Development Studies]. Roskilde Universitet.

Titeca, K. (2006). Political patronage and political values: The developmental role of political patronage and its impact on shaping political values in rural Uganda. *Afrika Focus*, 19(1), Art. 1, 43–67. https://doi.org/10.21825/af.v19i1.5414

Tripp, A.M. (2010). *Museveni's Uganda: Paradoxes of power in a hybrid regime*. Boulder: Lynne Rienner Publishers.

Ulriksen, M.S. and Katusiimeh, M.W. (2014). *The history of resource mobilization and social spending in Uganda* (UNRISD Working Paper No 2014-6). United Nations Research Institute for Social Development (UNRISD). http://hdl.handle.net/10419/148730

Veit, A., Schlichte, K., and Karadag, R. (2017). The social question and state formation in British Africa: Egypt, South Africa and Uganda in comparison. *European Journal of Sociology / Archives Européennes de Sociologie*, 58(2), 237–64. https://doi.org/10.1017/S0003975617000108

Vokes, R. and Wilkins, S. (2016). Party, patronage and coercion in the NRM'S 2016 re-election in Uganda: Imposed or embedded? *Journal of Eastern African Studies*, 10(4), 581–600. https://doi.org/10.1080/17531055.2016.1279853

Zacka, B. (2017). *When the State Meets the Street: Public Service and Moral Agency*. Cambridge, MA: Belknap Press.

4

Street-level bureaucrats in environments of systemic corruption: sources of influence

Oliver Meza, Elizabeth Pérez-Chiqués, and Anat Gofen

Introduction

This chapter seeks to contextualise predatory and other corrupt behaviours by SLBs by switching the focus beyond individual-level factors to one that accounts for the different levels of influence that weigh on SLBs in contexts of systemic or widespread corruption. To do so, this chapter addresses levels of influence that are present in systemic corruption dynamics involving SLBs, including and going beyond individual-level factors, and influence from colleagues, direct managers, and political principals. Although the literature has recognised these factors as influencing street-level work (for example, May and Winter, 2009), these studies overwhelmingly reflect conditions in developed countries or in contexts where corruption does not constitute the context for street-level work (Gofen et al, 2022). Corruption at any one of the levels of influence or at all levels poses questions related to the impact of these contextual factors on street-level work and policy implementation. What can be observed or perceived as predatory behaviour from SLBs might rather reflect the role of SLBs in contexts of corrupted politics, management, and peers, where SLBs are tools for pursuing private interests. Rather than analysing street-level corruption as petty corruption or isolated corruption, in this chapter we aim to reinterpret predatory or corrupt behaviours of SLBs as part of wider patterns of systemic corruption.

Street-level corruption in environments of systemic corruption

Street-level corruption has been defined as 'corruption by a public official who carries out routine activities at a lower level of the public administration' (Nieuwbeerta et al, 2003, 140). Exercised by SLBs, street-level corruption emphasises that well-documented unique characteristics of street-level implementation, mainly SLBs' discretionary power and direct interaction with citizens, provide a convenient opportunity for SLBs to pressure a citizen by 'withholding a service to which the citizen is legally entitled, reporting an offense which the citizen did not commit, or reporting an offense that is commonly committed but generally not reported' (Nieuwbeerta et al, 2003, 140). Street-level corruption is frequently limited to extortion type in the context of public official-citizen interactions, is considered less harmful than corruption at higher levels of the bureaucracy, and is depicted as occurring in environments where public officials have lost their grip on lower-level officials (Rose-Ackerman, 1999; Nieuwbeerta et al, 2003). Additionally, these studies often portray SLBs as the initiators of the corrupt activity (Nieuwbeerta et al, 2003) or use the rotten-apple approach to corruption, in which the behaviour of a corrupt individual spreads to others. Policy prescriptions based on this view of SLB corruption, generally include the need for increased administrative oversight or other means to gain control – decreasing the discretion, supervising the discretion, increased prosecution – of street-level workers (Nieuwbeerta et al, 2003).

Although this approach might be adequate for environments in which SLB corruption is an exception, it is wholly inadequate for understanding and addressing SLB corruption in countries facing weak institutional contexts where corruption might be pervasive or systemic and of a completely different nature (Mungiu-Pippidi, 2011, 2006; Arellano-Gault, 2016; Marquette and Peiffer, 2018; Arellano-Gault and Rojas, 2021):

> [W]hat we term corruption in these countries is not the same phenomenon as corruption in developed countries. In the latter, the term corruption usually designates *individual* cases of infringement of the norms of integrity. In the former, corruption actually means 'particularism' – a mode of *social organisation* characterized by the regular distribution of public goods on a non-universalistic basis that mirrors the vicious distribution of power within such societies. (Mungiu-Pippidi, 2006, 86–7)

Peeters and Campos (2022) identify predatory behaviour and corruption as one of several SLB responses to conditions pervasive in weak institutions; we zoom in on the sources of influence and the consequent dynamics involving SLBs in contexts of systemic or widespread corruption. In weak institutional environments where corruption is systemic, behaviours that might be classified as corrupt are embedded in dense cultural understandings and constitute a mode of social organisation with important social functions (Scott, 1972; Mungiu-Pippidi, 2006, 96; Arellano-Gault, 2016, 2017; Marquette and Peiffer, 2018; Jancsics, 2019). Additionally, in the developing context, corruption can serve as an important tool for political leaders, given that it helps them overcome some of the fiscal constraints that they face (Marquette and Peiffer, 2018). It can also serve as a means to access services for citizens (Arellano-Gault, 2016; Bauhr, 2017) and as a route for social mobility (Scott, 1972).

Systemic corruption is sustained by informal and formal rules and can become the norm (Mungiu-Pippidi, 2006; Arellano-Gault, 2016). For example, Gofen et al (2022) address street-level corruption as a phenomenon that is embedded in systemic corruption and find that, although organisational corruption and street-level corruption can be conceptually distinguished, these phenomena are interrelated, with corruption among superiors and colleagues increasing tolerance among SLBs regarding inappropriate interactions with citizens. Similarly, Vega and Maya (2021) refer to public service health workers in Mexico as captives of corrupt systems. The authors show how the work of health SLBs is shaped by the logics of systemic corruption, and how workers both contribute and are subjected to it (Vega and Maya, 2021, 5). In another example, a recent study on the predatory behaviour of police officers in found that the behaviour was organisationally condoned; that it was part of institutionalised informal requirements for officers to be promoted and to have overall better career prospects. In addition, these contexts are often characterised by clientelist practices and feature SLB involvement in activities such as vote-buying and delivery of services or benefits to groups based on particularistic criteria. Furthermore, these corrupt behaviours can be the response or coping mechanism of SLBs resulting from deficiencies in the institutional environment such as precariousness of work conditions and resource scarcity, among others (Peeters and Campos, 2022). These studies help contextualise and understand predatory behaviour by SLBs, SLB corruption, and SLB involvement in clientelist or extortive practices as part of wider organisational and institutional patterns – as behaviour in function of or aligned with wider organisational and institutional informal goals.

In the developing country context, SLB corruption as well as other organisational dynamics cannot be understood in a decontextualised manner, nor neatly and artificially separated from higher-level corruption, other informal governance patterns, or from wider institutional factors (Peeters and Dussauge Luna, 2021; Gofen et al, 2022; Lotta, Lima-Silva, and Favareto, 2022; Lotta, Pires, Hill, and Møller, 2022; Peeters and Campos, 2022). In contexts of systemic corruption, we should think about corruption as a structural aspect that determines and sets the conditions for SLB's work, that limits or shapes their discretion and directs street-level implementation. We approach corruption not as what SLBs do but as the environment SLBs live and operate in.

Sources of influence: a typology

While SLBs are agents, and therefore they take decisions and are responsible for them even if they enact them within a weak institutional context where corruption is systemic, the following section seeks to focus on the many sources that influence SLBs' decision-making. A two-dimensional space is produced considering the main sources of influence: hierarchical (top-down or bottom up/sideways) and as internal or external to the organisation (from inside or from outside). This two-dimensional space is an attempt to organise the multiple and often co-existing sources and levels of *corrupted* influence weighing upon SLBs operating in contexts of systemic corruption.

A classic approach towards the study of SLBs is the dimension of hierarchy. Top-down is a source where actors such as politicians, top- and mid-level managers among other similar authorities within an organisation exert some kind of influence over SLBs. However, when the sources of influences are top-down but come from outside, we might think of other institutions such as local traditions and culture, or social expectations which exert influence as an informal institution. In contrast, the street level as a source of influence is termed here as sideways or bottom-up. These dimensions interact both with the locational dimension, which could be either within or outside the organisation. A street-level source of influence within the organisation is the one exerted by colleagues, but from the outside these influences would come from the interactions being produced between citizens–clients and SLBs themselves.

The typology is based on fieldwork observations in Mexican municipalities for the elaboration of the corruption consolidation framework (Meza and Pérez-Chiqués, 2021). The framework unveils four analytical dimensions which serve to investigate the features of corruption 'as the rule' in local governments. One of these dimensions is named organisational mechanisms, which refer to the forms and ways that corrupt network members engage with other people to either force them to participate or inhibit them to whistle blow. Directly inspired by this grounded work, we believe that sources of influence affecting SLBs' behaviour, attitudes, and proclivity towards corruption come from various places within and from outside the organisation and also either from above or sideways. We take on these sources in Table 4.1 to exemplify some of the existing mechanisms based on relevant literature and on the aforementioned fieldwork; however, they are not exhaustive but indicative of where to look to understand these influences.

a) Top-down and from inside

SLBs's propensity for corrupt behaviour is frequently conditioned by the organisational features in place. A first and obvious source of influence over SLBs comes from within their organisation and is exerted by managers, and the formal and informal rules. Organisation is therefore an important key set of institutions that signal what is important, and what is not, and how

Table 4.1: Sources of influence

	From inside	From outside
Top-down	Politicians Managers Rules/norms/organisational culture	Social traditions Social expectation Civic/political culture
Sideways – bottom-up (street-level)	Colleagues' peer pressure Colleagues' attitudes Colleagues' knowledge Subordinates	Bureau–client interactions Citizens' expectations

things are done. SLBs are especially observant of these behavioural cues (Gofen et al, 2022).

Within organisations, a growing set of evidence suggests that ethical leadership has a bearing on employee behaviour (Meyer-Sahling and Mikkelsen, 2022). This evidence is clearer in the context of the US (Hassan et al 2014; see also Wright et al, 2016). Therefore, there is an expectation that high-level management offers behavioural cues to SLBs. The literature even suggests that leadership does not need to engage in corruption in order to foster it. It is a matter of condoning, ignoring, facilitating either explicitly or not, intentionally, or not (Ashforth and Anand, 2003).

Second, and perhaps even more important is the managerial influence over SLBs. This is a well-studied source of influence. Managers may embed corruption in organisational practices in at least two forms: as technicisation and as cover-up for higher authorities. The first is related to the specialised area of managerial work where they attempt to either legalise or simulate 'going by the rule' to undertake a corrupt action. Frequently, these corrupt actions fall within the interest of authorities, politicians-in-office for example, and delegate the technicalities of the procedure to mid-level managers. In systemic corruption contexts, this procedure is recurrent and accompanied with a fierce control of check and balances from politicians in order to avoid getting caught or increase the probability of impunity (Jávor and Jancsics, 2016; Meza and Pérez-Chiqués, 2021).

The case described in the accounts by Odevaine in Italy offers a clear example of the entanglement between politicians' electoral interest and use of public resources on the one hand, and the collaboration of higher and mid-level managers on the other to commit corrupt acts which they, themselves, could also benefit economically from: 'Public contracts were awarded to a select group of third-sector organizations that were willing to pay bribes, and that, in turn, employed local people in exchange for political votes' (, 161). However, when the impunity strategy fails, mid-level managers participate by assuming responsibility, for example, facing the jury or the penalty. This latter behaviour refers to the second function of mid-level managers, which is one where they are drawn to cover elites' misbehaviours.

Within public organisations, higher echelons in the hierarchy have implications in SLBs' behaviour. As seen before, a direct link is seen as pressure from high-ranking officials toward employees, and therefore SLBs, to conduct illegal behaviour. Refusal to engage in the behaviour may result in job loss or sanctions (Needleman and Needleman, 1979), including fewer opportunities for job promotions (Meza and Pérez-Chiqués, 2021). Some public employees expressed the uncertainty of their positions, their vulnerability, and their fear of operating in environments in which they found themselves having to participate in illegal or unethical actions; they felt they had no option but to participate. Others, especially those involved in or knowledgeable of very routinised corruption expressed a certain matter-of-factness regarding the involvement of different hierarchical (administrative and political) levels in corrupt transactions:

> 'So, let's say, the lower level is the inspectors ... next are their bosses, their director, the mayor as the responsible of all the administration, and then the municipal assembly. There has always been talk of a chain, meaning that, the director asks the inspectors for a quota [from bribes], this can be monthly, weekly, or daily. Then, of that which is collected, the director also has to give a part of it to the mayor, and then, the mayor has to distribute among the aldermen ... that inspector is being part of a chain of corruption. Yes, because what the inspector is interested in is maintaining his work ... and if his work implies giving that contribution, well, he's going to do it; but overall, he is being part of the chain. (Int. 190805_004)

Other times top management may cause SLB corruption by setting unrealistic goals that are not achievable using legal procedures (Ashforth et al, 2008). This was exemplified by an interviewee that expressed distress because of the many illegal actions that were taken in order to achieve goals but at the same time recognises that these actions were necessary because they responded to a higher rationale: winning elections. As another municipal employee explained, you do not question instructions, "even though you have a regulation, if it comes from above, you do it or you do it, they are not asking you".

A less direct source of influence has impact through perception. Gofen et al (2022) observed that SLBs' higher perception of organisational corruption is associated with (1) greater willingness to collaborate in corrupt actions, (2) a lower perception of corruption in corrupt acts, (3) higher willingness to rationalise a corrupt act, and, (4) less willingness to report the corrupt act.

Beyond actors, there are also institutional mechanisms that shape SLBs' experiences and their opportunity structure for participating in corruption. Among these are internal checks and balances, such as the municipal comptroller's office, the implementation or lack thereof of transparency legislation, and implementation of merit-based hiring, among others. In environments where corruption is consolidated, these institutional features are often weakened, co-opted, or non-existent. For example, in one of the municipalities studied, the municipal comptroller explained how it was impossible to effectively monitor the municipal police force: "There is a wall." And it is considered too dangerous given that the police force does not necessarily respond to the municipal administration but to criminal groups. An interviewee explained how SLBs, especially police and employees who have inspection tasks, are often recruited and hired because of the interference or infiltration of criminal groups in municipalities. The case of municipal police is illustrative of how institutional weaknesses virtually disable sectors of the municipal workforce, and how SLBs can be both victimisers and victims in corruption dynamics (see also, Vega and Maya, 2021).

Relatedly, weaknesses in personnel management influence SLBs. According to interviewees, the majority of the workforce including SLBs are not hired based on merit but rather based on their prior political work, political affiliation, or personal connections. The lack of job security and high personnel turnover – characteristic of politicised management of public employees – in addition to weaknesses in whistle-blowing processes and protections contribute to leaving SLBs unprotected from coerced participation in corruption schemes. They participate because they want to keep their jobs, because of fear, or because of loyalty to the individual, party, or external element that hired them. This makes SLBs a great resource for participating in vote buying and other clientelist practices as well as in extractive types of corruption (for example, extortion of citizens). As an interviewee expressed: "The street, that's the area that lends itself to the most corruption."

These accounts offer a glimpse of what could be happening in a context of systemic corruption. In contexts as such, both direct and indirect links reinforce each other offering clear behavioural cues to SLBs about what is needed, what is appropriate, and what is expected.

b) Top-down and from outside

A top-down source of influence over SLBs to commit corruption may come from outside of the organisation. A well-studied manifestation of this phenomenon is political corruption. This refers to political offices becoming an instrument for achieving personal benefits (World Bank, 1997). Political corruption is beyond organisational means and corporate frontiers. It is a political system itself; a corrupt system that stems and entangles political authority with private actors in pursuit of the basest private interests (Bozeman et al, 2018). The influence of political corruption over SLBs could also occur indirectly through the effect of citizens' and private agents' willingness to transact with them. Citizens' perception is influenced by the perceived levels of political corruption which provides them with powerful messages regarding the types of engagement that are deemed appropriate; many times, both citizens and government officials believe that corrupt transactions are appropriate or acceptable. Recurrent manifestations of these causal mechanisms may seem clear in the presence of high governmental failure where corruption is rationalised as a means of access to public services (for example, Jancsics, 2019). However, this line of influence will be addressed later in a subsequent section.

A second line of influence between political corruption and SLBs' agency is perhaps subtler. Political corruption can somehow imply a series of parallel situations that will serve as conditioners that inhibit corruption-deterrence efforts. Igiebor (2019) lists some of them: (1) a weak enforcement of control mechanisms, (2) a lack of transparency and accountability efforts, (3) a lack of citizen participation in governmental decisions, and (4) the use of public resources under the guise of nepotism, clientelism, and the seeking of electoral victories. While Igiebor's list is used to describe Nigeria, this situation is closely related to the findings of Meza and Pérez-Chiqués (2021) when explaining the features of corruption consolidation in local governments in Mexico. There too, weak, absent, or co-opted checks and balances, high levels of opacity coupled with simulation of transparency, and the use of public office and resources to benefit political parties or private interests, serve to severely curb anti-corruption efforts. These institutional mechanisms have both internal (see prior section) and external versions (for example, state or federal auditing offices would be considered external checks and balances, while municipal comptrollers are considered internal).

A third and less well-studied manifestation of a top-down and external source of influence over SLBs and corruption comes from other social interactions. In the literature, females have been assumed as being less corrupt than males. The research has encountered, however, critical exceptions to this assumption. Among these is the fact that cultural threats affect the relation between gender and corruption-proclivity. Following gender studies' stream of thought, arguably, SLBs are gendered humans that according to Stensöta et al (2015) are asymmetrically exposed to varying intensities of attributes of social structures. Young (2002) defines such attributes as (1) sexual division of labour, (2) normative heterosexuality, and (3) hierarchies of power. Stensöta et al (2015) propose that females' life experience of these social structures is different with respect to males' experience, and that such attributes affect women's personality affecting their proclivity to engage in corruption-prone actions. Stensöta and colleagues test this theoretical proposition by looking at the mediating effect of institutions. They conclude that the association between women and corruption exists but is, however, altered depending on institutional features within the working environment.

c) Sideways from colleagues (internal bottom-up)

Key sources of influence may come from peers and subordinates. In the case of SLBs, peer pressure and peer attitudes are crucial to understand behaviour. Organisational corruption can be influenced in a bottom-up way, where individuals are the primary beneficiaries of the corruption at the expense of the organisation (Pinto et al, 2008).

Socialisation and social influence are said to affect people to engage in corrupt actions. The mechanisms widely vary. For instance, a popular mechanism is that of peer-pressure. In-group members socialise or educate newcomers as to what is and what is not the correct way to proceed (Ashforth and Anand, 2003). Subsequently, it was found by researchers that perception of peers' behaviour is also associated with individuals' own proclivity to act in a corrupt way (Zey-Ferrell et al, 1979; see also Belle and Cantarelli, 2017).

Evidence also suggests a subtler mechanism of peer-led influence using narrative-based idiosyncratic frames. The concept of accepted zones of non-compliance (Meza and Zizumbo-Colunga, 2021) elaborates on the relation between narrative frames commonly used in the public sector and among peers to persuade each other to step into a non-compliance zone. An example the authors offer is the story of made-up expenditures, such as coffee expenditures instead of travel expenses because it would help to balance the budget between the organisational units. In other words, as an act of self-managed compensation for belonging to a less well-off unit within a public organisation, public officials could agree to make up expenditure figures from one item to another.

Peers can also influence participation of other SLBs by more pecuniary means. exemplify the mechanism with a case in Budapest. In a public swimming pool facility, employees in charge of giving access to people would work around the entry process to keep certain entrances under their control for their own gain. To assure the participation of peers, a profit-sharing scheme was developed between them. In the work of Meza and Pérez-Chiqués (2021), the influence exerted by peers and by subordinates is also featured. Interviewees narrated how if someone did not want to participate in corrupt actions, they were deemed untrustworthy by their peers, "it's natural [corruption] and if you don't do it, you're the one who's wrong". The influence of subordinates came up in a discussion about the different corruption styles of political parties that had governed a municipality. While one of the political parties was considered to take care of those lower-level employees ("they always distribute [the gains of corrupt acts] to the ones below"), another political party was considered to act with greed and ambition: "they kept everything for themselves. They did not give anything to the ones who were the worst off, they were considered to be the worst, the most unfair," because they did not allow others to participate in or benefit from acts of corruption. The interviewee considered this discontent to be one of the reasons that the political party was unable to stay in power.

d) Sideways from citizen–clients (external bottom-up)

Within a context of systemic corruption, rational expectations of citizen's interactions with bureaucracy arise in the form of complacent dyadic corruption. The concept of social bribes has been used, also, to describe scenarios where corrupt interactions occur as part of a 'normal' relationship. Such embedded expectations, contrary to many theoretical accounts, involve high levels of trust. More specifically, inter-agent and individual type of trust (Pérez-Chiqués and Meza, 2021).

Rational expectations may also arise in day-to-day interactions. Corruption becomes the 'grease of wheels' and, therefore, a necessary mechanism to make the government function. At a certain point, this approach was popular within certain streams of thought that affected the perception of corruption: instead of a malady in society it was seen as a necessity within contexts of state-failure. Certainly, in cases where corruption has become the rule, such idiosyncrasy prevails. Corruption is expected and citizens and SLBs alike are actively engaged, as an interviewee expressed: "It takes two to clap." Surveys in local governments in Mexico capture this notion by asking people, and public officials, their agreement with a series of popular sayings resulting in the following numbers. Agree and strongly agree: 49 per cent with 'He/she who does not cheat, does not get ahead', 38.5 per cent with 'Sometimes it's justified to pay a bribe', and 51 per cent with 'it's very normal to bribe' (Meza and Pérez-Chiqués, 2021). Moreover, citizens' rational expectations to engage in corrupt transactions with SLBs increase as denouncing corruption in municipal governments is considered worthless (33 per cent), 21 per cent think it takes too long, and 15 per cent fear reprisals (Meza and Pérez-Chiqués, 2021). Additionally, people prefer to game the system by using a leverage instead of voicing their discontent with public services (Peeters et al, 2020).

Belle and Cantarelli (2017) suggest a group of mechanisms called social influences, which could also apply here to explain sources of influence towards SLBs. Their meta-analysis identifies two key mechanisms. One is the empathy–altruism hypothesis. It relates to the proclivity to act towards someone if it elicits empathetic emotions (Batson et al, 1991). The mechanism applies even for unethical decisions or actions (the next paragraph connects back to this point). Furthermore, within the social influence group of mechanisms, another prevalent one is the social identity hypothesis. This concerns the possibility of imitation within group members (even when one is in the organisation, say a public organisation, and the other one is not). According to research, this imitation mechanism may apply even with unethical practices or decisions.

Finally, and as in all forms of influences previously discussed, subtle expressions of these mechanisms are also possible. For instance, in the form of language and narratives. Even in places with systemic corruption, the tales we tell about our actions are key to persuading ourselves and others that we are still good people and behave correctly. This partially explains why we use nicknames for certain misbehaviours such as using *palancas* (leverages) in Mexico or *Jeitinho* in Brazil. The bottom line is that humans, SLBs, and citizens are never really ready to mis-represent themselves. They are ready to misbehave but not so much so that it affects their notion of being a *good person* (Feldman and Halali, 2019; see also Zamir and Sulitzeanu-Kenan, 2018). However, SLBs, citizens, and humans in general do misbehave, and do engage in corruption. To perform these activities, they frequently use alternative frames such as narratives. Therefore, citizens in their pursuit of a favour, instead of asking an SLB to perform an action for their sole benefit, sometimes an illegal one, prefer to frame it with a different narrative. The aforementioned concept of accepted zones of non-compliance (Meza and Zizumbo-Colunga, 2021) refers to a situation where a narrative is used to cover up what could be considered a corrupt action. The application of such narratives to public officials, and SLBs, in their interactions with citizens, affect their perception with respect to justify a corrupt act, and their proclivity to participate in it as long as it helps, for example, vulnerable sectors of the population (Meza and Zizumbo-Colunga, 2023;).

Conclusion

This chapter aimed to contextualise predatory and other corrupt behaviours by SLBs by switching the focus beyond individual-level factors to factors that account for the different levels of influence that weigh on SLBs in contexts of systemic or widespread corruption. Aided with dimensions of top-down and bottom-up, and in and outside the organisation, we have developed a matrix to analyse the different sources of influence that weigh upon SLBs. The discussion of the matrix presented here is not meant to be exhaustive but to be indicative of sources that should be further studied and considered. The matrix yields sources different from those that the literature has pointed to before. Corruption coming from any one of the sources of influence poses questions related to the impact of these contextual factors on street-level work and policy implementation. What can be observed or perceived as predatory behaviour from SLBs might rather reflect the role of SLBs in contexts of corrupted policies, politics, management, and peers, where SLBs are tools for the pursuit of private interests.

References

Arellano-Gault, D. (2016). Understanding the trap of systemic corruption. *Governance* 29(4), 463–5. https://doi.org/10.1111/gove.12236

Arellano-Gault, D. (2017). Corruption as organizational process: Understanding the logic of the denormalization of corruption. *Contaduría y Administración* 62(3), 827–42. https://doi.org/10.1016/j.cya.2016.01.005

Arellano-Gault, D. and Rojas, G.S. (2021). Dealing with the 'original contradiction' in fighting corruption in countries with systemic corruption: A critique of the cases of Brazil and Mexico and their multiorganizational strategies. In J. Pozsgai-Alvarez (ed), *The Politics of Anti-Corruption Agencies in Latin America*. London: Routledge, pp 155–75.

Ashforth, B.E. and Anand, V. (2003). The normalization of corruption in organizations. *Research in Organizational Behavior*, 25, 1–52. https://doi.org/10.1016/S0191-3085(03)25001-2

Ashforth, B., Gioia, D., Robinson, S., and Trevino, L. (2008). Re-viewing organizational corruption. *Academy of Management Review*, 33(3), 670–84. https://doi.org/10.5465/AMR.2008.32465714

Batson, C.D., Batson, J.G., Slingsby, J.K., Harrell, Kevin L., Peekna, H.M., and Matthew, T.R. (1991). Empathic joy and the empathy-altruism hypothesis. *Journal of Personality and Social Psychology*, 61(3), 413–26. https://doi.org/10.1037/0022-3514.61.3.413

Bauhr, M. (2017). Need or greed? Conditions for collective action against corruption. *Governance*, 30(4), 561–81. https://doi.org/10.1111/gove.12232

Belle, N. and Cantarelli, P. (2017) What causes unethical behavior? A meta-analysis to set an agenda for public administration research. *Public Administration Review*, 77(3), 327–39. https://doi.org/10.1111/puar.12714

Bozeman, B., Molina Jr., A.L., and Kaufmann, W. (2018). Angling for sharks, not pilot fish: Deep corruption, venal corruption, and public values failure. *Perspectives on Public Management and Governance*, 1(1), 5–27. https://doi.org/10.1093/ppmgov/gvx002

Feldman, Y. and Halali, E. (2019). Regulating 'good' people in subtle conflicts of interest situations. *Journal of Business Ethics*, 154, 65–83. https://doi.org/10.1007/s10551-017-3468-8

Gofen, A., Meza, O., and Pérez-Chiqués, E. (2022). When street-level implementation meets systemic corruption. *Public Administration and Development*, 42(1), 72–84.

Gonzalez-Ocantos, E. and Oliveros, V. (2019). Clientelism in Latin American politics. In G. Prevost and H.E. Vanden (eds), *Oxford Encyclopedia of Latin American Politics*. New York: Oxford University Press, pp 1–28. https://doi.org/10.1093/acrefore/9780190228637.013.1677

Hassan, S., Wright, B.E., and Yukl, G. (2014). Does ethical leadership matter in government? Effects on organizational commitment, absenteeism and willingness to report ethical problems. *Public Administration Review*, 74(3), 333–43. https://doi.org/10.1111/puar.12216

Igiebor, G.O. (2019). Political corruption in Nigeria: Implications for economic development in the Fourth Republic. *Journal of Developing Societies*, 35(4), 493–513. https://doi.org/10.1177/0169796X19890745

Jancsics, D. (2019). Corruption as resource transfer: An interdisciplinary synthesis. *Public Administration Review*, 79(4), 523–37.

Jávor, I. and Jancsics, D. (2016). The role of power in organizational corruption: An empirical study. *Administration & Society*, 48(5), 527–58. https://doi.org/10.1177/0095399713514845

Lotta, G., Lima-Silva, F., and Favareto, A. (2022). Dealing with violence: Varied reactions from frontline workers acting in highly vulnerable territories. *Environment and Planning C: Politics and Space*, 40(2), 502–19.

Lotta, G., Pires, R., Hill, M., and Møller, M.O. (2022). Recontextualizing street-level bureaucracy in the developing world. *Public Administration and Development*, 42(1), 3–10.

Marquette, H. and Peiffer, C. (2018). Grappling with the 'real politics' of systemic corruption: Theoretical debates versus 'real-world' functions. *Governance*, 31(3), 499–514.

May, P.J. and Winter, S.C. (2009). Politicians, managers, and street-level bureaucrats: Influences on policy implementation. *Journal of Public Administration Research and Theory*, 19(3), 453–76.

Meyer-Sahling, J-H., and Mikkelsen, K.S. (2022). Codes of ethics, disciplinary codes and the effectiveness of anti-corruption frameworks: Evidence from a survey of civil servants in Poland. *Review of Public Personnel and Administration*, 42(1), 142–64. https://doi.org/10.1177/0734371X20949420

Meza, O. and Pérez-Chiqués, E. (2021). Corruption consolidation in local governments: A grounded analytical framework. *Public Administration*, 99(3), 530–46. https://doi.org/10.1111/padm.12698

Meza, O. and Zizumbo-Colunga, D. (2021). Constructions of noncompliance: Narratives and contexts in the case of administrative corruption. *International Public Management Journal*, 24(5), 623–45. https://doi.org/10.1080/10967494.2020.1793041

Mungiu-Pippidi, A. (2006). Corruption: Diagnosis and treatment. *Journal of Democracy*, 17(3), 86–99.

Mungiu-Pippidi, A. (2011). Contextual choices in fighting corruption: Lessons learned. *Norwegian Agency for Development Cooperation*, Report 4/2011. https://ssrn.com/abstract=2042021

Mutahi, N., Micheni, M., and Lake, M. (2022). The godfather provides: Enduring corruption and organizational hierarchy in the Kenyan Police Service. *Governance*, 36(2), 401–19. https://doi.org/10.1111/gove.12672

Needleman, M.L. and Needleman, C. (1979). Organizational crime: Two models of criminogenesis. *The Sociological Quarterly*, 20(4), 517–28. https://doi.org/10.1111/j.1533-8525.1979.tb01232.x

Nieuwbeerta, P., De Geest, G., and Siegers, J. (2003). Street-level corruption in industrialized and developing countries. *European Societies*, 5(2), 139–65.

Peeters, R. and Campos, S.A. (2022). Street-level bureaucracy in weak state institutions: A systematic review of the literature. *International Review of Administrative Sciences*, https://doi.org/10.1177/00208523221103196

Peeters, R., Gofen, A., and Meza, O. (2020). Gaming the system: Responses to dissatisfaction with public services beyond exit and voice. *Public Administration*, 98(4), 824–39. https://doi.org/10.1111/padm.12680

Peeters, R. and Dussauge Laguna, M.I. (2021). Acting out or playing along: A typology of citizens' low trust responses to public organizations. *Governance*, 34(4), 965–81. https://doi.org/10.1111/gove.12631

Pérez-Chiqués, E. and Meza, O. (2021). Trust-based corruption networks: A comparative analysis of two municipal governments. *Governance*, 34(4), 1039–56. https://doi.org/10.1111/gove.12554

Pianezzi, D. and Grossi, G. (2018). Corruption in migration management: A network perspective. *International Review of Administrative Sciences*, 86(1), 152–68.

Pinto, J., Leana, C.R., and Pil, F.K. (2008). Corrupt organizations or organizations of corrupt individuals? Two types of organization-level corruption. *Academy of Management Review*, 33(3), 685–709.

Rose-Ackerman, S. (1999). *Corruption and Government: Causes, Consequences, and Reform*. Cambridge: Cambridge University Press.

Scott, J.C. (1972). *Comparative Political Corruption*. New Jersey: Prentice Hall.

Stensöta, H., Wängnerud, L., and Svensson, R. (2015). Gender and corruption: The mediating power of institutional logics. *Governance*, 28(4), 475–96. https://doi.org/10.1111/gove.12120

Vega, R.A. and Maya, A.P. (2021). Operating at the edge of il/legality: Systemic corruption in Mexican health care. *The Journal of Latin American and Caribbean Anthropology*, 26(1), 46–64. https://doi.org/10.1111/jlca.12513

Wright, B.E., Hassan, S., and Park, J. (2016). Does a public service ethic encourage ethical behaviour? Public service motivation, ethical leadership and the willingness to report ethical problems. *Public Administration*, 94(3), 647–63. https://doi.org/10.1111/padm.12248

World Bank. (1997). *World Development Report 1997: The State in a Changing World*. New York: Oxford University Press. https://openknowledge.worldbank.org/handle/10986/5980.

Young, I.M. (2002). Lived body vs gender: Reflections on social structure and subjectivity. *Ratio*, 15(4), 410–28.

Zamir, E. and Sulitzeanu-Kenan, R. (2018) Explaining self-interested behavior of public-spirited policy makers. *Public Administration Review*, 78(4), 579–92.

Zey-Ferrell, M., Weaver, K., and Ferrell, O.C. (1979). Predicting unethical behavior among marketing practitioners. *Human Relations*, 32(7), 557–69. https://doi.org/10.1177/001872677903200702

Zizumbo Colunga, D. and Meza, O. (2023). Flying under the radar: How frames influence public officials' perceptions of corruption. *Political Behavior*, 45, 995–1014. https://doi.org/10.1007/s11109-021-09745-3

PART II

Exploring institutional contexts

5

Weak institutions and dangerous working conditions: coping by the wiremen of public electricity distribution utility in India

Sneha Swami and Subodh Wagle

Introduction

Fulfilling its energy needs is a precondition for the economic development of any country. Energy in the form of electricity has a vital role to play in improving the quality of life of citizens as well as in the industrial development of the country. Further, meaningful access to adequate and appropriate electricity services to households and industries requires adequate, reliable, quality, and affordable electricity supply. In this regard, India claims to have achieved near-complete electrification, which means almost all households and firms are connected to the electricity network; however, due to various reasons, the electricity supply remains unreliable, inadequate, and of low-quality in most parts of the country (Bhattacharyya, 2010; ESMI, 2019).

In the electricity sector, the organisation responsible for supplying electricity to consumers in the last leg of the electricity network – identified as the distribution of electricity – is called electricity distribution utility or EDU. EDU is entrusted with the responsibility of providing electricity services to consumers as well as of collecting revenue – that is, payment for these services – from consumers for financially supporting the entire value chain of electricity supply. In India, electricity distribution in most parts of the country is handled by state-owned public electricity distribution utilities (hereinafter called PEDU). Indian PEDUs historically suffer from high financial losses and low levels of public trust. While high financial losses are primarily attributed to non-payment of electricity bills and political interference at the state or local levels, the poor performance of lower-level employees is cited as one of the leading causes underlying low public trust (Min and Golden, 2014). Further, this poor performance of lower-level employees of PEDUs, in turn, is often attributed to corruption, indiscipline as well as lack of capacities, accountability, and motivation among these employees (Bhattacharya and Patel, 2011; Sharma et al, 2016; Sarangi, et al, 2021). For example, Smith (2004) discusses the role of utility employees in corrupt practices such as electricity theft and deliberate mistakes in data collected from electricity meters. Thus, the poor performance of the workforce of the PEDUs, especially frontline workers, is seen as the bane of PEDUs as well as the electricity sector in India.

The frontline workers working in the field offices of Indian PEDUs are called wiremen, who are salaried and 'permanent' employees of the PEDUs. The eligibility criteria for selection as a wireman include satisfactory performance in the school certificate examination and earning a diploma from any industrial training institute (ITI); no interview or screening test is conducted while recruiting wiremen. After recruitment, wiremen are given training for one to two weeks. The majority of wiremen in India are male, but there are few female field-staff who are also identified as 'wiremen'. However, the female wiremen do not go to the field to attend to consumer complaints or for technical work. These wiremen – supervised by an Assistant Engineer or AE – are responsible for all the frontline tasks involved in the last-mile of provisioning of electricity services to electricity consumers, including restoring interrupted supply, maintaining infrastructure, recovering arrears of bills from defaulting consumers, addressing consumer complaints, and providing new electricity connections. Thus, the wiremen of Indian PEDUs effectively work as policy implementers who deliver policy benefits related to electricity distribution. Further, they are in direct contact with consumers and enjoy some discretion while making everyday decisions. These key attributes of the tasks of wiremen fit them into the category of street-level bureaucrats (SLBs as defined by Lipsky [1980]).

Though they handle such critical tasks, the working conditions of the wiremen in Indian PEDUs are marked by work pressures exerted by higher authorities to complete the policy targets, resolve consumer complaints, and address supply interruptions with the highest priority. Another source of work-stress are the threats of physical injury created by dangerous working conditions surrounding their regular tasks such as erection, maintenance, and repair, especially of the high-voltage distribution network. Wiremen adopt diverse coping strategies to survive these stressful and dangerous working conditions.

With this background, this chapter looks into the issue of the occupational hazards and dangers faced by wiremen of an Indian PEDU, which are rooted in the institutional lacuna characterised in the literature as the weak institutional environment. The main proposition of the chapter is that the weak institutional environment creates dangerous working conditions – that is, working conditions that pose threats of physical injuries – to which the wiremen of the Indian PEDU respond with certain coping actions. These coping actions are of public and academic concern due to their adverse impact on the wiremen, electricity consumers, PEDUs, and on the public in general. After this introductory section, the next section in the chapter reviews literature relevant to the proposition of the chapter for framing the proposition and situating it in the existing literature. The following section presents the evidence supporting the proposition that emerged from a field research project. The fourth section compares some findings of this research with relevant findings from the literature. The last section presents some concluding remarks.

Coming to the research methods, the evidence presented in this chapter is based on the analysis – using the thematic analysis technique – of qualitative data collected for a qualitative–interpretivist research project with a broader scope. The data were collected through extended, immersive fieldwork of about four months' duration conducted at seven field-level offices (called Section Offices) of an Indian PEDU – called here MPEDU – located in two districts in the state of Maharashtra, India. The main data collection method was in-depth, multi-round, unstructured, and semi-structured interviews of 42 wiremen (five of them female), who were the frontline workers employed by the MPEDU. In addition, data were also collected through informal interactions with consumers and wiremen, as well as through participant and non-participant observation in the field-level offices and at various field sites where the wiremen carried out their tasks.

Frontline workers and occupational dangers

The proposition of the chapter mentioned before involves three substantive themes – weak institutional environment, street-level bureaucracy theory, and occupational hazards and dangers of physical harm to SLBs. The introductory chapter of the book presents a detailed review of the first two of these three themes. Hence, this section presents a review of the literature on the third theme in some detail.

Serious occupational dangers and dangerous work conditions have received considerable attention in academic research (Chau, et al, 2007; Liu and Tsai, 2012; Zolnikov et al, 2018). The issue of occupational health is of greater concern for certain occupations or in certain sectors because the work in these sectors or occupations inherently involves occupational dangers – that is, the threat of physical harm, such as diseases, physical wounds, mental trauma, or fatal or non-fatal accidents. Such sectors and occupations include construction, manufacturing, mining, healthcare, energy, agriculture, and sanitation (Dodoo et al, 2019). However, in each of these sectors, different factors create dangerous working conditions, posing different types of dangers. For example, health professionals are at the risk of physical injury, infectious diseases, mental trauma, or psychological disorders (Tipayamongkholgul et al, 2016), which are often rooted in causal factors like inadequate staff, lack of adequate or appropriate training, and inadequate, inappropriate, or faulty equipment. They are also vulnerable to physical and verbal abuse by patients or patients' relatives (Angland et al, 2014). The factors at the root of such abuse include poor security measures, overcrowding of patients, as well as inexperienced and inadequate human resources, resulting in lower-than-expected service levels or excessive waiting times for patients. The workers from the sanitation sector face health hazards like exposure to harmful gases, cardiovascular degeneration, infections and skin problems, respiratory diseases, or even social atrocities (Tiwari, 2008). However, these workers are often not provided with the necessary safety gear or proper equipment (Darokar, 2019). Even street-sweeping workers are exposed to road dust and other contaminants leading to respiratory problems (Patil and Kamble, 2017). Similarly, police officers face a range of dangers at work, including homicide, assaults, communicable diseases, injuries, or abuse (Mayhew, 2001).

The tasks of wiremen or the SLBs of PEDUs include the erection, maintenance, or repair of infrastructure for electricity distribution, which involves working with electrical wires and equipment carrying live electricity at high voltages as well as located at a significant height. As a result, they constantly face a serious risk of electric shock, accidental falls, strikes by falling objects, and collapsing of support equipment; all of which lead to physical injuries or sometimes death (Lu et al, 2021). Lu et al (2021) identify and broadly categorise the sources of dangers, especially in the case of the electricity distribution sector, in four different types of factors: personal, object-related, environmental, and managerial. The personal factors include work skills, knowledge, mental state, work mood, and team cooperation. The object-related factors involve specifics of equipment and tools used by the personnel and the specifics of their work sites. The environmental factors are weather conditions, safety culture, and organisational commitment to safety. Finally, the managerial factors include resource allocation, workload, work duration, work pressure, training given to the staff, abilities to handle accidents, degree of accountability for accidents, and presence of work leaders on site. The significance attached to the organisational and managerial factors in the literature indicates that the sources of dangers and the resultant dangers are often rooted in institutional environments.

Another study by Päivinen (2006) elaborates on the different types of dangers faced by electricians working in the electricity sector (that is, wiremen) and the sources of these dangers. Apart from facing risks of accidents while working with hand tools, electricians face unique and severe dangers created by the cold, slippery, or dark conditions in which they are often forced to work. Further, objects falling from poles is the most frequent cause of accidents for electricians. Electricians' work calls for manual handling of dangerous materials and lifting of heavy equipment. Interestingly, the study mentions that slipping, climbing, and other dangers pertaining to tasks performed at significant heights are all deemed dangerous, but falling from these heights is not explicitly mentioned (Päivinen, 2006). The task of climbing poles is seen as a highly dangerous and physically demanding task, and it comes with the risk of uncontrollably slipping down or being left dangling at a height in the safety harness, which, in turn, poses the risks of serious physical harm. Further, the tasks performed at height are seen as involving circumstances and postures that are both physically demanding and highly risky. Any incidence of sliding or slipping on wet or snowy terrains would lead to hitting forcefully against nearby structures or dropping a hand tool, both of which pose a further risk of serious physical injuries. Thus, as per the literature, the nature of work, working conditions, and behaviour of SLBs, together, pose dangers of fatal or non-fatal physical injuries for SLBs in the electricity distribution sector.

In the background of this discussion, this chapter discusses and establishes the proposition that the weak institutional environment creates dangerous work conditions – that is, conditions that pose risks or threats of serious physical injury – for the wiremen, that is, the SLBs in the Indian PEDU, who respond to these dangers by adopting certain coping actions. These coping actions, in turn, impact the policy outcome, functioning, and interests of the PEDU or the well-being of wiremen and consumers.

Weak institutions, dangers, and coping by wiremen

This section establishes the above-mentioned proposition of the chapter by presenting evidence that emerged from the field research project mentioned previously. It demonstrates how the dangerous working conditions are created by institutional weaknesses; how these conditions lead to the threats of physical injuries to the wiremen; and how wiremen respond to these threats with diverse coping actions. This section, except the last subsection, discusses the dangerous working conditions created by institutional weaknesses such as lacunas in the administrative and organisational capacities – institutional void and institutional dysfunctionality, resource constraints, accountability gaps, professional lacunas, and political interference. The last subsection presents an analysis of the coping actions adopted by wiremen in response to these dangerous working conditions.

Institutional void and institutional dysfunctionality

The Indian PEDU, called MPEDU, suffers from two specific but interrelated manifestations of the lack of administrative capacities – institutional void and institutional dysfunctionality – that create dangerous working conditions. While institutional void pertains to the absence of explicitly articulated rules or the effective freedom to not follow non-mandatory or discretionary rules, institutional dysfunctionality refers to non-compliance with mandatory rules as well as to the lack of effective enforcement in response to such non-compliance.

A good example demonstrating such institutional void and institutional dysfunctionality in the case of MPEDU pertains to the tasks related to the maintenance of infrastructure. Two types of maintenance tasks are defined by MPEDU – preventive maintenance tasks and breakdown maintenance tasks. The preventive maintenance tasks – implying proactive and prior efforts to pre-empt faults in the electricity supply in future – include tasks like cutting down branches of trees that would obstruct the electric lines or tightening of sagging distribution wires. And the breakdown maintenance tasks include all tasks pertaining to restarting the electricity supply interrupted because of faults in the electricity distribution infrastructure. Thus, breakdown maintenance essentially involves the repair of such faults in a post-facto manner. While a utility cannot easily escape from the responsibility of breakdown maintenance, preventive maintenance, though critical for continued smooth operations of the network over a long period, remains an organisational choice. It is noteworthy that MPEDU does not prescribe any mandatory rules regarding the frequency, process, or quality criteria for preventive maintenance. MPEDU has a higher budget for breakdown maintenance than that for preventive maintenance. Thus, the management of MPEDU gives less importance to the preventive maintenance of its electric infrastructure. Similarly, MPEDU employees do not pay much attention to infrastructure maintenance until and unless some component of the electric infrastructure fails. With the absence of norms or enforcement of a preventive maintenance schedule, MPEDU field offices carry it out at their convenience and not as per the predetermined plan. Even when wiremen plan for preventive maintenance activities, their plans often remain unexecuted due to interference with other unplanned tasks – such as revenue recovery – that are given a higher priority by their superiors. The immediate supervisors often pressurise wiremen to work on the tasks prioritised by higher authorities at the cost of routine, planned tasks such as preventive maintenance. Thus, while there is an institutional void in the form of a lack of mandatory rules governing preventive maintenance, the neglect of preventive maintenance by wiremen and their higher authorities demonstrates institutional dysfunctionality.

The result of this institutional void and dysfunctionality is the neglect of preventive maintenance that makes the distribution network technically precarious; as a result creating dangerous work conditions for wiremen. For example, due to the neglect of pre-monsoon preventive maintenance, fast-growing vines climb over electricity poles, switch-boxes, and transformers while thickets of bushes and shrubs completely cover the surrounding areas

Figure 5.1: Vines and vegetation thickets surrounding a distribution transformer during monsoon

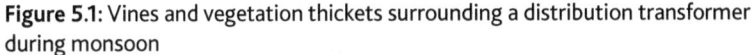

(Figure 5.1). These conditions pose serious risks of bites and attacks by honey bees, snakes, lizards, larvae, and mosquitoes while performing the repair work. The wiremen report sightings of wild animals in the thickets around transformers located near the forest areas.

Another example of the lack of administrative capacity, more specifically in the form of an institutional dysfunctionality, relates to the failure of higher authorities to control the rampant non-compliance by wiremen with the rules prescribing the use of safety equipment. Wiremen are supposed to wear rubber hand gloves and protective helmets as well as use an earthing rod while working on the 'live' distribution wires conducting electricity. Most wiremen use rubber gloves, but not all wiremen use helmets or earthing rods (Figure 5.2). As there is a lack of monitoring of field tasks carried out

Figure 5.2: Rubber gloves used by wiremen

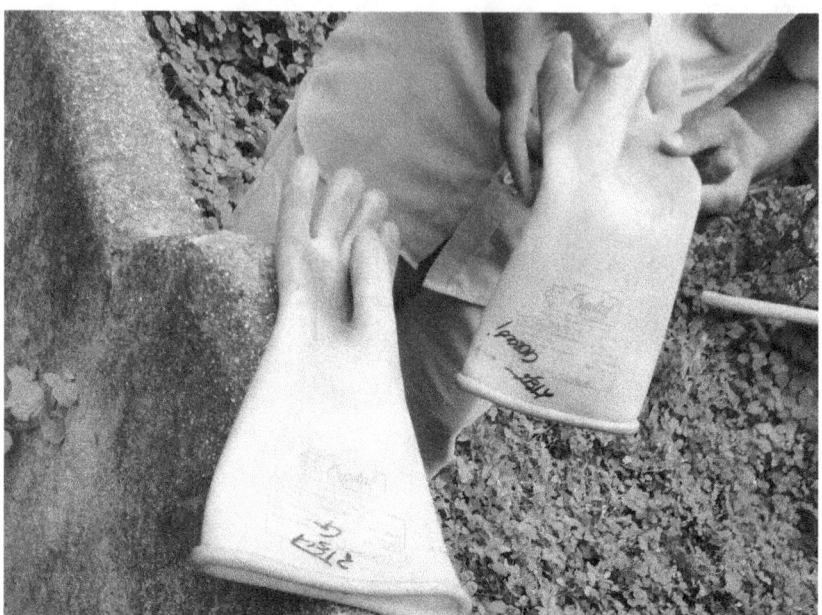

by wiremen, there is no enforcement of rules prescribing the use of safety equipment. This certainly increases the dangers for wiremen while working on the distribution lines carrying live electricity supply.

Resource constraints causing dangers

A major precondition for effective, timely, and efficient delivery of electricity services by SLBs is the timely availability of adequate and appropriate resources such as human resources, material resources – especially equipment, tools, and materials needed for maintenance and repair – and financial resources to purchase required material from the market. As supply interruptions of any type may occur at any instance, these resources are expected to be readily available at field offices all the time; however, this is not the case on most occasions. As a result, when the electric supply is interrupted, the wiremen, on their own, have to make extra efforts to arrange all the required resources in a short time and as per the need of the technical problem.

For attending to supply interruptions, wiremen need tools and instruments like rubber gloves, gumboots, testers, and other hand tools for working

Figure 5.3: Ladder purchased by staff of a section office to climb on a smooth pole

on the live electricity distribution lines. However, often, these tools are not available in a timely manner. MPEDU provides some tools – such as rubber gloves, engineering helmets, and testers – in a limited quantity, but other essential tools especially related to safety – like hand tools, raincoats, and gumboots – are not provided. The lack of availability of such safety equipment poses the danger of electric shock to wiremen while working on the live electric wires.

MPEDU does not provide a ladder to wiremen, which is required to climb the smooth metal poles (of about 15 to 20 centimetres diameter) on which the distribution lines are hung above the ground at a height of more than 4 metres (Figure 5.3). In the initial period of their employment, the wiremen are expected to learn to climb up such poles without the use of any equipment. However, it is physically challenging and dangerous, especially

Figure 5.4: Swing-like contraption used by wiremen

for elderly wiremen, to climb these poles. MPEDU also does not provide any safety harness. Hence, there is always a serious risk of falling off the smooth pole while climbing it or while working at the top of the pole. After climbing the pole, wiremen, while working on the electric connections located at the top of the pole, sit on a swing-like contraption made of a loop of a thick rope tied to the pole (Figure 5.4). Wiremen cited instances of failure of this contraption, causing wiremen to fall down from the top of the pole and suffer severe injuries.

Not only the safety equipment but also the appropriate material resources – like poles, wires, conductors, or insulators – required for attending to interruptions or carrying out the repairs are not supplied by MPEDU in adequate quantity and on a regular basis. Wiremen have to frequently purchase such materials from the market and apply for reimbursement of the money spent. As these reimbursements come with many delays, wiremen prefer to compromise on the quantity or quality of the material while making these purchases in order to save money, though they are well aware of the dangers involved.

During the pandemic (that is, during the extended periods in 2020 and 2021), field offices were fully functional as the electricity supply was supposed to be maintained continuously. Wiremen had to go to various consumer locations to resolve supply-related problems. Even though they did not have to go inside the houses of consumers, wiremen had to enter areas that were sealed by health authorities due to the presence of a large number of COVID-19 cases. However, MPEDU did not make any special efforts to provide additional protection – apart from what was provided by masks and sanitisers – to wiremen to deal with the risks of infection they faced during such operations. During this entire period, wiremen were given a one-time special allowance of INR 1,000 (equivalent to US$12.5) to buy masks or the sanitiser. This amount was woefully inadequate to buy these basic protective materials for the extended duration of the pandemic, forcing wiremen to purchase such essential equipment with their own money or have the risk of infection. For hospitalisation and medical expenses, every wireman had insurance coverage of INR 500,000 (approximately US$6,250). However, MPEDU paid only 40 per cent of the premium for this insurance; the remaining 60 per cent of the premium was deducted by MPEDU from the salaries of wiremen. The wiremen who were infected by the COVID-19 virus had to bear the cost of about half of the hospital bills from their own pockets. Depending on the treatment, such expenses were almost two to three times their monthly salary.

Accountability gaps causing dangers

MPEDU prescribes certain standard operating procedures (SOPs) and standard technical specifications governing the tasks pertaining to the erection of the infrastructure for the distribution system. For example, such specifications are prescribed for insulators or switches on electric transformers, for conductors as per the technical requirements of the supply load, and for the depth of the pits for laying the foundations of poles. However, the contractors or wiremen involved in these tasks do not follow many such standards while installing or repairing. Such non-compliance with technical specifications is also widespread in the purchase of material, which results in the purchase of non-standard material that costs less but which is of a different specification or even of inferior quality. However, there are no effective accountability procedures to curb such practices, reflecting a significant accountability gap – that is, the lack of an explicit and effective system of enforcing accountability – and, thus, a lacuna in the administrative capacity of MPEDU. This accountability gap often leads to non-compliance with SOPs and the use of non-standard material, which, in turn, leads to the creation of dangerous work conditions for wiremen.

The oft-cited reason for such non-compliance with standards is the resultant savings in expenditure. However, it is agreed that such non-compliance often leads to the creation of dangerous work conditions that pose threats and risks to wiremen. For example, non-compliance with SOPs governing the erection of electric poles by private contractors increases the risk that these poles may fall due to the weight of the wiremen working at the top of the pole carrying live wires. However, there are no monitoring or accountability procedures in place to regulate such non-compliant behaviour of private contractors, which could be seen as the basic requirement of the practice of outsourcing services to private contractors. In another instance of such accountability gaps creating dangers for wiremen, private contractors compromise the quality standards for certain components while installing the distribution equipment. Such substandard components create serious risks for wiremen working on maintenance or repair of these equipment. Under AE's supervision, wiremen are expected to monitor these tasks carried out by the private contractors. However, due to the lack of time or motivation, wiremen do not rigorously monitor the performance of such tasks by the contractors. When wiremen or AE notice such low-quality components at a later point in time, they ask the contractors concerned to replace the sub-standard components. However, in many instances, the private contractors successfully avoided such replacement, citing different excuses. In one instance, the contractor exerted political pressure on higher officials of MPEDU to release payments for these tasks without making such replacements. Thus, wiremen suffer serious risks due to the accountability gaps that allow private contractors to escape their responsibilities.

Inadequate professionalisation leading to dangers

Another type of factor characterising weak institutions are the lacunas in the professional aspects of the work of the SLBs. A critical factor that leads to dangerous working conditions for the wiremen is the failure on the part of the wiremen themselves to adhere to professional norms and practices. Even when some safety equipment is available, wiremen do not make use of the safety equipment. In the presence of their superiors, however, wiremen use all the available safety equipment. In another example, whenever the underground cables (which are invisible from above the ground) are connected to switches in the pillar boxes, the professional norm is to clearly record these connections in the written form inside the pillar boxes. This helps wiremen to quickly identify later the faulty connections and repair them without any risk. Unfortunately, almost as a general practice, MPEDU personnel involved in installation or repair do not make such written records, posing dangers to wiremen, especially new and inexperienced wiremen, attempting to repair faults in these cables.

A major area of MPEDU's work affected by the lack of professionalism is the interactions between the wireman and consumers. These interactions form a large part of the tasks carried out by wiremen. The two main types of occasions for most consumers–wiremen interactions are, first, 'revenue recovery' (or recovery of arrears of electricity bills) from defaulting consumers and, second, addressing complaints about the interruptions or low quality of electric supply. Both these types of interactions involve contestations and have the potential for serious conflict as both parties involved in these interactions are not just irritated but perceive themselves as victims and the other parties as villains. As a result, most of these interactions lead to verbal exchanges that soon aggravate into aggressive behaviour on the part of both parties but mainly consumers. However, the wiremen, who act as representatives of MPEDU in these interactions, do not receive any training on how to handle this vital component of their daily work, apart from a general instruction to always speak politely with consumers. Due to the professional failure of wiremen to handle such situations tactfully, on many occasions, such interactions end in physical altercations. In such an eventuality, wiremen need protection, but no such protection is provided to them by MPEDU. Wiremen reported many instances when consumers had hurt them physically, and they had to report such cases to local police stations.

Undue political interference posing dangers

The discussion in the first chapter on the political factors as aspects of weak institutions primarily refers to the undue influence of political actors on the functioning of SLBs. For wiremen of MPEDU, a major source of danger are the politically connected consumers. The wiremen often face conflicts in the field due to contentious situations or cantankerous consumers, as explained before. Consumers are irritated by repeated interruptions caused by chronic technical problems that are often rooted in diverse institutional weaknesses. In other situations, defaulting consumers get agitated when wiremen are at their doorsteps to recover arrears or disconnect the supply of the consumers with frequent payment defaults. In many such situations, consumers argue, use bad language, or even enter into verbal altercations. However, consumers who have political connections or are active in politics try using physical force to stop the wiremen from performing these tasks. These consumers seek help from local politicians-cum-musclemen to confront wiremen physically.

One such consumers' group is farmers or agricultural consumers in rural areas who have strong, politically active associations. As agricultural consumers depend on electricity for watering their farms, the timely and regular electricity supply of appropriate voltage is their critical need for ensuring proper crop growth. As a result, local farmers or agricultural consumers of MPEDU and their associations are quite active and vocal in matters related to timely and quality electricity supply. With political power behind them, farmers often resort to strong-arm tactics against wiremen. The risks of being victims of physical violence by politically active, militant farmers are further complicated by the social pressures on wiremen as most of these wiremen belong to local areas, have family or kinship connections with many of their farmer-consumers, and also have to deal with local politicians in their daily lives.

In some cases, consumers and local political activists resort to attacking and ransacking MPEDU's field offices. In such situations, the wiremen face the danger of serious physical injuries due to the violent actions of politically influential consumers.

Dangers due to natural disasters

Another interesting set of observations pertains to the dangers faced by wiremen due to natural disasters – such as floods, thunderstorms, or torrential monsoon rain spells. While these natural disasters act as sources of serious danger to wiremen, they are also found to further aggravate the dangers created by the weak institutional factors mentioned before. During floods, wiremen have to travel to different locations in the flooded areas to either disconnect or restore the electricity supply, depending on the changing flood situations. They even have to take dangerous rides in small rescue boats along with their unwieldy equipment to disconnect the supply and eliminate the danger of electrocution to the local population. The wiremen shared that, in certain instances, the small boats carrying wiremen and their equipment to flooded regions capsized, and wiremen were caught in strong flood currents, facing the danger of drowning. While attempting to disconnect or reconnect the electric supply, the major danger is the risk of electrocution by the electric current flowing through water. The unpredictability of such dangers further aggravates the stress due to these threats. Moreover, the limited human resources available with MPEDU force wiremen to stay put in their field offices for days to deal with emergencies created by such natural disasters. This leads the wiremen to suffer from acute fatigue and excessive stress, which makes them more vulnerable to dangers caused by calamities. Thus, this lacuna in the administrative capacity – shortage of human resources – aggravates further the dangerous working created by calamities.

In another example of a natural disaster, the heavy winds and torrential rains during the monsoon season pose the danger of injuries due to falling trees or due to breaking and falling of live electricity distribution wires while wiremen are working under these wires. Also, in the monsoon season, moisture seeps into the old equipment carrying live electricity current, putting the wiremen at risk of electrocution by the leaked electric current. During these natural calamities, the occurrence of such dangerous situations and conditions is highly unpredictable. MPEDU lacks the planning procedures and norms required to deal effectively with such events. The lack of planning – a manifestation of a professional type of institutional weakness – for such natural disasters aggravates the dangers for the wiremen. As a result, wiremen have to work with acute precautions and have to remain in 'alert mode' all the time.

Thus, the five types of institutional weaknesses – institutional void and dysfunctionality, resource constraints, accountability gaps, political interferences, and professional lacunas – create diverse types of dangerous work conditions, putting the wiremen at risk of serious physical injuries or even death.

Broad coping strategies of wiremen

To deal with these dangerous work conditions, the wiremen of MPEDU deploy some broad coping strategies. The first such oft-deployed broad coping strategy is 'taking extra precautions' to respond especially to the dangers created by natural factors such as wild animals as well as live electricity. For example, the wiremen always check such dangerous areas thoroughly before entering them. Using long sticks, they tap the poles and switch-boxes from afar before opening the boxes to shoo away lizards or snakes. The wiremen quite frequently use mosquito repellent creams to protect themselves from insect bites. To deal with such dangers, wiremen also use another broad coping strategy of 'providing mutual support' to fellow wiremen; they take extra efforts to protect their colleagues dealing directly with these dangers. They usually go in a group of three or four to work at the sites in forests or bush areas. At night, they carry torches so that the thickets surrounding pillars can be thoroughly inspected before entering, and the light from the torches will force wild animals to flee. The wiremen also resort to these two broad strategies for dealing with local politicians or politically dominant consumers like farmers. Their thorough knowledge of local politics and politicians helps the wiremen to identify consumers with close political connections beforehand. Wiremen then try to handle such consumers carefully. While communicating with these actors, wiremen are very cautious and use very polite language. Further, to protect each other from violence, the wiremen go in a big group rather than going individually or in pairs while taking action against such consumers.

The higher authorities often take a high-handed approach, forcing wiremen to neglect critically essential tasks such as preventive maintenance and jeopardising the safety of wiremen. The wiremen seem to be helpless in the face of these pressures and resort to another broad coping strategy, called here 'reconciled acquiescing' or 'reconciled acquiescence', which implies passive acceptance or submission – out of helplessness – to dangerous situations created by the repressive behaviour of dominant actors. This strategy of 'reconciled acquiescing' is also resorted to by wiremen while facing another set of dominant actors, the politicians and politically dominant consumers, whose inordinate demands are fulfilled readily and on priority by wiremen, even at times by suspending norms and rules.

To deal with dangers caused by resource constraints, a broad coping strategy frequently used by the wiremen is the strategy of 'self-financing safety' – that is, spending from their own pockets to deal with danger and buy safety equipment. For example, the wiremen buy necessary equipment from the market by spending their own money. There is no financial provision with field offices to reimburse such expenses. At one field office, a group of wiremen gifted a set of hand tools to a wireman from the same office on his birthday so that they could use these gifted hand tools. Essential equipment like a ladder to climb the poles is often not provided by MPEDU. As the ladder of the adequate size and appropriate type was a significant price (around INR 12000, equivalent to US$150), all wiremen and the Assistant Engineer in one field office pooled together INR 500 to 600 (equivalent to about US$7) each to buy the ladder (Figure 5.3). It was reported that this ladder made their work a lot easier. However, employees attached to one field office could only afford to buy one ladder. As a result, when tasks requiring the ladder occurred simultaneously at different locations, wiremen at one location could use the ladder, but at the other locations, they had no other option but to accept the risks involved in climbing the pole without the ladder, which can be seen as another instance of 'reconciled acquiescence'.

However, when wiremen cannot deploy the strategy of 'self-financing safety' due to limited financial capacity on their part to deal with dangers due to resource constraints, they resort to the other two previously mentioned broad coping strategies that they can manage without extra finances– 'providing mutual support' and 'taking extra precautions'. Wiremen are aware of risks caused by the poor-quality components and equipment supplied by MPEDU or purchased by them to save money. Hence, they always take precautions and make multiple checks on components and equipment before initiating any repair or maintenance work. Similarly, when performing risky tasks, different wiremen in a team continuously and simultaneously watch different components and equipment while continuously communicating with and warning each other.

When self-financing is impossible, wiremen also resort to another broad coping strategy of 'contriving contraptions' that involves creating a low-cost alternative to the standard equipment or standard material using locally available and free (or very low-cost) material. For example, when low-voltage insulators are not available, the wiremen often use a piece of discarded rubber footwear in place of such insulators. Another example is the make-shift covers built by wiremen for the switch-boxes on electricity poles – to replace the original metal covers stolen by miscreants – using the discarded wooden pieces that were locally available at no cost. In local parlance, this is called a jugaad (Singh et al, 2012).

But when even these three broad strategies cannot be deployed, for instance, when the ladder is not available, cannot be purchased, and cannot be built, the wiremen have no other option but to bear the risks involved in climbing the pole without the ladder. In essence, in such situations, the wiremen silently submit themselves to the dangers involved in the tasks allotted to them – an instance of the broad strategy of 'reconciled acquiescing'. In certain interesting situations, wiremen integrate two broad coping strategies – that is, 'self-financing safety' and 'reconciled acquiescence'. As MPEDU significantly delay the reimbursement of expenditure made by wiremen from their own pockets, wiremen compromise on the quantity or quality of the material purchased and used. This is done in order to save money, though they are aware that this would potentially lead to danger. Thus, on one hand, wiremen try to protect themselves from danger by resorting to the strategy of 'self-financing safety'. But, on the other hand, when the self-financing becomes impossible, wiremen resort to the strategy of 'reconciled acquiescence' by submitting to the dangers caused by lower quantity or quality of materials purchased and used by them, which is the result of the delays in reimbursement caused by their higher authorities.

Apart from these frequently used broad coping strategies, wiremen employ some other interesting coping strategies. While wiremen do not often use safety equipment even if it is available, however, in the presence of their superiors, they resort to 'feigned compliance' and use the available safety equipment. While dealing with difficult or politically dominant consumers, they engage in the strategy of 'diverting the dangers' by sending such consumers to their superiors (typically Assistant Engineers). Many senior wiremen, while working under such dangerous working conditions over long durations, resort to 'substance abuse', becoming addicted to tobacco or alcohol. As another coping strategy, the wiremen often rely on 'collective action'. Almost all wiremen are members of labour unions or trade unions that often fight with MPEDU management for protecting the labour rights of their members or against any injustice to wiremen at the individual or group levels. The unions protect and support their members against the pressures and actions of dominant consumers or higher officials.

Thus, the wiremen facing the dangers that threaten their safety resort to diverse broad coping strategies. Some of the frequently used broad coping strategies include: providing mutual support, taking extra precautions, self-financing safety, reconciled acquiescing (to dominant actors), and jugaad or contrivance. At times, these are supplemented by other coping strategies such as diverting dangers, feigned compliance, collective action, or substance abuse.

The costs of coping strategies like self-financing safety, providing mutual support, and reconciled acquiescing are borne primarily by the wiremen themselves. Some coping strategies, like taking extra precautions, lead to significant delays in the timeline of repair and maintenance work, primarily affecting the overall performance of MPEDU and service delivery to consumers of MPEDU. Similarly, the 'reconciled acquiescence' of the wiremen by suspending norms to give priority to the demands of the politically dominant consumers often takes a significant toll on the interests of other electricity consumers. However, when as part of the combined strategy of 'self-financing safety' and 'reconciled acquiescence', wiremen purchase and use less than the required quantity of material or low-quality material for repair or maintenance of electric infrastructure, it not only leads to dangerous situations for wiremen but also to frequent requirement of repair, thus, affecting the well-being of both wiremen and consumers.

Dangers and coping by wiremen: drawing parallels

The discussion in the previous section on the dangerous working conditions faced by the wiremen of MPEDU and the coping strategies they adopt in response have some parallels from the other sectors that are discussed in the literature. As mentioned before, the literature identifies four categories of sources of dangers faced specifically by workers in the electricity distribution sector – personal, object-related, environmental, and managerial (Lu et al, 2021). The wiremen working with MPEDU face dangers from all these four categories of sources. While their attitudes – a personal attribute – shape their non-adherence to safety-related norms, which put them in danger, the live electricity flowing through the wires with which they work is the second type of (the object-related) source of danger. Similarly, natural calamities and politically dominant consumers form the third type of sources that pertain to environmental causes, whereas the weak institutional setting surrounding their work exposes them to the fourth category of sources of dangers. The discussion in the previous section also established that the wiremen in MPEDU face most of the dangerous working conditions that are reported in the study by Päivinen (2006).

Resource constraints, as the manifestation of lacunas in the administrative capacity (Gibson, 2004), are identified in the SLB literature as one of the obstacles to effective policy implementation, and the use of available resources is one of the reasons for the use of discretions by SLBs (Lipsky, 1980). Resource shortages are seen in the literature as predetermining the informal practices (that is, coping actions) of SLBs in diverse sectors, which may result in denial of service or poor quality service delivery to citizens (Brodkin, 2012). In addition to poorly equipped offices and limited facilities like communication facilities, the resource constraints in terms of scarcity of certain key resources – such as drugs in the health sector – are cited repeatedly in the literature as a major problem (Walker and Gilson, 2004). Similarly, in the case of wiremen working with MPEDU, resource shortages, especially shortages of safety equipment, pose dangers to their life. The lack of essential equipment like a ladder forces wiremen into both physical drudgery and danger. Often, wiremen have to share the essential protective equipment like rubber gloves that protect them from electrocution, causing instant death.

The bureaucracies in developing countries and post-authoritarian regimes are found to be politicised more often. In such situations, politicians have a variety of options available to them for influencing and controlling the bureaucracy (Cornell and Lapuente, 2014). A study by Iyer and Mani (2012) finds that politicians working under electoral pressures and using their formal and informal powers try to interfere and control bureaucrats who, in turn, are concerned about their career prospects. The adverse implications of widespread, undue political interference in the functioning of the Indian PEDUs is well documented in the literature (Golden and Min, 2013; Min and Golden, 2014; Baskaran et al, 2015). In the case of Indian PEDUs, politicians influence the transfers and promotions of the frontline workers and their superiors (Cornell and Lapuente, 2014), but the more frequent mode of interference adopted by politicians is to put pressure on SLBs to suspend or abandon enforcement of rules to serve the politically connected consumers. The wiremen are more concerned about the physical harm caused by violent mobs instigated by local politicians if they resist such demands made by politicians. In response, wiremen favour politically influential consumers to avoid the risk to their careers and their lives. Lameck and Hulst (2020) observed that the skewed distribution of resources as well as differing ground conditions, especially in rural contexts as compared to urban contexts, aggravated organisational challenges and posed additional or particular challenges for frontline workers. In the present study, the electricity distribution infrastructure is found to be comparatively more ill-maintained in rural areas; as a result, there is a higher incidence of dangers of physical harm to wiremen from wildlife or insects in rural or forest areas.

Coming to the coping strategies by SLBs, in the study reported by Lavee (2021), participants informally spend their own personal resources for their customers in order to complement insufficient, formally provided work materials. In a similar vein, to cope up with such resource constraints, wiremen of MPEDU engage in the coping strategy of 'self-financing safety' by spending money from their own pockets. To cope with dangers in their work environment, police officers were found to be consuming alcohol and tobacco at rates higher than the general population (Smith et al, 2005). In a similar observation, many senior wiremen in the study, suffering from high blood pressure and other health problems due to working under severe stress for many years, are also addicted to tobacco and alcohol due to work stresses. Leung et al (2003) observe such addiction and habit of overeating among construction professionals, which they term 'behavioural expression of unpleasant emotions'. These scholars call this coping strategy 'emotional discharge'. Such behaviour is also called by other scholars 'emotion-focused coping' (Follkman et al, 1979; Lambert et al, 2004; Leung et al, 2006).

Päivinen (2006) reports that electricians in the electricity transmission and telecommunication sector, like wiremen of MPEDU, engage in contrivance or jugaad by modifying their hand tools in order to increase the utility of tools as well as to enhance their own comfort and convenience. In demonstrating the strategy of 'mutual support' adopted by the wiremen, the healthcare workers are found to mutually support each other by taking on extra duties if a fellow worker does not turn up for taking over the next shift (Etim et al, 2015). The wiremen of MPEDU, frustrated with the delaying tactics of habitual defaulters of electricity bills, often engage in aggressive behaviour. Such coping is called as 'confrontive coping' by Chang et al (2006), which refers to 'aggressive efforts to alter a stressful situation and includes a certain degree of hostility and risk-taking' (p 135). Many of the broad coping strategies used by wiremen of MPEDU – such as taking extra precautions, providing mutual support, self-financing safety, jugaad – can be brought under the meta category of 'planful problem solving', which 'refers to self-initiated, overt attempts to deal directly with the problem and its effects' (Chang et al, 2006, 135). Thus, the broad coping strategies adopted by the wiremen working with MPEDU do have many parallels with the coping strategies adopted by frontline workers in other sectors, as reported by other scholars.

Conclusion

The analysis presented in the chapter indicates that weak institutional settings led to dangerous work conditions creating different implications for the SLBs, consumers, and the utility. This demands immediate and significant improvement in institutional weaknesses. One solution suggested and partly tried in different countries, including India, is sectoral reform (Jamasb, 2005; Verma et al, 2020). The reform measure like outsourcing core services is often suggested as a remedy to deal with the weak institutional setting of publicly owned utilities (Andersson and Jordahl, 2011). However, there is evidence that this measure has not succeeded in bringing significant improvements at the ground level in the sector (Thakur et al, 2005; Victor et al, 2015).

Another suggested response is to reduce the discretion available to wiremen and thereby improve their performance by increasing monitoring of their functioning. Since 2000, the emphasis has been on technological measures such as specially designed mobile phone applications that comprehensively monitor the SLBs' functioning (Bovens and Zouridis, 2002; Lindgren et al, 2019). It is not possible to make effective use of such measures in work conditions marked by severe resource constraints like those faced by PEDU wiremen. Further, as evidenced in similar studies in other sectors, such measures turn counter-productive as SLBs respond to such measures with 'creative compliance' or 'feigned compliance' (Fisher and Monahan, 2008; Charbonneau and Doberstein, 2020; Wu, 2021; Camarena and Fusi, 2022). These observations underscore the need to eschew ad-hoc or 'escape-route' type measures and make concerted efforts to address the institutional weaknesses in public agencies.

References

Andersson, F. and Jordahl, H. (2011). *Outsourcing Public Services: Ownership, Competition, Quality and Contracting.* IFN Working Paper No. 874, https://ssrn.com/abstract=1868279.

Angland, S., Dowling, M., and Casey, D. (2014). Nurses' perceptions of the factors which cause violence and aggression in the emergency department: A qualitative study. *International Emergency Nursing*, 22(3), 134–39. https://doi.org/10.1016/j.ienj.2013.09.005

Baskaran, T., Min, B., and Uppal, Y. (2015). Election cycles and electricity provision: Evidence from a quasi-experiment with Indian special elections. *Journal of Public Economics*, 126, 64–73. https://doi.org/10.1016/j.jpubeco.2015.03.011

Bhattacharyya, S.C. (2010). Energy access problem of the poor in India: Is rural electrification a remedy? *Energy Policy*, 34, 3387–97. https://doi.org/10.1016/j.enpol.2005.08.026

Bhattacharya, S. and Patel, U.R. (2011). Does the exuberance in the Indian power sector have legs?. *Global Economy and Development Working Paper*, 45.

Bovens, M. and Zouridis, S. (2002). From street-level to system-level bureaucracies: How information and communication technology is transforming administrative discretion and constitutional control. *Public Administration Review*, 62(2), 174–84.

Brodkin, E.Z. (2012). Reflections on street-level bureaucracy: Past, present, and future. *Public Administration Review*, 72(6), 940–9. https://doi.org/10.1111/j.1540-6210.2012.02657.x

Camarena, L. and Fusi, F. (2022). Always connected: Technology use increases technostress among public managers. *The American Review of Public Administration*, 52(2), 154–68. https://doi.org/10.1177/02750740211050387

Chang, E.M., Daly, J.W., Hancock, K.M., Bidewell, J., Johnson, A., Lambert, V.A. et al (2006). The relationships among workplace stressors, coping methods, demographic characteristics, and health in Australian nurses. *Journal of Professional Nursing*, 22(1), 30–8.

Charbonneau, É. and Doberstein, C. (2020). An empirical assessment of the intrusiveness and reasonableness of emerging work surveillance technologies in the public sector. *Public Administration Review*, 80(5), 780–91. https://doi.org/10.1111/puar.13278

Chau, N., Gauchard, G.C., Dehaene, D., Benamghar, L., Touron, C., Perrin, P.P. et al (2007). Contributions of occupational hazards and human factors in occupational injuries and their associations with job, age and type of injuries in railway workers. *International Archives of Occupational and Environmental Health*, 80(6), 517–25. https://doi.org/10.1007/s00420-006-0158-8

Cornell, A. and Lapuente, V. (2014). Meritocratic administration and democratic stability. *Democratization*, 21(7), 1286–1304. https://doi.org/10.1080/13510347.2014.960205

Darokar, S. (2019). Manual scavengers: A blind spot in urban development discourse. In M. Madhushree and R. Carciumaru (eds), *Including the Excluded in South Asia*. Singapore: Springer, pp 209–18. https://dx.doi.org/10.1007/978-981-32-9759-3_13

Dodoo, J.E. and Al-Samarraie, H. (2019). Factors leading to unsafe behavior in the twenty first century workplace: A review. *Management Review Quarterly*, 69(4), 391–414. https://doi.org/10.1007/s11301-019-00157-6

Etim, J.J., Bassey, P.E., Ndep, A.O., Iyam, M.A., and Nwikekii, C.N. (2015). Work-related stress among healthcare workers in Ugep, Yakurr Local Government Area, Cross River State, Nigeria: A study of sources, effects, and coping strategies. *International Journal of Public Heath, Pharmacy and Pharmacology*, 1(1), 23–34.

ESMI (Electricity Supply Monitoring Initiative) (2019). *Watch your Power Quality, Prayas Energy Group*. http://watchyourpower.org/uploaded_reports.php

Fisher, J.A. and Monahan, T. (2008). Tracking the social dimensions of RFID systems in hospitals. *International Journal of Medical Informatics*, 77(3), 176–83.

Follkman, S., Schaefer, C., and Lazarus, R.S. (1979). *Cognitive Processes as Mediators of Stress and Coping*. New York: John Wiley.

Golden, M. and Min, B. (2013). Distributive politics around the world. *Annual Review of Political Science*, 16(1), 73–99. https://dx.doi.org/10.1146/annurev-polisci-052209-121553

Gibson, D. (2004). The gaps in the gaze in South African hospitals. *Social Science & Medicine*, 59(10), 2013–24. https://doi.org/10.1016/j.socscimed.2004.03.006

Iyer, L. and Mani, A. (2012). Traveling agents: Political change and bureaucratic turnover in India. *Review of Economics and Statistics*, 94(3), 723–39. https://doi.org/10.1162/REST_a_00183

Jamasb, T. (2005). *Electricity Sector Reform in Developing Countries: A Survey of Empirical Evidence on Determinants and Performance (Vol. 3549)*. Washington, DC: World Bank Publications.

Lambert, V.A., Lambert, C.E., Itano, J., Inouye, J., Kim, S., Kuniviktikul, W. et al (2004). Cross-cultural comparison of workplace stressors, ways of coping and demographic characteristics as predictors of physical and mental health among hospital nurses in Japan, Thailand, South Korea and the USA. *International Journal of Nursing Studies*. 41(3), 671–84.

Lameck, W. and Hulst, R. (2020). Explaining coping strategies of agricultural extension officers in Tanzania: The role of the wider institutional context. *International Review of Administrative Sciences*, 86(4), 749–64. https://doi.org/10.1177/0020852318824398

Lavee, E. (2021). Who is in charge? The provision of informal personal resources at the street level. *Journal of Public Administration Research and Theory*, 31(1), 4–20. https://doi.org/10.1093/jopart/muaa025

Leung, M.Y., Liu, A.M.M., and Wong, M.K. (2006). Impacts of stress-coping behaviors on estimation performance. *Construction Management and Economics*, 24(1), 55–67.

Leung, M.Y., Wong, M.K., and Oloke, D. (2003). *Coping Behaviors of Construction Estimators in stress management*. Proceeding of 2003 Conference of the Association of Researchers in Construction Management, ARCOM, 3–5 September, Vol. 1, pp 271–7.

Lindgren, I., Madsen, C.Ø., Hofmann, S., and Melin, U. (2019). Close encounters of the digital kind: A research agenda for the digitalization of public services. *Government Information Quarterly*, 36(3), 427–36.

Lipsky, M. (1980). *Street-Level Bureaucracy: Dilemmas of the Individual in Public Services*. New York: Russell Sage Foundation

Liu, H.T. and Tsai, Y.L. (2012). A fuzzy risk assessment approach for occupational hazards in the construction industry. *Safety Science*, 50(4), 1067–78. https://doi.org/10.1016/j.ssci.2011.11.021

Lu, D., Xu, C., Mi, C., Wang, Y., Xu, X., and Zhao, C. (2021). Establishment of a key hidden danger factor system for electric power personal casualty accidents based on text mining. *Information*, 12(6), 243. https://doi.org/10.3390/info12060243

Mayhew, C. (2001). Occupational health and safety risks faced by police officers. *Trends and Issues in Crime and Criminal Justice* (no. 196). Canberra: Australian Institute of Criminology.

Min, B. and Golden, M. (2014). Electoral cycles in electricity losses in India. *Energy Policy*, 65, 619–25. https://doi.org/10.1016/j.enpol.2013.09.060

Päivinen, M. (2006). Electricians' perception of work-related risks in cold climate when working on high places. *International Journal of Industrial Ergonomics*, 36(7), 661–70. https://doi.org/10.1016/j.ergon.2006.04.005

Patil, V.P. and Kamble, R.K. (2017). Occupational health hazards in street sweepers of Chandrapur city, central India. *International Journal of Environment*, 6(2), 9–18. https://doi.org/10.3126/ije.v6i2.17358

Sarangi, G.K., Pradhan, A.K., and Taghizadeh-Hesary, F. (2021). Performance assessment of state-owned electricity distribution utilities in India. *Economic Analysis and Policy*, 71, 516–31.

Sharma, T., Pandey, K., Punia, D.K., and Rao, J. (2016). Of pilferers and poachers: Combating electricity theft in India. *Energy Research & Social Science*, 11, 40–52.

Singh, R., Gupta, V., and Mondal, A. (2012). Jugaad – From 'making do' and 'quick fix' to an innovative, sustainable and low-cost survival strategy at the bottom of the pyramid. *International Journal of Rural Management*, 8(1–2), 87–105.

Smith, D.R., Devine, S.U.E., Leggat, P.A., and Ishitake, T. (2005). Alcohol and tobacco consumption among police officers. *The Kurume Medical Journal*, 52(1–2), 63–5. https://doi.org/10.2739/kurumemedj.52.63

Smith, T.B. (2004). Electricity theft: A comparative analysis. *Energy Policy*, 32(18), 2067–76. https://doi.org/10.1016/S0301-4215(03)00182-4

Thakur, T., Deshmukh, S.G., Kaushik, S.C., and Kulshrestha, M. (2005). Impact assessment of the Electricity Act 2003 on the Indian power sector. *Energy Policy*, 33(9), 1187–98.

Tipayamongkholgul, M., Luksamijarulkul, P., Mawn, B., Kongtip, P., and Woskie, S. (2016). Occupational hazards in the Thai healthcare sector. *A Journal of Environmental and Occupational Health Policy*, 26(1), 83–102. https://doi.org/10.1177/1048291116633871

Tiwari, R.R. (2008). Occupational health hazards in sewage and sanitary workers. *Indian Journal of Occupational and Environmental Medicine*, 12(3), 112. https://doi.org/10.4103%2F0019-5278.44691

Verma, M., Mukherjee, V., Yadav, V., and Ghosh, S. (2020). Indian power distribution sector reforms: A critical review. *Energy Policy*, 144, 111672.

Victor, O.E., Aziz, N.A., and Jaffar, A.R. (2015). Privatization of electricity service delivery in developing nations: Issues and challenges. *International Journal of Built Environment and Sustainability*, 2(3), 202–10.

Walker, L. and Gilson, L. (2004) 'We are bitter but we are satisfied': Nurses as street-level bureaucrats in South Africa. *Social Science & Medicine*, 59(6), 1251–61. https://doi.org/10.1016/j.socscimed.2003.12.020

Wu, Y. (2021). *Compliance Ethnography: How Small Businesses Respond to the Law in China*. Singapore: Springer.

Zolnikov, T.R., da Silva, R.C., Tuesta, A.A., Marques, C.P., and Cruvinel, V.R.N. (2018). Ineffective waste site closures in Brazil: A systematic review on continuing health conditions and occupational hazards of waste collectors. *Waste Management*, 80, 26–39. https://doi.org/10.1016/j.wasman.2018.08.047

6

Underserving the disadvantaged: institutional failures and their consequences for frontline workers and vulnerable publics

Roberto Pires, Maria Paula Santos, Beatriz Brandão, and Luiza Rosa

Introduction

When making decisions about how to provide services, frontline workers are decisively influenced by the institutional setting under which they perform their work. In this chapter, we call attention to the ways frontline workers experience the state, in a context of institutional failure. Implementation gaps, failures, or deficiencies in materialising policies as originally designed are quite common when public policies are put into practice (Pressman and Wildavsky, 1973).[1] Failures in implementation processes have long been associated with frustration and deviation from stated policy goals, used as a common explanation for poor government performance (Hill and Hupe, 2014; Sher-Hadar, 2020). However, we still lack a better understanding of how frontline workers deal with implementation gaps and how this ultimately affects the ways public service users are treated (Dubois, 2015). When frontline workers are placed in situations in which they face limitations and cannot rely on the tools or level of resources officially recognised as essential, their possibilities for action become severely restricted, and users might have to cope with service provision that is far from ideal – ranging from insufficient to potentially harmful.

We conceive implementation gaps as a consequence of institutional weakness. As proposed by Brinks et al (2020), 'institutional weakness' refers to situations in which formal institutions fail to work as intended in terms of regulating – prescribing or forbidding – social, economic, and political behaviours. The concept provides an analytical angle of situations that are very common in (albeit not limited to) developing countries, allowing for a characterisation of levels of institutional development in comparative perspective. Institutional weakness leads to the perception of the state as a patchworked institutional landscape (McDonnell, 2017), in which legal and bureaucratic reach is functionally and territorially uneven, producing unequal and selective enforcement (Perelmiter, 2022), as well as service provision.

Lotta, Nieto Morales, and Peeters (in their introduction to this volume) take a step forward from these insights and propose connecting the notion of weak institutions to the analysis of policy implementation. According to them, the concept allows for an institutional analysis of how elements in the working conditions and organisational contexts create incentives and constraints that shape frontline workers' behaviour, ultimately affecting how citizens are treated by public services on an everyday basis. As frontline workers inhabit state institutions (Hallet and Ventresca, 2006), their ordinary behaviours and interactions with service users are profoundly influenced by the institutional context. In weak institutional settings, frontline workers must make decisions about how to provide services in situations in which they lack resources to allow everyone to be treated fairly.

In this chapter, we follow this cue and use the case of the National Policy on Care for Users of Alcohol and other Drugs, as implemented in two Brazilian cities (Rio de Janeiro and Brasília), as a substantive context for empirical examination. The case is illustrative of many other situations in which a policy aimed at providing universal access to care (for drug abuse problems) is implemented in the context of a country (Brazil) characterised by systemic resource shortages in the public sector and structural social inequalities (Lotta and Pires, 2023). Moreover, given the uneven implementation of this policy across cities and territories, the case offers a unique opportunity for analysing the repercussions of a concrete implementation gap – the absence in some territories of hosting units formally designed to cater for the needs of the most vulnerable segments of the clientele.

Our goal is to investigate how these gaps in the implementation of the formal design of the referred policy shape frontline workers' behaviours in the provision of lower levels of access and precarious forms of care to the most vulnerable segments of the target population. In societies characterised by structural social inequalities, looking deeper into these dynamics provides a relevant way to advance our understanding of ongoing processes of inequality reproduction. It helps uncover how policy implementation in weak institutional settings may lead to perpetuating (rather than mitigating) inequalities, by reinforcing unequal access to public services.

We believe this type of analysis could offer important contributions to ongoing debates on street-level bureaucracy. Although the repercussions of frontline agency to the disadvantaged have received growing scholarly attention (Lotta and Pires, 2019; Pires, 2019), a focus on implementation gaps is still quite limited in current analytical efforts. We could point out to at least three different streams in which this claim is valid: (1) studies focused on SLBs' coping strategies, discretionary decisions, and their distributive consequences (Lipsky, 1980); (2) sociological perspectives on frontline workers' agency, which have brought attention to interactions with service users, the reinforcement of differences in social status, knowledge, and power positions (Dubois, 1999; 2010), as well as to the role of moral judgements, the enactment of stereotypes, subaltern identities, and forms of prejudice inscribed in social norms (Maynard-Moody and Musheno, 2012, 2022); and, finally, (3) discussions about the onuses of interacting with public policies and administrative burdens, which have emphasised the procedures and practices that complicate access to public services and benefits (Herd and Moynihan, 2019; Peeters and Nieto-Morales, 2020; Peeters, 2020).

As a result, there is a lacuna in our understanding about how implementation gaps contribute to the institutional production of harm to disadvantaged groups, in terms of their access and experiences with public services. In order to advance scholarly knowledge about how policy implementation leads to 'bureaucratic disentitlement' (Lipsky, 1984) or 'administrative exclusion' (Brodkin and Majmundar, 2010), we argue it is necessary to focus on how implementation gaps shape frontline working conditions, the particular ways the job gets performed under these conditions, and the how interactions with the public unfold. By doing so, we may gain analytical leverage on the modes through which publics are effectively governed and subjects are institutionally processed (Lövbrand and Stripple, 2015), leading to selective, unequal access, and precarious forms of care to the most vulnerable segments of the target population.

In sum, this chapter aims at contributing to ongoing debates by bridging discussions on institutional weakness and implementation gaps with concerns about how frontline work affects disadvantaged social groups. In order to do so, we first present the case of the National Policy on Care for Users of Alcohol and other Drugs that will provide the empirical support for the analysis and then lay out our research design and strategies. The case is useful because it involves service provision to users with different levels of socioeconomic deprivation and presents variations across sites in terms of implementation gaps, in the contexts of Rio de Janeiro and Brasília. Following from that we discuss the main findings, resulting from comparisons across and within the two cities. Finally, we present our conclusions and point out the implications of the present study in terms of a broader research agenda focused on understanding street-level bureaucracy in weak state institutions.

Implementation gaps in care for people experiencing drug problems in Brazil: case and context

The National Policy on Care for Users of Alcohol and other Drugs (NPAUD) was launched in 2002 by the Brazilian Ministry of Health. Since then, the National Health Care System (*Sistema Único de Saúde* – SUS) consolidated[2] the public provision of specialised services to people in active addiction all over the country. NPAUD resulted from the Psychiatric Reform that took place in Brazil in the preceding decades and embodied four fundamental principles: (1) deinstitutionalisation (or dehospitalisation) and the shifting of care from closed institutions onto open services operating under community-based treatment approaches; (2) psychosocial attention, implying forms of care that go beyond the focus on a 'disease' located in the subjects' physical body and psychic structures, emphasising the subjects' experiences of suffering in relation to their social ties and environments; (3) integrated local service networks that articulate different forms of knowledge, attention, and care in each territory; and (4) harm reduction strategies aimed primarily at respecting patients' autonomy and engaging them into self-care and self-regulation practices and routines, rather than focusing exclusively on the abrupt interruption (abstinence) of drug consumption (Brazil, 2003).

In order to translate these guidelines into actual services, NPAUD and subsequent administrative acts[3] formally previewed a policy design anchored on local Networks for Psychosocial Attention (NPA), activated by Centers for Psychosocial Attention for Users of Alcohol and other Drugs (CPA-AD). As a substitute to asylums and treatment based on (often forced) internment and social isolation, CPA-AD are open-door services located in the many different places within a city where people in active addiction circulate. These centres are staffed with multi-professional teams – involving medical doctors, psychologists, social workers, occupational therapists, artists, educators, and so on – bringing together different forms of knowledge and care for the practice of psychosocial attention and harm reduction strategies. CPA-AD are also supposed to operate as strategic hubs for the articulation of a wide range of services in their territories, putting the NPAs in motion. NPAs, in turn, are formally designed[4] to include units providing: (1) basic healthcare; (2) emergency centres and complex health treatments (hospitals); (3c) mental healthcare; (4) psychosocial rehabilitation services; (5) cultural and social centres; and, finally, (6) hosting units (*Unidades de Acolhimento*) dedicated to drug users in situations of social vulnerability and in need of temporary protection.

NPAUD's principles and policy design have clearly changed the landscape of care for problematic users of substances in Brazil. Prior to 2003, treatment opportunities for drug users consisted of civil society offers, such as Narcotics Anonymous (NA) or Alcoholic Anonymous (AA) and other mutual-help groups; internments in psychiatric hospitals; or therapeutic communities and other religious-based treatments. By 2017, NPAUD's implementation reached 424 CPA-AD in operation in municipalities across the country,[5] promoting service networks in their respective territories. NPAUD's implementation led to both a quantitative and a qualitative expansion of care opportunities for people making harmful use of drugs. Prior to that, drug users belonging to the lower income classes had very few opportunities to access professional, specialised healthcare – as these were offered mostly through private clinics – and had to rely on spiritual or non-professional forms of treatment offered by religious institutions and mutual-help groups.

Even though there were advances in terms of the diffusion of CPA-AD up until 2019,[6] the full implementation of their local service networks (NPA), as formally envisioned by the federal government, has been a huge challenge for local governments. In Brazil, due to the federative arrangement defined by the Constitution of 1988, local governments are overburdened with the responsibility of providing multiple services (from healthcare, education, and social assistance to many other urban services). However, governments at the local level only take a smaller share of the total tax revenue distribution and are frequently dependent on political negotiations around transfers from state and federal governments (Gomes, 2009). This scenario perpetuates reduced administrative capacities at the local level, as compared to other spheres of government, in terms of human, technological, and financial resources (Marenco et al, 2017).

Given that local governments are pressed with overdemand for services and face resource limitations, deficiencies in putting NPA in full motion have been quite common. Chief among these implementation gaps is the lack of Hosting Units or Hus (*Unidades de Acolhimento*). Out of the 424 CPA-AD in operation in the country, only 65 (15 per cent) counted on HUs in their local service network. These HUs play a key role in the stabilisation of people undergoing situations of social risk and vulnerability, being also strategic to the objectives of social reinsertion, as they allow substance abusers to participate in society while in treatment.

Therefore, even though NPAUD's formal design seemed well suited for putting in practice inclusive, democratic, and rights-based care services for people suffering from substance abuse, CPA-AD and NPAs' actual implementation has not yet fully materialised policy makers' intentions. And we still know little about the actual implications of the absence of HUs for the way frontline workers perform their jobs and for how different users experience the service.

Research design and methods

In order to empirically explore the ways through which the HU gap shape frontline working conditions and interactions with service users, we conducted in-depth fieldwork on the daily operations of CPA-AD and their local networks in two Brazilian cities: Brasília (from June 2018 to July 2019) and Rio de Janeiro (from August 2019 to February 2020). The two cities represent different historical trajectories and institutional configurations for mental health policies. Historically, Rio de Janeiro was one of the hotbeds for social mobilisation and policy reformulation in the course of Psychiatric Reform. The city has a concentration of some of the most important schools and research institutions in mental health. Since the 1990s, Local authorities have been committed to deinstitutionalisation and the gradual foreclosure of psychiatric hospitals (Fagundes et al, 2016). By 2006, the local government had already established seven CPA-AD across the city's territory (the same number of centres that are currently in operation). In contrast, Brasília is a late NPAUD's adopter and, by 2006, had only one CPA-AD in place, ranking penultimate in country in terms of levels of population coverage by services (Brazil, 2006). Only in 2013, after the federal government stepped in and provided additional financial support, the district government expanded the number of CPA-AD to seven and reached the current service provision structure.

Even though the context for NPAUD's implementation is very different across cities, they both face a similar implementation gap related to HUs for people in treatment. While there are seven CPA-AD in each city, there are only two HUs in Rio and one in Brasília. Therefore, in both cities, there are local service networks in which HUs exist and operate, as well as other service networks that lack these facilities completely. Taking each CPA-AD and their service network as the unit of analysis, we can compare situations in which the HU is present and absent. Moreover, we can examine the repercussions of the presence and absence of HU under the different contexts of Rio and Brasília, examining how the actors involved make sense and express the 'logic of these situations' (Fischer, 1998).

In the course of fieldwork, we conducted observations of CPA-AD day-to-day activities and semi-structured interviews. In Brasília, we conducted observations in all the seven existing CPA-AD and performed 84 interviews with managers (7), frontline workers (44), and service users (32). In Rio de Janeiro, we conducted observations in four out of the seven existing CPA-AD and performed 51 interviews with managers (7), frontline workers (23), and service users (21).

The research process allowed us to explore the repercussions of the HU gap for frontline working conditions and for service interactions with vulnerable users, drawing from the experiences and interpretations of the actors involved. It provided the opportunity for both cross-case and within-case comparisons (Table 6.1), as we looked at situations in which the HU was present or absent in the same city, as well as across cities and their different implementation contexts.

From implementation gaps to unequal access: underserving the disadvantaged

The 11 CPA-AD units in which we conducted research have, on average, 41 staff members (ranging from 22 to 80) and provide services such as

Table 6.1: Comparisons within and across cities

	Implementation gap	
Implementation contexts	No	Yes
Rio de Janeiro	2 CPA-AD with HU	2 CPA-AD without HU
Brasília	1 CPA-AD with HU	6 CPA-AD without HU

Source: Authors' own

individual medical and psychological appointments, counselling from social workers, group psychotherapy, other therapeutic groups, health checks and tests, and cultural activities and leisure.[7] Intake procedures were also quite similar, basically involving an initial interview in which professionals ask about users' needs and run a quick assessment of their situation. As we repeatedly observed these initial contacts, something stood out. We noticed that, even though many people at intake declared very similar problems associated with drug abuse (that is, similar substances and repercussions to their health conditions and social life), they were assigned to very different therapeutic paths, in terms of the actual offers provided by the service. While some people initiated a therapeutic plan based on a schedule of activities provided by healthcare professionals in the CPA-AD, others were left awaiting or sometimes followed referrals to internments for unprofessional religious-based treatment at facilities in the cities' outskirts. As we questioned frontline workers about these differences, they commented that some level of variation is welcome and derives from their efforts of adapting therapeutic plans to the specific needs of different persons. However, they underscored that the differences we were observing did not result from these positive adaptation efforts. Rather, they were influenced by the lack of resources, tools, and options – such as the HUs – for dealing with users in situations of homelessness and other forms of intense vulnerability. The unavailability of HUs restricted the options available for CPA-AD frontline workers in the treatment of the most disadvantaged segment of the public, resulting in unequal access to people in different socioeconomic conditions. In what follows, we discuss service workers' experiences and interpretations about the consequences of the HU gap to the disadvantaged groups they serve.

Serving the disadvantaged: CPA-AD in the presence of Hosting Units

Both in Rio de Janeiro and Brasília, there were territories in which local service networks (NPA) included a CPA-AD and a HU in fine-tuned coordination. In these situations, the implementation gap under focus was absent. When this happened, we observed that the most vulnerable segments of the targeted public enjoyed full access to services, as envisioned by NPAUD's policy makers, engaging in treatment based on psychosocial attention and harm reduction strategies, while being free to come and go, circulating between other services, family members, and income opportunities.

These HUs were designed to provide shelter for substance abusers in situations of homelessness, under threat of violence, or lacking other forms of social support. The CPA-AD is responsible for signing up users to the HU in its jurisdiction. Once admitted, they may stay there from one day to six months.

More than just providing a place to stay, HUs become a key resource providing conditions for frontline workers at CPA-AD to design therapeutic plans customised to the specific needs of vulnerable patients, including activities taking place within CPA-AD's facilities (for example, medical appointment and group psychotherapy), as well as in the space of residence. So, HUs allow service users to experience treatment as coherent and continuous across spaces of care and residence.

As we observed in the two HUs in Rio de Janeiro, meetings with frontline workers at CPA-AD were frequent (weekly) in which they discussed and followed-up on each case individually, in order to make the necessary adjustments to therapeutic plans. One of these HUs was located right next door to its CPA-AD of reference, which allowed for intense circulation and continuous contact between workers and drug users under treatment.

Moreover, while in the house, users took advantage from streamlined articulations with other services in the local network. For example, we followed the case of Valesca,[8] a young woman, rejected by her mother because she was not born a boy. She had never met her father. She was initially raised by her grandmother, until Valeska threatened her with a knife and was abandoned by her grandmother to begin her life moving from shelter to shelter and wandering in the streets of downtown Rio. In the written reports about her case, it is stated that she has difficulties in establishing ties. Due to her aggressive behaviour, she does not stay for very long at the shelters. But, once she was admitted to the HU, CPA-AD's multi-professional team worked out her therapeutic plan. In addition to the activities in the HU, frontline workers initiated connections with other mental health and social assistance services specialised on the homeless, while also attempting to reach her family. Despite the continuity of her outbursts of aggressiveness towards workers and other residents, the mobilisation of these multiple resources and approaches has contributed to her stay at the house while her health conditions were being taken care of (Excerpt from field notes – multiple dates, 2019).

The main type of frontline worker in HUs are harm reduction agents. These agents had previous work experiences in non-governmental organisations or had been drug abusers themselves. They are trained to engage with drug abusers from a horizontalised perspective, aiming at respecting their autonomy and rights, by working out agreements with them about how the house is to be maintained, sharing, and living with others, and about when and how residents may go out. As declared by one of these harm reduction agents:

> 'It's a place of protection and an opportunity for them to stabilize and move ahead more lucidly ... many of them don't have a family or have lost their social connections. Those who were living on the streets have lost many social ties. And here the re-encounter a family home, a place of coexistence with other people, where we cry, laugh, and have work to do, a bathroom to clean, dishes to wash, beds to tidy up.' (Harm Reduction Agent in HU-1, Rio de Janeiro)

In Brasília, in one of our visits to the only HU available in the city, we noticed that most of the residents were out doing their own things, seeking jobs, or reconnecting to their families. They were expected to return and check in early in the evening. Among the few residents that were present at that moment, one was waiting for her appointment with the doctor at the CPA-AD next door. Two others were engaged in domestic work, following a schedule in which residents take turns on performing these tasks (Excerpt from field notes – 15 October 2018).

Freedom to come and go and the possibility to circulate across different spaces, while still in an environment of protection and care, make these HUs play the role of a "rehearsal for regaining their social lives ... we instigate them to go after their rights, seek support services, and so on ... in some sense, we lend them desire and provide assistance for pursuing those things" (Director of HU-2, Rio de Janeiro). The Director of the other HU in Rio narrated a case of an older man, who lived on the streets for many years and had very fragile physical health. Every now and then the man showed up, frequently intoxicated, and the team would take him in, call up the other services in order to provide care for him, an opportunity to rearrange his life, and get a new start. "There are some users that I am pretty sure would not be alive without the support provided by the CPA-AD and the HU. They would not have survived without this support" (Director of HU-1, Rio de Janeiro). In order to better understand the relevance of the HUs to frontline workers when attending to the needs of vulnerable clients, it is worth examining the situations in which HUs were not present and their repercussions to the ways users experience the service.

Underserving the disadvantaged: CPA-AD in the absence of Hosting Units

Side by side with territories in which CPA-AD were well connected to HUs, we also observed – both in Rio de Janeiro and Brasília – territories in which this situation did not occur, because HUs were simply not in place. Due to such implementation gaps, frontline workers had to bear with limitations in care offered to vulnerable segments of the targeted public, sometimes even referring them to other institutions and services providing forms of treatment that sharply diverged from NPAUD's values and guidelines. As we shall see later, HU gaps introduced clear discontinuities in the process of treatment between CPA-AD's offers and clients' places of residence. These discontinuities often led to incoherence, divergence, and tensions, culminating in reduced levels of attention and care to the disadvantaged.

Although the gap was equally present in some territories of both cities, we observed differences in the way CPA-ADs' professionals dealt with the absence of HUs when providing services to people in situations of intense vulnerability. In Rio de Janeiro, professionals would either advise clients to seek vacancies in the shelters ran by the Social Assistance Department[9] or provide whatever form of care possible on the streets where they currently stayed. In these situations, many of the frontline workers interviewed reported severe limitations to their capacities to interact with clients in the course of treatment and follow-up on their evolution, making it nearly impossible to constantly adjust the therapeutic plans in order to make them more customised and effective. Also, these situations imposed additional obstacles for engaging other networked services into the treatment of these clients, as the contacts between professionals and service users became more irregular and uncertain. As pointed out by a social worker "It is just much more challenging for clients to adhere to treatment when their life situations are not minimally stabilised" (CPA-AD 3, Rio de Janeiro).

In Brasília, in turn, CPA-AD's frontline workers filled in the HU gap through systematically referring clients in situations of vulnerability to Therapeutic Communities (TCs). TCs are civil society organisations, often linked to religious groups, which offer care to substance abusers on a residential basis. In Brasília, TCs also enjoy government funding coming from the Justice and Public Order Department, rather than from the Health Care Department.[10] However, despite offering services to similar clienteles, TCs' approach to drug abuse treatment stands in sharp opposition to NPAUD's core principles and to CPA-ADs' offers. The TC model prescribes medium- to long-term internments (on average, six to nine months) in isolated facilities in the urban outskirts. In traditional forms of institutionalisation, substance abusers are supposed to disconnect from their social, community, and family lives during their treatments. Once inside, drug users must immediately commit to abstinence and abruptly stop the consumption of any psychoactive substance. Treatment is based on strict discipline and spirituality – mostly guided by evangelical churches (Santos, 2018).

The dissonances between TCs' model and NPAUD's guidelines were repeatedly affirmed by CPA-AD frontline workers and managers in Brasília.

The vast majority (83 per cent) of these interviewees declared at least one type of criticism towards TCs (Santos and Pires, 2020). Nevertheless, they still referred patients to TCs very frequently. When prompted about this apparent paradox, they argued that there are no other options available when dealing with people in situations of homelessness, under threat, or lacking any social support.

> 'I do refer patients to Therapeutic Communities. Not because I want to, but because there's simply no other option. If there were, of course it would be better for the patient to be closer to the city, able to access healthcare services, following treatments based on the respect for their rights, in accordance with the principles of the [National Health Care System] SUS. But there simply isn't such an option. So, we do send them to the Therapeutic Communities.' (Psychologist CPA-AD F, Brasília)

> 'Government has nothing else to offer. There is no plan b. There's only one Hosting Unit (Unidade de Acolhimento), which is way far from matching demands adequately. Also, the offer of shelters [run by the Social Assistance Department] in the Federal District needs to improve a lot. As a result, Therapeutic Communities take on an important role only because the policy [NPAUD] does not work as it should in Brasília.' (Manager CPA-AD C, Brasília)

Moreover, we repeatedly heard from CPA-AD frontline workers in Brasília that, once they referred patients to TCs, it was really hard to keep contact and follow up on the evolution of each individual's treatment. With only a few exceptions, most TCs refused to bring their internees to appointments and regular therapeutic activities in the CPA-AD. CPA-AD professionals, in turn, could not visit patients in TCs, due to lack of time and poor logistical capacities.

These situations imposed discontinuities not only in terms of following through a coherent treatment but also in terms of users' experiences of treatment as something confusing and subject to a lot of tension. The controversies we observed around the administration of medication are very illustrative. In some cases, deeply religious TCs substituted CPA-AD prescription of medication for prayers. "They resist the administration of medication because they believe prayers will actually cure the person" (Nurse CPA-AD C, Brasília).

Misadministration of medication is another salient problem. As reported by many CPA-AD patients who had previously been TC internees (interviews with group of users, Brasília), once in the TC, medical prescriptions are reinterpreted by unprofessional staff, medicines are confiscated, and redistributed to other internees at will. CPA-AD frontline workers insisted that the unsupervised medication use, as well as its abrupt suspension, can lead to serious physical harms and to triggering new episodes of mental health crises.

Finally, the operation of TCs is not subject to regular inspections[11] and complaints about human rights violations in these facilities abound (CFP, 2011; CFP/MNPCT/MPF, 2018). Our interviews with users that underwent treatment in TCs corroborate these views about the operation of some TCs in Brasília. Also, these complaints reach back to frontline workers at CPA-AD. As narrated by a psychologist, "they complain a lot about the poor quality of the food and mistreatment. But it's a delicate situation because they don't want us to file a complaint and move forward. They still need a place to stay, their families do not want them back" (CPA-AD F, Brasília)

In sum, both in Rio de Janeiro and Brasília, the lack of HU introduced discontinuities in the course of treatment, not only diverting actual service provision from the idealised formal policy but also impacting the levels and quality of attention provided to the vulnerable, ranging from less intense engagement to the offer of treatments based on radically different principles. When the HU gap is there, working conditions at CPA-AD deteriorate, forcing frontline workers into providing solutions they recognise as far from ideal. As a result, disadvantaged publics can hardly access drug abuse treatment based on psychosocial attention, harm reduction strategies, and freedom to circulate across social spaces.

Conclusion

In this chapter, we focused on the ways frontline workers experience the state as a weak institution and on how this context shapes the possibilities for action and interactions with service users. We investigated a specific but rather common consequence of institutional weakness: implementation gaps or failures in putting into practice elements of formal policy designs. Furthermore, we exposed how such failures affect the behaviours and actions of frontline workers, leading to the mistreatment of disadvantaged publics and experiences of inattention, exclusion, or even harm.

By connecting weak institutions and implementation gaps to frontline working conditions and patterns of response to disadvantaged users, we contributed to filling in a gap in ongoing debates. As discussed before, previous scholarly work on related topics has either focused on implementation without looking at their repercussions to frontline workers and service users, or focused on the effects on people's experience of services without looking at implementation gaps. The current analysis offered an interpretation that bridges these perspectives.

We used the case of the implementation of the NPAUD in two Brazilian cities as an empirical terrain in which we could observe the presence and absence of implementation gaps. Therefore, it offered conditions for exploring the connections between implementation gaps, frontline working conditions and practices, and the experiences of disadvantaged service users. By comparing Rio de Janeiro and Brasília, we noticed a common implementation gap related to the operation of HUs. Even though the context of implementation varied considerably across the two cities, the repercussions related to the absence of HUs were quite consistent, in terms of frontline workers' responses and levels and quality of access to the service. As observed in both cities, while the less vulnerable service users were able to enjoy specialised care in freedom, based on psychosocial attention and harm reduction strategies, the most vulnerable segment of the clientele was excluded from these possibilities. They could either fail entirely to access these public services or be forced to engage with them in precarious, less effective, or even perverse conditions.

While the case selected for empirical analysis has its own specificities, the interpretations constructed may serve as reference for the observation and analysis of frontline work and users' everyday experience of public services in contexts of institutional weakness in other policy domains or countries. What we take away as a more general point is that weak institutions fail to provide resources or tools that are essential to frontline workers in providing users with equitable access to public services. In such institutional settings, frontline workers must provide solutions that are perceptively far from ideal, especially harming the experience of the most disadvantaged groups with public services. While on the side of frontline workers, we see limited possibilities for action – such as 'this is the best we can do' or 'there simply is no other option' – on the side of disadvantaged users, we see lower levels and quality of access to public services. In between the two angles, we gain insight about how policy implementation in weak institutional settings may lead to the perpetuation of existing inequalities.

We believe such a line of inquiry is a fruitful way to advance our understanding of street-level bureaucracy in weak institutional settings. It provides us with two analytical advantages. First, it allows us to confront common sense and official views that tend to associate implementation gaps, deficiencies, and failures only with the general idea of poor government performance. By highlighting the consequences of implementation gaps for frontline workers and the people they are supposed to serve, we gain awareness of much broader repercussions of the phenomenon. Second, this perspective helps us to better understand the micro-level institutional processes that feed into the reproduction of unequal social structures and systems of domination. It connects the day-to-day experiences of frontline workers and the disadvantaged social groups they serve to the perpetuation of imbalanced power structures. Given the pervasiveness of gaps in policy implementation in weak institutional settings, we believe there is space and need for the development of a research agenda focused on comparatively exploring the political-institutional causes and social consequences of this phenomenon.

Notes

1. Pressman and Wildavsky (1973) introduced the idea of 'implementation deficit' in their analysis of the Economic Development Agency (EDA) projects. By focusing on what did not work as intended, they laid the grounds of what came to be recognised as the traditional top-down approach in implementation studies.
2. Before 2002, there were few local government experiments in providing public healthcare programs to substance abusers.
3. Ordinance N° 2.197/2004 – Ministry of Health.
4. Ordinance n° 3.088/2011, Ministry of Health.
5. Data provided by the Ministry of Health. www.saude.gov.br/noticias/693-acoes-e-progra mas/41146-centro-de-atencao-psicossocial-caps
6. Since 2019, the Bolsonaro government has shifted away support for the diffusion of CPA-AD and NPA, backpedalling on the emphasis on harm reduction strategies.
7. Some CPA-AD hold regular assemblies with service users. And, in Rio de Janeiro, some CPA-AD also develop outdoors activities in places that concentrate people engaged in risky use of substances.
8. All names are fictitious.
9. In these cases, CPA-AD do not formally refer but recommend clients to search for shelters by making themselves demands at Social Assistance Department's Centers (CRAS and CREAS).
10. In 2012, the TCs' national confederations successfully lobbied for TCs' formal inclusion in the list of services composing the Network for Psychosocial Attention (NPA), even against the resistance of the Mental Health Department at the Ministry of Health. However, despite the formal inclusion, the actual insertion of TCs in the local service networks is very controversial and contested by many mental health professionals, who argue that TCs directly confront the spirit of the Psychiatric Reform.
11. A consolidated regulatory framework for TCs is still pending and subject to disputes.

References

Brazil. (2003). *Ministério da Saúde. A política do Ministério da Saúde para a atenção integral a usuários de álcool e outras drogas.* Brasília: Ministério da Saúde.

Brazil (2006). Ministério da Saúde. Saúde Mental em Dados N.1. Brasília: outubro de 2006.

Brinks, D.M., Levitsky, S., and Murillo, M.V. (eds). (2020). *The Politics of Institutional Weakness in Latin America.* Cambridge: Cambridge University Press.

Brodkin, E. and Majmundar, M. (2010). Administrative exclusion: Organizations and the hidden costs of welfare claiming. *Journal of Public Administration Research and Theory*, 20 (4), 827–48.

CFP. (2011). *Relatório da 4ª Inspeção Nacional de Direitos Humanos: locais de internação para usuários de drogas / Conselho Federal de Psicologia.* Brasília: Conselho Federal de Psicologia.

CFP/MNPCT/MPF. (2018). *Relatório da Inspeção Nacional em Comunidades Terapêuticas – 2017.* Conselho Federal de Psicologia; Mecanismo Nacional de Prevenção e Combate à Tortura; Procuradoria Federal dos Direitos do Cidadão – Ministério Público Federal. Brasília: Conselho Federal de Psicologia.

Dubois, V. (1999). *La vie au guichet: relation administrative et traitement de la misère.* Paris: Economica. (Collection Études Politiques).

Dubois, V. (2010). Politiques au guichet, politiques du guichet. In B. Olivier and G. Virginie (eds), *Politiques publiques 2, changer la société.* Paris: Presses de Sciences-Po, pp 265–85.

Dubois, V. (2015). Critical policy ethnography. In F. Frank, D. Torgerson, A. Durnová and M. Orsini (eds), *Handbook: Introduction to Critical Policy Studies.* Cheltenham: Edward Elgar Publishing, pp 462–80.

Fagundes, H., Desviat, M., and Silva, P.R.F. (2016). Reforma Psiquiátrica no Rio de Janeiro: Situação atual e perspectivas futuras. *Ciência e Saúde Coletiva,* 21(5), 1449–60.

Fischer, F. (1998). Beyond empiricism: Policy inquiry in postpositivist perspective. *Policy Studies Journal,* 26(1), 129–46.

Gomes, S. (2009). Políticas Nacionais e Implementação Subnacional: Uma Revisão da Descentralização Pós-Fundef. *DADOS – Revista de Ciências Sociais,* 52(3), 659–90.

Hallett, T. and Ventresca, M.J. (2006). Inhabited institutions: Social interactions and organizational forms in Gouldner's 'Patterns of Industrial Bureaucracy'. *Theory and Society,* 35(2), 213–36.

Herd, P. and Moynihan, D. (2019). *Administrative Burden: Policymaking by Other Means.* New York: Russell Sage Foundation.

Hill, M. and Hupe, P. (2014). *Implementing Public Policy: An Introduction to the Study of Operational Governance.* London: Sage Publications.

Lipsky, M. (1980). *Street-Level Bureaucracy: Dilemmas of the Individual in Public Services.* New York: Russell Sage Foundation.

Lipsky, M. (1984). Bureaucratic disentitlement in social welfare programs. *Social Service Review,* (March), 3–27.

Lotta, G. and Pires, R. (2019). Street-level bureaucracy research and social inequality. In P. Hupe (ed), *Research Handbook on Street-Level Bureaucracy: The Ground Floor of Government in Context.* Cheltenham: Edward-Elgar Publishing, pp 86–101.

Lotta, G. and Pires, R. (2023). Public policy implementation in a context of extreme inequality: Between universalist ambitions and practical selectivity. In E. Lisboa, R. Gomes, and H. Martins (eds), *The Brazilian Way of Doing Public Administration.* Bingley: Emerald Publishing Limited, pp 219–31.

Lövbrand, E. and Stripple, J. (2015). Foucault and critical policy studies. In F. Fischer, D. Torgerson, A. Durnová, and M. Orsini (eds), *Handbook: Introduction to Critical Policy Studies.* Cheltenham: Edward Elgar Publishing, pp 92–110.

Marenco, A., Strohschoen, M.T., and Joner, W. (2017). Capacidade estatal, burocracia e tributação nos municípios brasileiros. *Revista de Sociologia e Política*, 25(64), 3–21.

Maynard-Moody, S. and Musheno, M. (2012). Social equities and inequities in practice: Street-level workers as agents and pragmatists. *Public Administration Review*, 71(1), 16–23.

Maynard-Moody, S. and Musheno, M. (2022). *Cops, Teachers, Counselors: Narratives of Street-Level Judgment*. Ann Arbor: University of Michigan Press.

McDonnell, E. (2017). *Patchwork Leviathan: Pockets of Bureaucratic Effectiveness in Developing States*. Princeton: Princeton University Press.

Peeters, R. (2020). The political economy of administrative burdens: A theoretical framework for analyzing the organizational origins of administrative burdens. *Administration & Society*, 52(4), 566–92.

Peeters, R. and Nieto-Morales, F. (eds) (2020). *La máquina de la desigualdad: Una exploración de los costos y las causas de las burocracias de baja confianza*. Ciudad de Mexico: CIDE/Colegio de México.

Perelmiter, L. (2022). 'Fairness' in an unequal society: Welfare workers, labor inspectors and the embedded moralities of street-level bureaucracy in Argentina. *Public Administration and Development*, 42(1), 85–94.

Pires, R. (ed) (2019). *Implementando Desigualdades: Reprodução de Desigualdades na Implementação de Políticas Públicas*. Rio de Janeiro: IPEA.

Pressman, J. and Wildavsky, A. (1973). *How Great Expectations in Washington Are Dashed in Oakland*. Berkeley: University of California Berkeley.

Santos, M.P. (2018). *Comunidades terapêuticas: temas para reflexão*. Rio de Janeiro: IPEA.

Santos, M.P. and Pires, R. (2020). Antagonismo Cooperativo na Provisão de Cuidado a Usuários de Drogas no Distrito Federal: conflitos e parcerias entre CAPS AD e CT. *Texto para Discussão IPEA* n.2604. Brasília: IPEA.

Sher-Hadar, N. (2020). Jamming with implementation research. *Critical Policy Studies*, published online: 24 September 2020. https://doi.org/10.1080/19460171.2020.1817762

7

Frontline implementation conditions of the Families programme: labour precarity and territorial gaps as aspects of weak state institutions in Chile

Taly Reininger, Gianinna Muñoz Arce, Cristóbal Villalobos, and Mitzi Duboy Luengo

Introduction

According to a 2017 report, Chile is one of the most centralised countries within the OECD (OECD, 2017). Although decentralisation efforts have grown in importance over the last two decades, the process has been slow and fragmented (Marshall, 2019). Centralised government institutions continue to concentrate power and resources, thus persisting with the historical dependence of regional and local governments on decisions made centrally (von Baer, 2009). Specifically, regarding local governments in Chile, municipalities are limited to the role of 'public service providers' (OECD, 2017, 21), implementing social policies designed at the national level utilising a vertical top-down policy design model. This policy design model has been described in the literature as a chronological and linear process model, divided into easily distinguished stages in which policy design precedes policy implementation (Hill and Hupe, 2014; Hupe and Hill, 2016).

Historically, top-down policy design proponents visualise the implementation of social policies as a mere administrative task in which local implementation professionals adhere to clear rules, regulations, and procedures to provide equal services to all (Li and Walker, 2021). Uniformity and congruence are the goals of vertical top-down policy design and implementation (Hupe, 2011). Thus, from this perspective, strict and correct adherence to rules and procedures in programme implementation should logically result in positive policy outcomes. However, the difficulties in reaching uniformity and congruence have been called into question by research utilising a bottom-up perspective, which has repeatedly demonstrated that the implementation of social policy is far from an a-political administrative task of simply applying rules and procedures (Lipsky, 2010). Research utilising a bottom-up perspective has revealed the importance of recognising that social policy is implemented by people (frontline workers), for people (users), and in very different contexts, all variables that have an essential impact on policy outcomes (for a review, see Hupe, 2019).

Focusing on the latter, the role of context in the implementation of social policy is critical to understanding policy outcomes; however, little research utilising a bottom-up perspective has included contextual macro-level factors such as local realities in its analysis (Sausman et al, 2016; Gofen et al, 2019; Peeters and Campos, 2022). Building on Lipsky's street-level bureaucracy approach, Rice (2012) introduces the importance of taking into consideration the institutional and systemic environments in order to grasp the complexities of policy implementation, presenting a micro-institutionalist model of policy implementation that includes three levels of analysis; the micro (caseworker–client interaction), meso (implementing organisation), and macro (broader societal context). This multilevel analysis is especially pertinent for examining policy implementation in Latin America, where structural and organisational conditions vary considerably from the regions where the great majority of street-level bureaucracy research has emerged (Lotta et al, 2022). In order to analyse the effect of implementing social policy in different structural and organisational conditions and contexts other than those with historically solid welfare states, the concepts 'weak institutions' and 'institutional weakness' have begun to appear in the literature on street-level bureaucracy (Peeters and Campos, 2022).

In the literature, weak institutions are defined as state institutions that function differently than intended, leading to policy implementation and outcome gaps, particularly prevalent in countries with historically unstable or recent social welfare systems. In a systematic review of the literature, Peeters and Campos (2022) identify four factors associated with institutional weakness: organisational/administrative, political, social, and professional. Organisational/administrative factors refer to administrative conditions of implementation and include state capacity and resources, supervision and control, and administrative competence, among others. Political factors refer to institutions' low bureaucratic autonomy and relate to issues such as patronage and clientelism, and the power of politics in hiring and firing decisions. In contrast, social factors refer to social-contextual characteristics, including low social trust, high social inequality, and high levels of violence, among others. Lastly, professional factors refer to issues related specifically to frontline professionals, such as precarious labour conditions, squalid workspaces, and the role of professional norms in decision-making. Although all four of the factors Peeters and Campos (2022) identify with weak institutions are helpful in analysing policy implementation in such institutions, in this chapter, our analysis will focus solely on two: professional and administrative/organisational factors. In Chile, the country's particular historical, political, social, and territorial contexts have shaped policy implementation, contributing to precarious frontline professionals' working conditions (professional factor) and implementation gaps due to regional differences (administrative/organisational factor).

The present chapter seeks to contribute to the literature on weak state institutions by analysing the tensions and challenges contractual and contextual differences pose to implementing one of Chile's central Social Protection programmes, *Programa Familias*. Under a social investment framework, this programme seeks to 'Provide families and individuals with comprehensive support to strengthen their capabilities and improve well-being in the areas of health, education, employment, income, and housing' (Ministerio de Desarrollo Social y Familia, 2023) Utilising individual and group interviews and descriptive results from a nationally representative survey of frontline professionals implementing the Families programme, tensions and challenges due to precarious employment conditions and territorial and contextual differences emerged as critical barriers to meeting the programme's objectives.

The chapter begins with a discussion on the relationship between precarious employment conditions, frontline professionals, and policy implementation in Chile, followed by a brief historical overview of Chile's Families programme and the social investment framework. A third section describes the study's methodology, followed by the findings that identify two interrelated difficulties frontline professionals face: precarious employment conditions and the challenges of implementing a universal programme in vastly diverse territorial contexts. We identify neoliberal fatigue (Lavee and Strier, 2018) as a widespread phenomenon among frontline professionals in Chile who work in weak state institutions, concluding with recommendations for policy makers.

Precarious employment, frontline professionals, and social policy implementation in Chile

In Chile, upon the return to democracy in 1990, the state rapidly and substantially increased funding for creating a wide range of new social policies and programmes, specifically focusing on 'fighting poverty'. Nevertheless, despite this increased interest in addressing social problems, the state continued with the neoliberal subsidiary model installed during the country's dictatorship (1973–89), limiting its role in the execution of social programmes and creating the need to outsource policy and programme implementation. While outsourcing is usually associated with the state contracting private institutions for programme implementation, in Chile, the state also created a second form of outsourcing by elaborating collaboration agreements with municipalities to implement policies designed on a central level.

The public–public outsourcing arrangement installed during the late 1990s and consolidated in the 2000s increased the contracting of fee-based workers in municipalities throughout the country. This particular modality of contracting workers establishes a commercial relationship between two parties, with the worker providing services to the organisation while stipulating temporality and worker independence. However, these conditions have been distorted in practice, with municipalities requiring fee-based workers to comply with set hours and duties, thus limiting the independence established in such contracts. Furthermore, through fee-based contracts, municipalities evade the regular contractual obligations that guarantee employees' rights to healthcare, vacation, maternal and paternal leave, and severance pay leading to highly precarious working conditions (Valdebenito, 2017). In these precarious contractual conditions, frontline professionals are expected to implement social policies and programmes targeted at those considered most vulnerable while paradoxically facing vulnerable conditions themselves.

The vulnerability and fragility frontline professionals face due to the widespread outsourcing model implemented in Chile has also brought significant stress loads for frontline professionals. On the one hand, due to the temporality of their fee-based contracts, they are constantly faced with uncertainty regarding the continuity of their employment. Fee-based contracts require constant renewal and since workers are considered independent, terminating contracts is much simpler than with workers who have stable long-term employment contracts since severance pay is not legally obligated. Previous research in Chile has identified the fear of losing one's job as a shared discourse among frontline professionals, significantly impacting physical and mental well-being (Muñoz-Arce et al, 2022). Adding to frontline professionals' stress levels, their role in making life-altering decisions (such as the approval of social benefits or the execution of punitive judicial measures) with service users further strains their physical and mental health in such unstable conditions (Mastracci, 2021). In Chile, these conditions have produced a professional subjectivity based on insecurity and precariousness (Villalobos et al, 2021).

Therefore, those who implement social programmes on the frontline in Chile find themselves in a 'liminal' space, an ambiguous position loaded with contradictions and tensions. In this scenario, professionals must respond to multiple mandates and superiors: those emanating from the central state level, those of the local organisations that implement the programmes, as well as the individual and collective professional visions and cultures within intervention teams (Schöngut-Grollmus, 2017). Likewise, the labour flexibility under which frontline professionals operate has blurred the limits between personal life and work, leading to self-exploitation, the fragmentation of social ties, social suffering, and the increase in 'moonlighting' due to insufficient wages (Bermúdez, 2015).

Also related to the latter, studies have identified the predominance of the 'entrepreneurial self' figure, which is at the base of most social programmes and which has promoted an individualistic and competitive identity not only among and between users but also among professionals who implement them (Reininger and Castro-Serrano, 2021). This neoliberal personal responsibility discourse and the unethical neoliberal climate (Weinberg and Banks, 2019) have permeated the decisions made by frontline professionals who often categorise families into worthy and unworthy of aid leading to 'neoliberal fatigue', a concept coined by Lavee and Strier (2018) in order to describe the emotional precarity frontline professionals face in their daily practice. The authors identify institutional abuse (lack of resources and institutional support), emotional overload (stress, anxiety, and helplessness of working with vulnerable families), and personal precariousness (the realisation that they, too, are vulnerable to poverty) as causal factors of neoliberal fatigue. This phenomenon is preoccupying not only regarding the well-being of frontline professionals but also regarding the negative impacts on service users, particularly the reproduction of inequalities (Lotta and Pires, 2019).

Chile's social protection system and the Families programme

In Chile, neoliberal reforms implemented during the dictatorship (1973–89) had profound political, economic, and cultural repercussions (Hall and Lamont, 2013). In 1990 with the return of democracy, the country faced a poverty rate close to 40 per cent, which was drastically diminished until the early 2000s when extreme poverty stagnated (Neilson et al, 2008). The government at the time, headed by President Lagos, made it one of its central missions to design a nationwide programme to end extreme poverty, leading to the creation of the Chile Solidario social protection system.

Passed into law in 2004, Chile Solidario consisted of three interrelated components: a psychosocial accompaniment programme (Puente), cash transfers, and preferential access to social services. Unlike traditional conditional cash transfer programmes (CCTs), which had rapidly advanced in Latin America during the 1990s and 2000s, Chile Solidario was considered a cash-plus programme due to its additional complementary components rather than solely cash transfers which was the dominant CCT policy model at the time (Roelen et al, 2017). Chile Solidario adopted a social investment framework, rapidly becoming the dominant welfare paradigm on an international scale, advocating for investment in human capital and actively promoting labour market participation to combat poverty (Laruffa, 2018). Chile Solidario, specifically through its Puente programme, sought to work individually with families through home visits with psychosocial professionals in identifying and strengthening family capabilities to eliminate the intergenerational transmission of poverty (Reininger et al, 2018).

Nevertheless, evaluations of Chile Solidario failed to demonstrate success in increasing family income and employment levels, thus leading to the systems reformulation in 2011 (Ingreso Etico Familiar) and once again in 2016 (Subsistema proteccion social Seguridades y Opportunidades y Programa Familias). Despite the system's reformulations, two interlaced elements have remained consistent throughout, the social investment framework and the psychosocial accompaniment component.

A unique characteristic of the social investment framework is the activating role it places on social policies (Laruffa, 2018; Staab, 2010). Thus, specifically in regards to the Families programme, psychosocial accompaniment professionals, or apoyos integrales, are expected to steer families towards actively investing in overcoming their situation of extreme poverty. Under this programme, extreme poverty is defined as a multidimensional phenomenon, the reason for which interventions with families are expected to address shortcomings in five dimensions: health, education, housing, income, and employment. In concrete terms, this involves translating goals into tangible achievable actions such as committing to regular child school attendance (education dimension), starting an entrepreneurship to increase family income (income), completing monthly health check-ups with infants (health), and so on. Due to its focus on individual and family human capital investment, essential territorial elements are disregarded by the Families programme, such as the availability, access, and quality of local services and opportunities (Urquieta, Labraña, and Salinas, 2021), a key aspect addressed recently in the literature on the social investment paradigm and its limitations in eradicating poverty (Bučaité-Vilké, 2022).

Methodology

The data analysed in this chapter are from an extensive three-year qualitative-quantitative sequential study (Creswell, 2015) that explored the implementation of social programmes from the perspective of frontline professionals. The interviews in this chapter corresponded to the data collected in the study's first phase and consisted of individual and group interviews with professionals implementing three different social programmes. For this particular chapter, only those interviews with professionals from the Families programme were analysed. These consisted of six semi-structured group interviews and 17 individual interviews with professionals in three regions: Atacama (north), Región Metropolitano (central), and Ñuble (South). Six municipalities were included in the sample to compare and contrast implementation contexts, including a rural and urban municipality from each region. Due to the COVID-19 pandemic, interviews were conducted online. Before each interview, participants were sent an informed consent form which was then signed and sent to the research team before each interview. The interviews were transcribed verbatim, and thematic analysis (Braun and Clark, 2012) was used to analyse the data.

During the study's second phase, an online survey was applied to frontline professionals working in the three programmes selected for the study. From the total universe of the study (4,868 people), a probability sample was constructed considering geographic location and programme (N=1694 valid responses). A link to the online survey was sent to frontline professionals through institutional mailings and was available for responses for eight weeks (August and September 2021). The survey was approved by the authorities of the programmes involved and by the Ethics Committee of the institution sponsoring the research. This chapter presents only the findings from the frontline professionals implementing the Families programme (total universe: 2,044; N=1,170 valid responses). The contractual and contextual challenges to implementation that emerged from the data are described in detail later.

Contractual tensions and challenges: outsourcing and precarious working conditions

The precarious working conditions of frontline professionals were manifested in multiple ways. On the one hand, frontline professionals tend to have more than one institution they have to report to (from the municipality and the ministry, and so on and, therefore, are accountable to different managers operating at different levels and different institutions. Each institution had its own objectives, logic, and accountability mechanisms, which also blurred the responsibilities regarding the programme's operating conditions. This institutional tension was also reinforced by the fee-based contract modality, in which most interviewees found themselves, as the following quote reveals: "(There are) many managers but only a single worker, many orders. When we complained about it, they have told us that the queue for those who want our position is long. We asked for a fixed contract, and there was no possibility; they blame each other (municipality and ministry)" (Individual Interview, Urban, Ñuble).

Added to the instability and double management frontline professionals faced were the squalid material conditions in which the programme was implemented. In various accounts, the interviewees reported a precariousness of all sorts: from not having a contract covering basic health and security rights, not being sure of pay dates, and lacking basic work materials for the programme's adequate implementation. The following quotes are testimonies of these precarious conditions: "We work in a supportive chain when someone is ill. We do it internally, among ourselves. We lack labour rights" (Individual Interview, Urban, Ñuble). "I did the impossible … we did not receive materials or anything from [state institution], the materials came out of our pockets" (Individual Interview, Urban, Region Metropolitana).

While the previous quotes address the contractual deficiencies frontline professionals face and the administrative and organisational faults that lead to the absence of materials needed for implementing the programme, the last interview excerpt is particularly powerful in demonstrating the manner in which frontline professionals use their own personal resources in order to 'patch up' administrative and organisational failings. This type of action by frontline workers in weak institutions has been identified as a form of policy improvisation since professionals seek solutions to structural deficiencies through individual localised actions (Peeters sand Campos, 2022). However, using individual private solutions is problematic since it not only increases the precarisation of frontline professionals but also conceals the administrative and organisational faults of the programme, thus not exposing the structural deficiencies that weak institutions reproduce (Lavee and Strier, 2019). Furthermore, the individual actions frontline professionals undertake to 'fix' administrative faults lead to long-term impacts on workers' physical and mental well-being (De la Aldea, 2019; Lavee and Strier, 2018).

The programmes' structural deficiencies also have an impact on service users who are subjected to receiving services in unworthy conditions and often lacking privacy:

> 'Before, we were in a shipping container where a maximum of three people fit, and there were five of us. We were completely overcrowded. ... Every two days, we go to work in our office, but we now work in a warehouse in the Municipality, where people often come looking for materials. We do not have the privacy of working by phone; there is noise. ... The municipality does not provide the best working conditions. This chair creaks all the time, and the furniture is very old or broken. One has to be constantly hammering nails to stabilise it.' (Individual Interview, Rural, Atacama)

Similarly, there is instability and insecurity regarding the continuity of the programme, which significantly affects the relationships between professionals and users: "There is tremendous job instability. Nobody tells you anything, if one is going to continue [implementing the programme the following year]. As for the payments, they paid us when they remembered, changing the payment date every month" (Individual Interview, Rural, Region Metropolitano).

Frontline workers also report the programme's high caseloads and administrative responsibilities as a cause of stress:

> 'Because how the methodology is proposed in the books or the guides they give us, but how it is actually applied on the ground is different. Because they [policy makers] do not consider the overload [number

of cases], they do not consider the administrative work, and they do not consider the time that one has to do follow-up tasks.' (Group Interview, Rural, Ñuble)

In Chile, research on frontline professionals has repeatedly identified neoliberal reforms and the implementation of new public management as causes of stress and mental health anguish (Muñoz-Arce, 2020; Muñoz-Arce et al, 2022; Reininger et al, 2021). Specifically, under New Public Management, frontline professionals are continuously and increasingly burdened with producing quantifiable results of their interventions, leading to a more significant amount of time completing paperwork and uploading data, which inevitably takes away from the time professionals could provide services.

The quantitative results of the survey confirm and delve into aspects related to frontline professionals' precarity. Thus, for example, 96 per cent of those surveyed who work full-time in implementing the programme are fee-based contracts indicating a lack of access to healthcare and other fundamental rights. To illustrate this lack of access, professionals declared that they could sometimes or never make use of medical leave (73 per cent), maternity or paternity leave (74 per cent), medical leave for children under one year of age (82 per cent), nor receive severance pay (95 per cent).

Another relevant aspect revealed by the survey results is the economic precarity frontline professionals face. In this regard, the majority of those surveyed declared that they were the main financial supporters of the household (72 per cent) and had someone in their care or economically dependent (70 per cent). Likewise, although an important part of the participants declared that the monthly income they received from work allowed them to cover basic needs and regular expenses, half of the participants overextended their credit card permanently and considered debt a naturalised economic management mechanism (Pérez-Roa, 2019).

Contextual tensions and contradictions: distance in policy design, rigidity in implementation, and territorial differences

Distance and rigidity were two aspects frontline professionals highlighted in the interviews, specifically regarding methodological and practical differences that emerged between national design and local implementation. The distance was understood as a lack of understanding of local contexts but also the lack of experience programme designers had in the 'real world':

'However, I believe the big problem with these social programmes is that they are designed behind four walls. ... What has happened in these years is that methodologies come to us, and we have to apply them.

And obviously, when we apply this methodology on the ground, it is totally different because on the ground it is not the same.' (Individual Interview, Urban, Atacama)

By describing programme design as undertaken 'behind four walls', a clear distance is established between formulation and design and local implementation. The four walls represent a physical barrier between policy designers and frontline professionals and a symbolic one of exclusiveness (only a few experts participate in design), privacy (behind closed doors), and a general lack of interest in including other voices in the programme's design. This distance and lack of voice create a significant challenge for programme implementation since the methodology applied in practice locally is vastly different from what was theoretically designed on a national level. This becomes apparent in frontline professionals' descriptions of the territorial contexts in which they are expected to operate:

'Sometimes you cannot carry out the number of [home] visits you have. In other words, it used to happen a lot to me; for example, sometimes I would visit a certain sector; I sometimes have six families in a sector, but due to time, I only manage to visit four. So, the other two [families] tell me, "Hey, but how, you passed by my house, and you did not visit me?" That is also something that generates a slightly negative feeling because sometimes in very remote sectors we never manage to visit all the families together [in one trip].' (Group Interview, Rural, Ñuble)

The Families programme establishes several mandatory home visits that psychosocial professionals must apply with each family assigned to their caseloads. Additionally, the programme's methodology pre-establishes the timing of these home visits, with the frequency of visits decreasing over the 24 months psychosocial professionals work with each family. The high caseloads and difficulties in meeting these home visit goals have been identified in previous research (Cisternas, 2021). As the previous quote describes, such pre-set goals are even harder to accomplish when considering interventions with families living in rural areas where distance is not considered. As the frontline professional implies previously, this lack of understanding or consideration of territorial differences in programme methodology leads to possible tensions with families since expectations cannot be met. These tensions can lead to friction in the relationship forged between families and frontline professionals, jeopardising the possibility that these relationships will act as a propeller of family change, as expected by the programme (Rojas, 2018).

The lack of attention to local realities is identified as a significant limitation of the Families programme, particularly the programme's ignorance of the realities of rural localities. In addition to such territorial differences, cultural and distinctive local features are also identified as essential, calling for a more bottom-up situated perspective in designing the programme:

> 'Ñuble has around 21 municipalities, and of the 21 municipalities, the vast majority are rural. It is a great limitation of the programme because as I explained to you … [the programme] does not consider the singularities, particularities, idiosyncrasies, and culture of each region and each municipality. This applies nationally to everyone equally.' (Individual Interview, Urban Ñuble)

However, perhaps the most challenging situation frontline professionals face due to territorial differences is the lack of local services and opportunities for families.

> 'Although there are many national [programme] collaboration agreements, here in the municipality they do not exist. People have less access to benefits, people who are part of the [social security] subsystem. So, in each family [intervention] plan, we can have many commitments, but if there are no programmes available [in the locality], it is difficult for us to complete that work with families because the benefits for that family do not exist or are very limited.' (Group Interview, Rural, Atacama).

As described previously, the Families programme consists of the psychosocial accompaniment component, cash transfers, *and* preferential access to public services. Nevertheless, stark regional inequalities exist regarding public services, especially in more rural areas. Frontline professionals face families in dire need of specific services; however, they can only secure such services if they exist. Referring families to other municipalities where such services exist requires more time and money and means challenges in establishing inter-municipal collaboration. This absence of local resources falls under the administrative/organisational factor of weak institutions, as identified by Peeters and Campos (2022) in the literature. In concrete terms and regarding the Families programme, this lack of services leaves families with unmet needs and promises, directly impacting programme outcomes. It is not surprising that families report frustration once the services they believed they would be able to access by programme participation are non-existent (Reininger y Castro, 2021). Furthermore, related to this administrative weakness, in addition to the absence of local services, is the limited number of quotas of existing services:

> 'However, for example, the programme that I told you about, the Apoyo al Plan Laboral, has so few quotas, and we participate in the

decision-making table, we try to make it a kind of reward for the most responsible people [who participate in the programme]. We strive so that they can apply, and since we are all present at the meeting, we try to get all of them selected [to the programme].' (Group Interview, Rural, Metropolitan region)

As described in the previous quote, to address limited quotas, frontline professionals proceed by pre-selecting candidates, focusing on those deemed most responsible and for whom being accepted in the programme would be understood as a 'prize'. This type of pre-selection utilises frontline professionals' moral criteria regarding those deemed 'worthy' of services. This process, best known as creaming, involves frontline professionals handpicking cases they believe will succeed (Lipsky, 2010; Guul, Pederson and Petersen, 2021). This type of discretionary action has been called into question since it is a manner in which social inequalities are reproduced in the implementation of social programmes (Lotta and Pires, 2019). This becomes a reality due to the limited quotas offered in which frontline professionals use their personal and moral evaluations of individuals to assign participation despite the supposed universal preferential access to services – what Weinberg and Banks (2019) identify as part of the unethical climate of neoliberalism. In conclusion, territorial differences are not only possible to observe through lack of services but also through the limited number of quotas. This is particularly prevalent in rural municipalities.

Conclusion

In conclusion, and as discussed throughout this chapter, policy implementation in Chile faces various challenges. Utilising Peeters and Campos's (2022) framework on weak institutions and a bottom-up perspective, we identified how administrative/organisational and professional factors significantly impact programme implementation. In the specific case of the Families programme, administrative/organisational factors include a lack of resources for programme implementation and the disregard for territorial differences. Our findings indicate that despite their own personal precarity, frontline professionals often use personal means in order to 'patch up' programme deficits due to the lack of resources. While these compensating actions have been 'normalised' they are problematic for two reasons: the emotional and physical toll such actions have on frontline professionals leading to neoliberal fatigue and burnout (Lavee and Strier, 2018, 2019) and the manner in which such actions provide a veil for structural programme deficiencies. By making up for programme deficiencies through individual compensatory actions, policy makers remain 'unaware' or can easily ignore structural faults, placing the blame for deficient outcomes on policy implementation rather than design, thus perpetuating and reproducing inequalities.

Our second finding in regard to administrative/organisational factors characteristic of weak institutions in Chile is the disregard for significant territorial differences. While Chile has a relatively small population (17 million) in comparison to other countries in Latin America, Chile's territory is highly diverse, including regions that are physically, historically, politically, economically, socially, and culturally varied. Yet, this rich diversity is not taken into consideration in policy design. Study participants indicated numerous problems due to the lack of attention to the country's diversity in the Families programme design, ranging from lack of public services to the use of quotas to assign 'meritorious' families to those few available local opportunities. Such faults and consequent creaming actions by frontline professionals reproduce the very inequalities the programme seeks to ameliorate.

Results from our study also revealed professional factors characteristic of weak institutions, specifically precarious employment conditions. Frontline professionals implementing the Families programme are hired through fee-based contracts that are temporary, unstable, and devoid of access to rights such as healthcare and severance pay. Despite the independence and temporality fee-based contracts offer workers, in practice, these 'advantages' only contribute to further worker precarity. In interviews, frontline professionals reported extremely precarious material, physical, and emotional employment conditions, ranging from multiple managers and unclear hierarchies to unpredictability in regards to pay dates. Such instability and lack of security have a toll on the physical and emotional well-being of frontline professionals which research has shown to have a negative impact on the relationships forged with programme participants and programme outcomes (Lavee and Strier, 2018; 2019; Muñoz-Arce, 2020; Reininger et al, 2021; Muñoz-Arce et al, 2022). One could argue the precarious conditions workers face are in fact a form of institutional abuse product of neoliberalism, specifically through outsourcing, the requirements of New Public Management, and the implantation of the personal responsibility discourse.

Considering the aforementioned tensions and challenges to implementing the Families programme in Chile due to weak institutions, recommendations for policy makers involve the inclusion of frontline professionals in place-specific programme design (Bučaité-Vilké, 2022), eliminating frontline professionals' precarious working conditions, and adopting an ethic of care (Mastracci, 2021).

The inclusion of frontline professionals in programme design allows for the use of situated local knowledge and the development of place-sensitive practices that take into consideration contextual challenges to successful programme implementation. Recent discussions on the social investment paradigm that has dominated the design of social policies over the last few decades reveal the need to invest resources in localities that lack services and opportunities in order for individuals to overcome situations of poverty (Bučaitė-Vilkė, 2022). While the social investment perspective has historically focused on individual human capital, these new developments call for investing in local capital, thus addressing structural barriers to overcoming poverty. However, this cannot be accomplished without the key situated knowledge frontline professionals have in regard to the localities within which they work.

Our second recommendation, eliminating precarious working conditions, is fundamental in order to improve programme outcomes. As discussed throughout the chapter, the instability and insecurity frontline professionals face daily impact their physical and emotional well-being leading to multiple negative programme outcomes. In order to improve programme outcomes, decent working conditions are a minimum requirement for frontline professionals who work with populations facing extreme vulnerabilities. Specifically, in Chile, this includes terminating fee-based contracts and providing all employees with basic rights to healthcare, vacation time, and severance pay.

Lastly, and related to the elimination of precarious working conditions, is the adoption of an ethic of care in state institutions. According to Mastracci (2021) certain state work, or what she terms 'emotional dirty work', has significant adverse impacts on workers such as stress, stigma, and burnout. In order to address the negative impacts of emotional dirty work, Mastracci (2021) argues that the state has the responsibility of providing care for its workers. Concretely, adopting an ethic of care implies providing employees with the services and conditions they need in order to do their job without developing negative physical and emotional repercussions. However, we are aware that needs to change in order for the adoption of an ethics of care in state institutions, especially in a country struggling with weak institutions.

References

Bermúdez, C. (2015). Trabajar en la cuestión social: Trabajo sobre los otros y transformaciones en los mundos del trabajo. *Tabula Rasa*, 22(22), 307–21.

Braun, V. and Clarke, V. (2012). Thematic analysis. In H. Cooper, P.M. Camic, D.L. Long, A.T. Panter, D. Rindskopf, and K.J. Sher (eds), *APA Handbook of Research Methods in Psychology, Vol 2: Research Designs: Quantitative, Qualitative, Neuropsychological, and Biological*. Washington, DC: American Psychological Association, pp 57–71. https://doi.org/10.1037/13620-004

Bučaitė-Vilkė, J. (ed) (2022). *Social Investment Policies and Territorial Inequalities: Mapping Policies and Services in the Baltic States*. Berlin etc.: Peter Lang.

Cisternas, J. (2021). *La coordinación intersectorial en el territorio. El caso del programa Familias Seguridades y Oportunidades.* [Master's thesis, Universidad de Chile].

Creswell, J.W. (2015). *A Concise Introduction to Mixed Methods Research.* London: SAGE Publications.

De la Aldea, E. (2019). *Los cuidados en tiempos de descuido.* Santiago: LOM.

Gofen, A., Sella, S., and Gassner, D. (2019). Levels of analysis in street-level bureaucracy research. In *Research Handbook on Street-Level Bureaucracy.* Cheltenham: Edward Elgar Publishing, pp 336–50.

Hall, P. and Lamont, M. (2013) *Social Resilience in the Neoliberal Era.* Cambridge: Cambridge University Press.

Hill, M.J. and Hupe, P.L. (2014). *Implementing Public Policy: An Introduction to the Study of Operational Governance* (3rd edn). London: Sage Publications.

Hupe, P.L. (2011). The thesis of incongruent implementation: Revisiting Pressman and Wildavsky. *Public Policy and Administration,* 26(1), 63–80. https://doi.org/10.1177/0952076710367717

Hupe, P.L. (ed) (2019). *Research Handbook on Street-Level Bureaucracy: The Ground Floor of Government in Context.* Cheltenham: Edward Elgar Publishing.

Hupe, P.L. and Hill, M.J. (2016). 'And the rest is implementation'. Comparing approaches to what happens in policy processes beyond *Great Expectations. Public Policy and Administration,* 31(2), 103–21. https://doi.org/10.1177/0952076715598828

Laruffa, F. (2018). Social investment: Diffusing ideas for redesigning citizenship after neo-liberalism? *Critical Social Policy,* 38(4), 688–706. https://doi.org/10.1177/0261018317749438

Lavee, E. and Strier, R. (2018). Social workers' emotional labour with families in poverty: Neoliberal fatigue? *Child & Family Social Work,* 23(3), 504–12. https://doi.org/10.1111/cfs.12443

Lavee, E. and Strier, R. (2019). Transferring emotional capital as coerced discretion: Street-level bureaucrats reconciling structural deficiencies. *Public Administration,* 97(4), 910–25. https://doi.org/10.1111/padm.12598

Li, M. and Walker, R. (2021). Need, justice and central–local relations: The case of social assistance in China. *Public Administration,* 99(1), 87–102. https://doi.org/10.1111/padm.12689

Lipsky, M. (2010). *Street-Level Bureaucracy: Dilemmas of the Individual in Public Services* (30th anniversary expanded edn). New York: Russell Sage Foundation.

Lotta, G. and Pires, R. (2019). Street-level bureaucracy research and social inequality. In P. Hupe (ed), *Research Handbook on Street-Level Bureaucracy.* Cheltenham: Edward Elgar Publishing, pp 86–101. https://doi.org/10.4337/9781786437631.00016

Lotta, G., Pires, R., Hill, M., and Møller, M.O. (2022). Recontextualizing street-level bureaucracy in the developing world. *Public Administration and Development,* 42(1), 3–10. https://doi.org/10.1002/pad.1968

Marshall, C. (2019, June). Centralismo y formas fluidas de planificación territorial en Chile: Mecanismos de gobernanza horizontal para la agenda urbana local. *XI Seminario Internacional de Investigación en Urbanismo, Barcelona-Santiago de Chile, Junio 2019*. Seminario Internacional de Investigación en Urbanismo. https://doi.org/10.5821/siiu.6713

Mastracci, S. (2021). Dirty work and emotional labor in public service: Why government employers should adopt an ethic of care. *Review of Public Personnel Administration*, 42(3), 1–16. https://doi.org/10.1177/0734371X21997548

Ministerio de Desarrollo Social y Familia (2023) *Programa Familias*. www.chileseguridadesyoportunidades.gob.cl/programa-familias

Muñoz-Arce G. (2020) 'Trabajo interprofesional en Chile', *RUMBOS TS Un Espacio Crítico Para la Reflexión en Ciencias Sociales*, (21), 87–108.

Muñoz-Arce, G., Duboy Luengo, M., Villalobos Dintrans, C., and Reininger, T. (2022). 'Oponerse sin perder el puesto': Tensiones y resistencias profesionales en la implementación de programas sociales en Chile. *Rumbos TS. Un Espacio Crítico Para La Reflexión En Ciencias Sociales*, 28, 89–108. https://doi.org/10.51188/rrts.num28.668

Neilson, C., Contreras, D., Cooper, R., and Hermann, J. (2008) The dynamics of poverty in Chile, *Journal of Latin American Studies*, 40(2), 251–73, http://doi.org/10.1017/S0022216X08003982

OECD. (2017). *Making Decentralisation Work in Chile: Towards Stronger Municipalities*. Paris: OECD. https://doi.org/10.1787/9789264279049-en

Peeters, R. and Campos, S.A. (2022). Street-level bureaucracy in weak state institutions: A systematic review of the literature. *International Review of Administrative Sciences*, 002085232211031. https://doi.org/10.1177/00208523221103196

Pérez-Roa, L. (2019). Consumo, endeudamiento y economía doméstica: una historia en tres tiempos para entender el estallido social. En K. Araujo (ed), *Hilos tensados. Para leer el Octubre chileno*. Santiago: USACH, pp 83–106.

Reininger, T. and Castro-Serrano, B. (2021). Poverty and human capital in Chile: The processes of subjectivation in conditional cash transfer programs. *Critical Social Policy*, 41(2), 229–48. https://doi.org/10.1177/0261018320929644

Reininger, T., Castro-Serrano, B., Flotts, M., Vergara, M., and Fuentealba, A. (2018). Conditional cash transfers: Social work and eradicating poverty in Chile. *International Social Work*, 61(2), 289–301. https://doi.org/10.1177/0020872816631601

Reininger, T., Muñoz-Arce, G., Villalobos, C. Morales Torres, C., and Campillo, C. (2021) Pandemic and social work in Chile: Precarity, precariousness and the quest for resistance in an uncertain world. *The British Journal of Social Work*, 52(8), 5105–5123, https://doi.org/10.1093/bjsw/bcac109

Rice, D. (2012) Street-level bureaucrats and the welfare state: Towards a micro-institutionalist theory of policy implementation. *Administration & Society*, 45(9), 1038–1062.

Roelen, K., Devereux, S., Abdulai, A., Martorano, B., Palermo, T. and Ragno, L (2017). How to make 'cash plus' work: Linking cash transfers to services and sectors, *Innocenti Working Paper 2017–10*, UNICEF Office of Research, Florence.

Rojas Lasch, C. (2018). Afecto y cuidado: pilar de la política social neoliberal *Polis, Revista Latinoamericana*, 49, 127–49.

Sausman, C., Oborn, E., and Barrett, M. (2016). Policy translation through localisation: Implementing national policy in the UK. *Policy & Politics*, 44(4), 563–89. https://doi.org/10.1332/030557315X14298807527143

Schöngut-Grollmus, N. (2017). Ensamblajes socio-técnicos para la producción de intervenciones psicosociales en un programa del Servicio Nacional de Menores de Chile. *Psicoperspectivas. Individuo y Sociedad*, 16(3), 41–51. https://doi.org/10.5027/psicoperspectivas-Vol16-Issue3-fullt ext-1049

Staab, S. (2010). Social investment policies in Chile and Latin America: Towards equal opportunities for women and children? *Journal of Social Policy*, 39(4), 607–26. https://doi.org/10.1017/S0047279410000243

Urquieta, A., Salinas, S. and Labraña, J. (2021). La improbabilidad de la transformación social efectiva: una reflexión en torno a los déficits de política pública en Chile. *Cuaderno de Trabajo Social*, 1(16), 115–32.

Valdebenito, S. (2017) *¿Cuántos trabajadores emplea el Estado de Chile? Problematizacion y orden de magnitud de la contratacion a honorarios. Documento de trabajo DT 005*. Santiago: Nueva Economia.

Villalobos, C., Wyman, I., Muñoz Arce, G., and Reininger, T. (2021). Trabajadores y trabajadoras sociales de primera línea frente al COVID-19. *Continuidades y transformaciones en Chile. Revista Intervención*, 10(2), 4–29. https://doi.org/10.53689/int.v10i2.97

von Baer, H. (2009). *Pensando Chile desde sus regiones* (1st edn). Temuco: Universidad de La Frontera.

Weinberg, M. and Banks, S. (2019) Practicing ethically in unethical times: Everyday resistance in social work. *Ethics and Social Welfare*, 13(4), 361–76.

8

Regime transitions and institutional weakness: the case of police reform in Poland in the early 1990s

Barbara Maria Piotrowska, Izabela Szkurłat, and Magdalena Szydłowska

Introduction

Regime transitions create a particular case of institutional weakness. The objectives and orientation, and alongside them the power relations in the entire state, change. If weak institutions are state institutions that fail to work as intended, transitions create weak institutions by changing the very objectives and the identity of those who define them. Therefore, even if a state transitions to a form that generally produces superior outcomes for citizens, such as during transitions to democracy, the period directly following the official regime change is often associated with significant institutional weakness and worse outcomes.

During regime transitions, some of the institutions that have to date performed well the tasks assigned to them can no longer operate as usual. This is further exacerbated in the case of institutions at the centre of the transition. And because authoritarian regimes are usually sustained or even led by their security apparatus, SLBs implementing policies associated with security maintenance find themselves at the very epicentre.

In police states, the secret police's and police's main role is to maintain regime stability and protect the state from social unrest. This contrasts with democracies, where the key objective of the security apparatus is to protect the citizens and their property. Hence, regime transitions mean a complete reorganisation of the very purpose of the state security apparatus. Institutions which were organised, staffed, and trained, to foster social stability maintenance, even if strong in an authoritarian setting, find themselves weakened as their prescribed objectives change. Hence, transitions create a special type of institutional weakness stemming from a change in circumstances, rather than weak fundamentals. This is because their design is optimised to work in a context that is no longer valid.

To illustrate how a relatively strong institution can quickly turn into a weak one, we consider a typical case of a police state that has transitioned into democracy. The Polish People's Republic was a communist country in Eastern Europe that, together with its police apparatus, has seen a successful transition to democracy that started in 1989. Just as in other states transitioning from a police state, the objective of the new democratic Republic of Poland was to depoliticise its security apparatus. This meant purging individuals with unpalatable pasts, recruiting a new force, and building a new image of the police as serving citizens, rather than the state. However, depoliticisation was only one of the hurdles faced by the reformers. Building trust among the population and developing skills helpful in fighting crime were the other two. And all of this happened in a context of rapidly increasing crime resulting from the police weakness. We discuss how these issues relate to four aspects associated with institutional weakness, framing them temporally as challenges stemming from the past (authoritarian legacies), from the present (the transition itself), and from new challenges (the increase in crime).

Our study is based on a historical case because, to fully understand the consequences of transition and the timescale required for institutions to recover their strength after the change in objectives, we need to take a long-term perspective. Hence, in contrast to the other studies presented in this book, we deviate from direct accounts of street-level bureaucrat behaviour and instead focus on the contextual factors surrounding their work and the gradual progression towards a new democratic equilibrium. The historical setting notwithstanding, this chapter offers several implications reaching beyond the Polish case to other post-authoritarian states, many of which are located in the Global South. First, the chapter suggests that administrative renewal is a complement to political transitions, as satisfaction with governance is linked to satisfaction with democracy. Second, more specifically, it highlights that authoritarian legacies common in many countries of the Global South continue to shape the SLB behaviour and their evaluation by the public even after regime formally changes. Finally, police reform is a key requirement of any democratic transition (Hassan, 2020) and the particular threats to police transformation identified in this chapter offer lessons for all countries transitioning to democracy.

Regime transitions and institutional weakness

Institutional weakness is often understood as intrinsic to the institutions or to the challenging settings within which they operate, making it difficult for them to work as intended. But what this perspective overlooks is that if institutional performance is evaluated relative to the objectives set out for the institution, these goals or intentions might change, affecting the institutional strength. This is particularly visible in the case of democratic transitions, as the mission of the government changes from maintaining the stability of the regime to prioritising the welfare of citizens. Institutions that were designed and staffed with the former goal in mind, will no longer be able to perform efficiently when their aim changes. Hence, we argue that regime transitions create a specific type of institutional weakness, one that is not intrinsic to the institution but rather to the changing circumstances in which it operates and which make the institution no longer fit for the new purpose.

Such a reorientation affects the work of different types of SLBs to varying extent. The work of healthcare personnel is unlikely to be significantly affected by a regime change. Schools might need to change their curricula (and the teacher training) and think about how to motivate teachers who joined their profession out of ideological conviction. But nowhere is the shift bigger than in the case of security services.

Under autocracy, security services allow the state to maintain its grip on power by suppressing the opposition (Barany et al, 2019). They are under the control of the regime, with close links between the ruling elite and the security apparatus giving them a central place (Hassan, 2020). Correspondingly, security sector reform is one of the first tasks that a newly democratic state needs to undergo (Barany et al, 2019). Security service reform takes on a different form in ex-military dictatorships and ex-police states. However, in successors to both types of autocratic regimes, successful reforms separate the functions of security agencies and introduce multiple effective oversight mechanisms, generally improving the ability of the agencies to promote security within their countries. But before this new improved institutional setting takes hold, the transition period is rife with uncertainty as rules, terms and conditions, and objectives of the new force are slowly redefined and internalised by both the police force and the citizens.

Given that protection of life and property is present even in the most minimal definitions of the state, the police force is not only one of the trickiest types of street-level bureaucracy to reform during transitions but also one of the most important to get right, as victimisation has been shown to undermine support for democracy in transition countries (Pérez, 2003).

Methodology

To show how the mechanisms of regime transition can turn a relatively strong police force into a weak one, even if the institution itself does not change, we need to take a long-term perspective that is best enabled by concentrating on a historical case. In this chapter, we analyse the case study of Poland. In many ways, it is a typical case of a police state that later underwent a successful transition to democracy. Between 1947 and 1989 Poland was an Eastern Bloc country referred to as the Polish People's Republic (PRL). It was a socialist one-party regime headed by the Polish United Workers' Party (PZPR) and led by a Marxist-Leninist government. The PZPR held dictatorial powers, being referred to in the 1976 amendment of the Constitution as 'the nation's leading force', and controlled the whole state, including the bureaucracy, the military, secret police, and the economy. In 1989, Poland underwent a triple (democratic, economic, and social) transition that changed the objectives of the state and the power relations within it.

We analyse the Polish case using process tracing, showing how in many ways the same forces that made security services strong under autocracy, contributed to their weakness in a democratic setting. This single-country case study allows us to explore the effects of temporal variation in the objectives of the state on the institutional strength of the police.

Reconstructing the effect of political and economic transition on the operation of the new democratic police in Poland requires triangulation of numerous quantitative and qualitative sources. In this chapter, we use historical newspaper articles from *Gazeta Wyborcza* archives, secondary literature, governmental reports and legislation, as well as survey data from the 1990s collected by CBOS (Centre for Public Opinion Research), to paint the picture of the challenges faced by the Polish police in the early 1990s. Therefore, unlike the other chapters, our approach in this section diverges from examining the perspective and behaviours of SLBs. This decision is guided by pragmatic and analytic considerations. From a practical standpoint, conducting interviews about this historical period today would introduce biases stemming from reconstructive memory. Theoretically, focusing on overarching trends and forces that may remain unnoticed by individuals allows us to grasp the broader influences shaping the work of SLBs during the transition period. However, we acknowledge that this choice of data and methodology constitutes a limitation of this chapter.

The Polish case

Before we move to the analysis of the effects of the democratic transition on the work of the police in Poland, we first need to understand the basis of operation of the old regime, and the role of the police within it. This enables us to identify the original objectives of the force and evaluate how well it performed prior to the transition, but also how its construction made it unfit to serve in a democratic society.

State security in the Polish People's Republic (PRL)

Being an authoritarian state, PRL relied on a heavy presence of security services to maintain stability and protect the state against frequent protests for improved living conditions and democracy. The two most prominent parts of the state security were the Security Service (*Służba Bezpieczeństwa*, SB) – the secret police, and the Citizens' Militia (*Milicja Obywatelska*, MO; henceforth: MO) – the 'police'. As MO was the body that later morphed more directly into the democratic police, this section concentrates on its role under the socialist government. However, in what follows, the coexistence of the two organisations becomes apparent, prompting occasional references to SB, where relevant.

The security service and the citizen's militia

The MO was founded in 1944 by the Polish Committee of National Liberation. Despite its initial autonomy, MO was quickly situated within the security department, an organisation whose main task was to terrorise and control the society, and 'the activity of militia [MO] bodies at all levels has been combined and linked with the work of the entire security apparatus' (Czop and Sokołowski, 2013). Even though its regional offices performed the usual policing tasks, such as peacekeeping and crime-solving, MO was also a key element of authoritarian power with its functionaries deeply involved in the repression of the opposition: terrorising the society, rounding-up guerrillas, and performing unlawful arrests, torture, and even executions. As a result, in public opinion they were perceived as an inseparable element of the communist repression apparatus, rather than a police formation (Karłowicz, n.d.).

MO and the opposition

Social unrest in the PRL manifested itself with frequent waves of strikes. The first prominent ones happened already in 1956 in Poznań, Bydgoszcz, and Szczecin. In response, the government strengthened the MO, creating a paramilitary force, the ZOMO (*Zmotoryzowane Odwody Milicji Obywatelskiej*, Motorised Reserves of the Citizens' Militia). This body was a rapid reaction division, equipped not only with firearms but also with rubber truncheons, and required to react in a mobile and immediate manner to any signs of citizen unrest.

ZOMO was deployed during the next wave of demonstrations in 1968 in Warsaw and, together with MO and the army, during the pacification of workers' strikes in 1970. The security services had a wide authorised leeway for their actions. Zenon Kliszko, a prominent politician of the party said at the time: "We are dealing with a counter-revolution, and a counter-revolution must be fought with force. Even if 300 workers die, the revolt will be crushed" (Garlicki, 1999). Hence, the security forces had the approval of the state to deploy brutal means of repression, further worsening their image among the population, and the opposition in particular.

This brutality became particularly prominent in the lead-up to and after the introduction of Martial Law in Poland in December 1981. The objective of the martial law was to put a lid on the further development of NSZZ 'Solidarność', an independent trade union acting as the main opposition force and an alternative centre of power. In the first 24 hours of its introduction, 3,173 opposition and Solidarność leaders were arrested by the MO forces and the SB (Majchrzak, 2021). While martial law was engineered predominantly against the members of Solidarność, given that the membership included more than a quarter of the population, the scope of repression was very broad.

During the martial law years, officers of the MO prevented any manifestations of public opposition, such as strikes and protests. The most popular preventive actions were warning calls, which were supposed to intimidate the opposition; harassment, which manifested in sending anonymous letters with threats, compromising rumours, calls to offices, and even the destruction of private property; arrests; and conscription to military service of active participants in anti-state activities (Ruzikowski, 2009).

To sum up, in its actions against the opposition, MO has proven to be a brutal force, effectively supporting the repression apparatus. Given the significant size of the opposition, this was known first-hand or indirectly to a sizeable proportion of the population, contributing to the general poor reputation and mistrust towards MO.

The triple transition

Martial law was called off in 1983. Despite its objectives, it did not manage to completely stifle the opposition and the ideals promoted by Solidarność. Over time, as the state lessened persecution of dissidents, society started feeling that the opposition was treated as a regular, albeit illegal, part of the socio-political reality (Mielewczyk, 2016).

In 1988, the state was weakened by an economic and social crisis, accompanied by successive waves of strikes. To stabilise society, the government decided to start preliminary talks with the opposition leaders, leading to the 31 August meeting between the opposition representative, Lech Wałęsa, and a government representative, General Kiszczak. After the meeting, the strikes ceased (Wilczak, 2014). Further negotiations took two forms. The first were the closed meetings held in the fall of 1988 and early 1989. Under a preliminary consensus the authorities guaranteed the rapid legalisation of Solidarność, while the opposition approved the package of political changes and promised to participate in 'non-confrontational' elections to the Sejm (parliament) (Skórzyński, 2019). The second one was the official Round Table deliberations, running from 6 February 1989 to 5 April 1989. The main compromise was the agreement to hold free elections to the Senate, as well as partially free elections to the Sejm. These two institutions were to then elect the president of the People's Republic collectively. The resulting June 1989 parliamentary election saw a resounding victory of the opposition and allowed for the creation of a cabinet led by Solidarność members. The peaceful transition to democracy was confirmed after the free presidential election of 1990 and the free parliamentary elections of 1991.

While MO was still present during the regime change in 1989, it was dissolved soon after. On 10 May 1990, the Security Service and the Civic Militia ceased to exist. By the Police Act of 6 April 1990, a new Policja was established, created as 'a uniformed and armed formation intended to protect the security of citizens and to maintain public safety and order' (Ustawa z Dnia 6 Kwietnia 1990 r. o Policji, 1990).

An important part of the transition is that it involved not only a move from authoritarianism to democracy. The second aspect of the transition included a rapid transformation of the economy from socialism and state ownership to a capitalist market economy, dubbed "Shock Therapy". Among other effects, it was associated with a massive increase in unemployment and the privatisation of state-owned enterprises. We discuss the link between these two developments to the operation of the police in the following sections. The third and final aspect of the transition was the changes happening in society, which needed to accept the new rules of the game and adjust its mentality to the new democratic and free-market reality.

The previous section demonstrates that the role of MO in the authoritarian regime has been that of a fully-fledged member of the repression apparatus. It was competent in fulfilling its primary goal - fighting the opposition and pacifying strikes and other forms of unrest, making it a relatively strong institution with respect to that function. However, MO did not get many opportunities to concentrate on the goals relevant to the operation of democratic police, such as solving crimes. Moreover, as a side-effect of its brutality, the public did not see it as a police force that could be trusted with resolving crimes. All of this has left a crushing legacy for the new police organised under the democratic government, significantly contributing to its institutional weakness.

Institutional weakness faced by the police during the transition

This book identifies four aspects associated with institutional weakness (organisational capacities, political influence, social trust and inequality, and bureaucratic professionalisation). Polish police in the early 1990s experienced all of them: as the new state was no longer a police state, the force needed to deal with lower importance and fewer resources; it no longer held political influence; the trust towards the new force was relatively low, especially among the former opposition; and the police did not have the skills required to deliver the new objective of fighting crime. Analysis of these challenges, and their link to the institution's performance under authoritarianism, is the central topic of this chapter. However, because at the point of transition the state faced challenges stemming from the legacies of the old regime (the past), the process of transition itself (the present), and new problems (the future), we choose to classify these institutional weaknesses temporally.

The past: authoritarian legacies

Despite the enthusiasm surrounding the turn of the page on the communist rule in Poland, over forty years spent under autocratic rule have had a lasting effect on everyday lives, as well as on institutions. Two prominent ways in which they impacted building a new democratic police force concerned citizens' low trust towards the police, as well as difficulties with the recruitment of new functionaries.

Working in a context of low trust

Citizen trust is key to the proper operation of the police: if the citizens do not believe that the force wants and can help them, they will not report a crime. If the crime is not reported, it cannot be resolved, leading to a further decrease in the feeling of safety and decreased trust in police.

As described earlier, because of its authoritarian history including prioritising the stability of the regime over the security of the citizens, the Polish pre-transition police force, MO, did not have a good reputation. And while the new state tried reforming this image, starting with the official objectives of the police and its renaming as *Policja Państwowa*, a change in perceptions and belief in the new objectives could not happen overnight.

Of the five Eastern European countries surveyed in the second wave (1990-1994) of the World Values Survey, Poland, at 29.3 per cent had the highest proportion of respondents who said that they have "none at all" confidence in the police. To better understand the dynamics of confidence in police in Poland, we use data from CBOS (*Centrum Badania Opinii Społecznej*; Centre for Public Opinion Research sourced from Polskie Archiwum Danych Społecznych), which asked the respondents to evaluate the work of the police in many of its monthly surveys running from 1990. We start by zooming in on the situation in the 1990s.

Figure 8.1 shows that confidence in the work of the police initially increased in the early 1990s. However, as the organisation was rebuilding itself and crime was rising, the evaluation of police started falling again after 1993. To complete the picture, we also consider the long-term trend data from later CBOS surveys (Figure 8.2). Here, we can see that the fall in the

Figure 8.1: Evaluation of the police in the early 1990s (annual average)

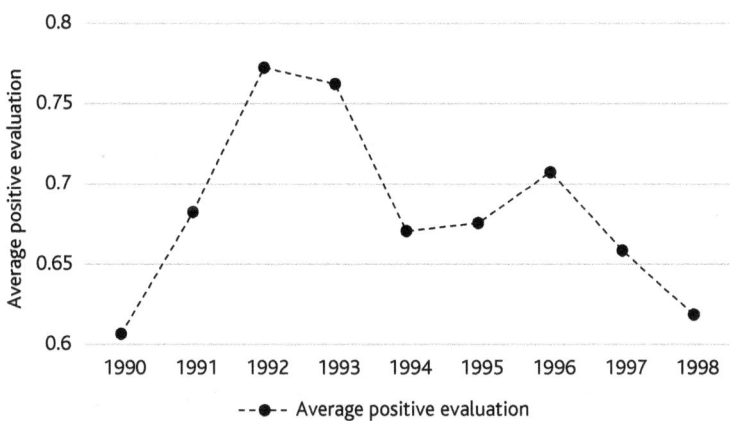

Source: data: CBOS

Figure 8.2: Survey evaluation of the police on a longer time scale

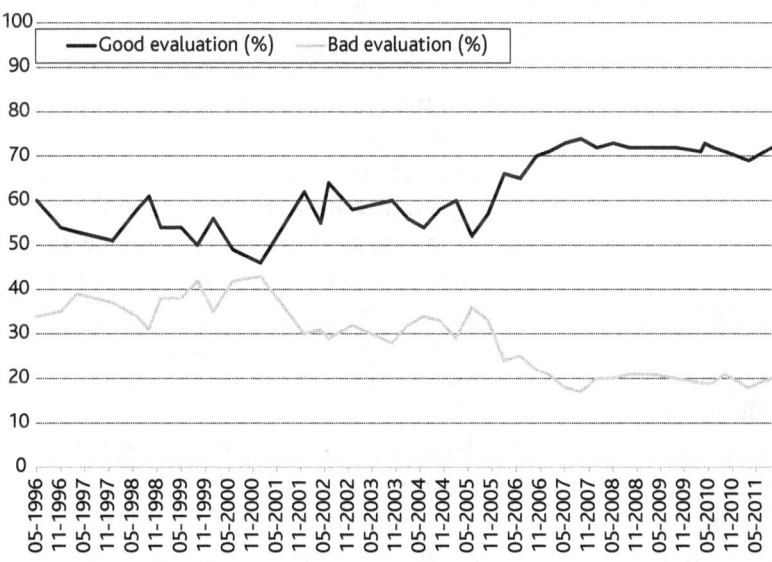

Source: CBOS from Policja.pl, 2011

trust after 1996 was a harbinger of a new low-trust equilibrium, hovering at c.a. 60 per cent. This has finally been overcome in the mid-2000s. Since then, around 70 per cent of respondents have consistently evaluated the police positively. Hence, even though the security organisation officially changed its objectives in the early 1990s, it took several years for the citizens to positively evaluate its performance.

Figure 8.3: Positive evaluation of the police among those who were and were not members of Solidarność

Source: data: CBOS

As discussed earlier, a particular challenge in terms of building trust in the Polish police stemmed from the size of the pre-transition opposition. With such a populous social movement (and the network of connections associated with it), the stories of repressive behavior could travel far and fast, even if they were not reported by the censored media.

Likely because of this wide network that could provide access to information about security apparatus abuses, former members of the opposition were generally even less confident in the police than the public. CBOS data allow us to disaggregate the trends in police evaluation between those who were and were not members of Solidarność in 1981. Graphing these trends demonstrates that there was a differential evaluation as long as the data on membership in Solidarność was collected (until 1999) (Figure 8.3).

Hence, in the early 1990s, the new democratic police struggled with low citizen trust, which made its proper operation difficult. The poor reputation of the force stemming from its pre-transition activities had wider effects, affecting recruitment, as we will see in the next section.

Personnel issues – verification and recruitment

Resource shortage is almost a defining feature of street-level bureaucracies, such as police (Lipsky, 2010). Even in ordinary times, officers worldwide complain about staff shortages. Regime transitions exacerbate this problem. Even a minimal security sector reform includes staff turnover, frequently caused by personnel purges. Thus, created vacancies need to be filled in an environment where the institution does not have the best reputation. The situation in Poland in the early 1990s was no different.

First, the communist security personnel, including both the secret police (SB) and MO, saw different levels of screening. The purge, or verification, of SB personnel was performed by 49 regional (and one central) commissions that reviewed 14,034 applications. In making a positive or negative recommendation the commissions evaluated the candidates with respect to their collaboration with the previous regime and loyalty to it, as well as skills that could be useful in the new democratic reality (Kozłowski, 2019). Hence, where verification costs were high, high levels of pre-transition repression could mean that some individuals would be found unfit to serve, even if some skills would be lost in the process (Nalepa and Piotrowska, 2022). Eventually, 10,439 officers (over 75 per cent) were verified positively. This meant that these individuals were allowed to *apply* to work for the new democratic security services. However, the success of the application was not ensured.

Because of the scale and complicated nature of the enterprise, MO, in general, has not been purged (Kozłowski, 2019). However, the personnel have been reviewed, with 3,027 of the c.a. 100,000 ex-MO fired (Letkiewicz and Mejer, 2016), mostly "for the benefit of the organization". However, in the last years of the regime, many of the SB officers, nicknamed "parachuters" (Kozłowski, 2019, 59) had foreseen the upcoming transitions and moved (or were transferred) to MO to avoid a presumed purge. Aware of that, the legislators included in the verification law a provision for some of the former SB officers to be scrutinised. Moreover, part of the positively verified officers of SB could, and did, apply to work for the police. Hence, the purges affected the personnel in both forces, albeit to a different extent.

Second, the new force needed new recruits, people not compromised by working for the previous regime and trained in the modern methods of policing. As the minister of interior and administration, Krzysztof Kozłowski, observed: "I hear: 'Well, let's hire honest, reliable, professional people'. The whole point is that this system [authoritarianism] was destroying them, preventing their self-realisation, and knocked them out, distorting them" (Kozłowski, 2019, 71). Hence, the problem with recruitment stemmed from the previous set of incentives that made the pool of existing specialists largely inappropriate for the service. Moreover, working for the security apparatus was seen unfavourably in many families. Fortunately, in Poland, this prejudice has to some extent decreased with the transformation of MO into police. A newspaper article from April 1990 describes the surprise of the recruitment officers at the number of applicants for work in the police (Burek, 1990). However, its author sees the causes of increased interest in burgeoning unemployment, an incentive possibly overriding any reservations about working for the security apparatus.

Even when new people could be hired, the training period necessary to reconstruct the relevant capabilities of security services was estimated at 8–10 years (Kozłowski, 2019). While the training time, at three years divided into basic and professional training, was significantly shorter for the police, the time required to train them still meant an elevated number of vacancies in the early 1990s (Gazeta Wyborcza, 1990; Ustawa z Dnia 6 Kwietnia 1990 r. o Policji, 1990). In Warsaw in 1989 there were 2,000 vacancies. By 1990, the number had grown to 3,100 (Gazeta Wyborcza, 1990). The rise in crime led to a further increase in the number of vacancies that needed filling. Consequently, the government increased the number of desired posts from 80,000 in 1990 to 105,000 in 1993 (Niebieski, 2019), in which year around 30,000 of new recruits needed training (Letkiewicz and Mejer, 2016). Moreover, the new recruitment system faced its own challenges. A 1999 report conducted by the Polish supreme audit institution outlines the weaknesses of officer recruitment in the mid-1990s, pointing out the importance of motivation demonstrated in studies showing that 50 per cent of policemen did not identify with police service (Najwyższa Izba Kontroli, 1999).

Summing up, because of the need to purge and difficulties with recruitment, security services in 1990 saw a high level of vacancies. The situation in the police was also dire, with the increase in crime further inflating the demand for new policemen. Hence, the personnel shortages usual in the work of SLBs were further exacerbated by the transition.

The present: the transition

The transition itself meant that the defining roles of the security apparatus changed dramatically. This necessitated a new mindset, as well as a new skill set.

The change in objectives

The first set of challenges stemmed from the complete change of mission of the security services and their power within the system. Under communism, the role of MO in supporting the state was stated clearly in its oath: 'I vow to faithfully serve the socialist homeland – the Polish People's Republic, the Polish nation, and the Polish United Workers' Party, to protect the constitutional principles of the state and its security' (Dziadul, 2019). The new oath states instead:

> I, a citizen of the Republic of Poland, aware of the duties of a police officer, swear to: serve the nation faithfully, protect the legal order established by the Constitution of the Republic of Poland, protect

the security of the State and its citizens, even at the risk of my life. (Dz.U. z 1990 r. nr 30, poz. 179)

Three major differences stand out. First, policemen were no longer swearing loyalty to any political party. In fact, party membership was no longer allowed, in line with the prescribed apolitical character of the police (Kruk, 2018). This was a big change in regions such as Katowice, where around 80 per cent of the MO functionaries and all the officers were members of the PZPR (Dziadul, 2019). Second, the new oath included protection of citizens, a point not included prominently in the pre-democratic version. Third, while both formulae referred to the protection of the constitutional order, the constitutional documents have in the meantime changed. In particular, the Small Constitution of 1992 outlined the basis of the new democratic system, and the 1997 Constitution that followed included new types and scope of citizen's rights, as compared to the 1952 socialist document (Szymaniak, 2001). Generally, this meant that the police were now expected to serve the citizens, rather than the party. This change in mission and depoliticisation needed to be internalised by all the functionaries.

Moreover, work in the security apparatus no longer received good remuneration. While in 1980 a functionary of SB and MO received some 120 per cent of average pay, in 1990 this amount was significantly below the average (Burek, 1990; Kozłowski, 2019). In addition to affecting recruitment, described previously, it meant that the perks and potentially some prestige of the work were no longer its in-built feature.

Skill compatibility

The change in emphasis from maintaining the stability of the state and protection of the interest of the party, to taking care of the security of the citizens was no trivial challenge. It required a change in priorities, as well as the development of new skills. Authoritarian states often seem to have very effective policing systems. However, the security maintenance and citizen protection functions should not be confused. Scoggins (2021) describes how in China the government has prioritised 'stability maintenance' at the expense of other aspects of policing, to project an image of a strong security state. As a result of limited resources, corruption, ambiguous responsibilities, and divided control, the regular police force struggles to deal with everyday crime. Kozłowski (2019) notices a similar problem in Poland where the political police were supported and maintained at the expense of the criminal police. Hence, the skill set available to the police force was constructed with a goal in mind that has shifted during and after the transition. This made some of the training no longer relevant and shifted values to other abilities.

The change in priorities meant that the police force lacked the skills necessary to fight everyday crime. Scoggins (2021) substantiates this with an account of a Chinese interviewee who could be seen as well-trained: 'You don't learn anything. ... Ninety-five percent is just political thinking ... not really any practical examples you can use' (Scoggins, 2021, 78). MO saw a similarly intensive ideological training: between 1945 and 1951, the number of hours devoted to ideology reached up to 39.3 per cent of all training time (Pączek, 2017). This meant that a transition to democracy in Poland was associated with a need for a new curriculum in policing courses that the new recruits could be educated in. This was exacerbated by the increase in new forms of crime in the 1990s.

The future: new challenges

The transition in its three aspects fed into increasing levels of crime. This can be disaggregated into two different challenges: an increase in the types of crime that the police force was familiar with, and in new types of, mainly organised, crime.

Increase in crime

Analysing the statistics related to regular crime reveals a clear increase. Between 1989 and 1990, the number of criminal offenses increased by about 350,000, around 64 per cent. This would imply that on any given day in 1990 there were 1,000 more crimes than in the previous year (Czabański, 2010). However, these numbers cannot be trusted, as before the democratic transition, the state manipulated crime statistics (Kury et al, 1996). Hence, concentrating on specific crimes provides a more reliable picture. For example, the number of homicides increased by as much as 30 per cent, with a similar rise in the number of assaults. Theft increased by around 50 per cent and robberies increased by almost 80 per cent compared to the previous year (Czabański, 2010). Police resources were completely inadequate to address this volume of crime. Nationally, between 1990 and 1993, only 49.1 per cent were resolved, with significant regional variation (for example, in 1990 in Warsaw this number was only 12 per cent (Gazeta Wyborcza, 1990; Kury et al, 1996)). This increase was not limited to the transition year, which could be affected by questionable figures. Crime statistics document a steady increase until the early 2000s (Czabański, 2010).

New types of crime

On top of the increase in more familiar types of crime, the early 1990s saw the emergence of organised crime, virtually non-existent pre-1989, including the phenomenon of the so-called Polish 'mafia'. This originated from two sources. The first one was the takeover of parts of the economy by corrupt officials or politicians. The second one was the organisation of petty criminals into powerful groups taking control of economic activities. Both the first and second forms of criminal activity were closely linked to the power-business relationship (Domański, 2013).

To understand the origin of these groups, consider the circumstances of the rise to prominence of two mafia groups: Wołomin and Pruszków. The groups specialised in crimes such as racketeering, kidnapping for ransom, and theft of luxury cars. While the members of both had been already committing crimes before 1989, the transition caused a massive increase in their activity. First, the reorganisation of security services in 1990 meant that the control over organised crime had to be reassigned to newly established branches of the service. The police initially did not even have a directorate responsible for fighting economic crimes, something that was present in MO. It took until 1994 for the Office for Combating Organized Crime to be funded. The criminals could also capitalise on the weakness of the police stemming from the factors described earlier to grow and internationalise their operations. Second, with the opening of borders, Poland has become a transit country for products such as contraband alcohol (Wasilewski, 2018).

Discussion: regime transitions as institutional weakness

The previous discussion has given us an overview of how the Polish regime transition in the early 1990s created institutional weakness for one particular street-level bureaucracy: the police. While generally a typical case, Poland is unusual for two reasons. First, the transition had a triple character (political, economic, and social), creating challenges for the police that would not be present in a transition of only one type. Second, because of the significant number of members of the main opposition and those related to it, the proportion of citizens who have had a negative experience with the MO was higher than in authoritarian countries where repression is more targeted. Both factors made the task of creating a new trustworthy and effective democratic police force even more difficult than in other cases.

However, authoritarian legacies are prevalent (and will become relevant after any future transitions to democracy) also in countries of the Global South. Hence, despite the idiosyncrasies described earlier, the situation of the Polish security sector is redolent of challenges faced by many other transition countries and offers broader implications.

First, it highlights that one way in which these legacies continue to impact the post-transition states is through SLB behaviour and through their interactions with the citizens. While the politicians in power may change during regime transitions, the SLBs are unlikely to see a fundamental turnover. And in the everyday life of the citizens, it is the SLBs, rather than the political elites, that are the most visible face of the state. Therefore, post-transition countries need to pay particular attention to managing SLBs to convince the citizens that the regime change can be reconciled with personnel continuity. Second, institutions that do not deliver on their objectives frustrate government's ability to deliver and damage the perceptions of government effectiveness. The latter, in turn, is associated with lower satisfaction with democracy (Dahlberg and Holmberg, 2014). Hence, bureaucratic renewal is an essential complement to political transitions in fostering democracy. Finally, security service reform specifically is a particularly important requirement of any democratic transition (Hassan, 2020). Whether in the post-military regimes of Latin America or in the ex-police states in Africa, military and police reforms often accompany the constitutional transitions (Pérez, 2003 ;Barany et al, 2019). Hence, singling out particular threats to police transformation identified on the example of Poland offers lessons for all countries transitioning to democracy.

Conclusion

This chapter highlights that institutional weakness should be evaluated with respect to organisational objectives. Transitions to democracy amplify this point, as they are associated with a rapid shift of the mission, potentially weakening formerly strong institutions, as they adjust to the new goals. If weak institutions are state institutions that fail to work as intended, transitions cause this weakness by redefining the very objectives of work of institutions such as the police.

We show how institutional weakness stemming from regime transition mechanics affects the operation of a specific street-level bureaucracy: the police, analysing a typical case of a police state that transitioned to democracy. Security services including both the secret police (SB) and the Citizens' Militia (MO) formed the foundation of the repressive apparatus of the authoritarian Polish People's Republic and played a key role in supporting its survival. After the transition to democracy, they were dismantled and new democratic equivalents, including democratic police, were created. However, the police faced challenges stemming from institutional weakness caused by the transition. Its authoritarian past caused low esteem of the new police force, especially among the opposition members, which could make performing basic policing difficult. It also meant that all personnel needed to be reviewed in order to remove those unsuitable for serving the newly democratic country, and recruits needed to be trained according to newly defined criteria. The transition itself caused issues too. First, the very definition of the role of the police shifted dramatically from protecting the party to protecting the citizens. Second, this shift in emphasis meant that those educated under the old regime received an education that placed excessive emphasis on ideology and insufficient on the new goal: fighting crime. Finally, the police faced new challenges: its weakness, combined with the relative weakening of border controls meant that crime, particularly organised crime, soared. Hence, the Polish police during the transition faced all the types of institutional weakness outlined in the introduction.

References

Barany, Z., Bisarya, S., Choudhry, S., and Stacey, R. (2019). *Security Sector Reform in Constitutional Transitions*. Oxford: Oxford University Press.

Burek, T. (1990). Pójdź Stachu do milicji. *Gazeta Wyborcza,* 17 April 1990.

Czabański, J. (2010). Ocena bezpieczeństwa w Polsce w latach 1989–2009. In J. Kochanowski and M. Kuruś (eds), *Quo vadis Polonia. W drodze do demokratycznego państwa prawa. Polska 1989–2009*. Warszawa: Biuro Rzecznika Praw Obywatelskich, pp 179–90.

Czop, A. and Sokołowski, M. (2013). Historia polskich formacji policyjnych od ii wojny światowej do czasów współczesnych. *Kultura Bezpieczeństwa. Nauka–Praktyka–Refleksje,* 13, 28–47.

Dahlberg, S. and Holmberg, S. (2014). Democracy and bureaucracy: How their quality matters for popular satisfaction. *West European Politics,* 37(3), 515–37.

Domański, M. (2013). Przestępczość zorganizowana w RP po 1989 roku. *Securitologia,* 18(2), 85–95. https://doi.org/10.5604/18984509.1130060

Dziadul, J. (2019, 1 October). Jak policjanci powstali z milicjantów i dlaczego historia toczy się kołem. *Polityka.* www.polityka.pl/tygodnikpolityka/ spoleczenstwo/1926800,1,jak-policjanci-powstali-z-milicjantow-i-dlacz ego-historia-toczy-sie-kolem.read

Garlicki, A. (1999, 28 August). Towarzysz Zenon. *Polityka.* www.polityka. pl/archiwumpolityki/1878614,1,towarzysz-zenon.read

Gazeta Wyborcza. (1990, 20 April). Biedna milicja. *Gazeta Wyborcza.* https:// classic.wyborcza.pl/archiwumGW/6018236/BIEDNA-MILICJA

Hassan, M. (2020). *Regime Threats and State Solutions*. Cambridge: Cambridge University Press. https://doi.org/10.1017/9781108858960

Karłowicz, Z. (n.d.). 'Solidarność' – Milicja Obywatelska (MO). Brama Grodzka: Teatr NN. https://teatrnn.pl/leksykon/artykuly/solidarnosc-milicja-obywatelska-mo/

Kozłowski, T. (2019). *Koniec Imperium MSW. Transformacja Organów Bezpieczeństwa Państwa 1989–1990*. Warszawa: Instytut Pamięci Narodowej.

Kruk, M. (2018). Prawne aspekty apolityczności Policji. *Studia Nad Bezpieczeństwem,* 3, 145–60. https://doi.org/10.01.2018

Kury, H., Krajewski, K., and Obergefell-Fuchs, J. (1996). Obraz przestępczości w Niemczech oraz w Polsce w okresie transformacji ustrojowej (wybrane aspekty). *Archiwum Kryminologii,* XXII, 7– 41.

Letkiewicz, A. and Mejer, P. (2016). *Polska Policja. Wyższa Szkoła Policji w Szczytnie.* https://info.policja.pl/inf/historia/policja-w-iii-rp/policja-w-iii-rzeczypo/67621,Policja-w-III-Rzeczypospolitej-19902010.html

Lipsky, M. (2010). *Street-Level Bureaucracy: Dilemmas of the Individual in Public Services.* New York: Russell Sage Foundation.

Majchrzak, G. (2021, December 13). *Kryptonim 'Jodła', czyli internowania.* Przystanek Historia. https://przystanekhistoria.pl/pa2/tematy/stan-wojenny/88171,Kryptonim-Jodla-czyli-internowania.html

Mielewczyk, M. (2016). Polska transformacja ustrojowa i fenomen 'Solidarności' a sytuacja międzynarodowa w latach 80. XX w. *Gdańskie Studia Międzynarodowe*, 14(0), 88–110. https://doi.org/10.5604/01.3001.0010.1229

Najwyższa Izba Kontroli. (1999). *Informacja o wynikacj kontroli systemu naboru kadr w Policji i wykorzystania okresu służby przygotowawczej do ukształtowania zawodowego policjanta (Inf 1471).* Nr ewid. 206/99/P98079/DON. Warszawa: Najwyższa Izba Kontroli.

Nalepa, M. and Piotrowska, B.M. (2022). *Clean Sweep or Picking Out the 'Bad Apples': The Logic of Secret Police Purges with Evidence from Post-Communist Poland.* https://www.researchgate.net/publication/360374842_Clean_sweep_or_picking_out_the_%27bad_apples%27_the_logic_of_secret_police_purges_with_evidence_from_Post-Communist_Poland

Niebieski. (2019, August 1). *Wymiana pokoleniowa w Policji. Milenialsi w służbie.* Niebiescy997. https://niebiescy997.pl/wymiana-pokoleniowa-w-policji-milenialsi-w-sluzbie/

Pączek, T. (2017). Szkolenie zawodowe i polityczne szeregowych oraz podoficerów Milicji Obywatelskiej w latach 1945–1954. In W. Bagieński, P. Chmielowiec, Dziurok Adam, W. Frazik, D. Iwaneczko, R. Klementowski, R. Leśkiewicz, P. Skubisz, and M. Stefaniak (eds), *Aparat Represji w Polsce Ludowej 1944–1989*, 1(15), 103–26.

Pérez, O.J. (2003). Democratic legitimacy and public insecurity: Crime and democracy in El Salvador and Guatemala. *Political Science Quarterly*, 118(4), 627–44.

Policja.pl. (2011, 23 September). *72 Proc. Polaków Dobrze Ocenia Policję (Wrzesień 2011).* Statystyka.Policja.Pl. https://statystyka.policja.pl/st/opinia-publiczna/70276,72-proc-Polakow-dobrze-ocenia-Policje-wrzesien-2011.html

Ruzikowski, T. (2009). *Stan wojenny w Warszawie i województwie stołecznym 1981–1983.* Warszawa: Instytut Pamięci Narodowej.

Scoggins, S.E. (2021). *Policing China.* Ithaca, NY: Cornell University Press. https://doi.org/10.1515/9781501755606

Skórzyński, J. (2019, 7 February). Tajemnica Magdalenki, czyli spiskowa historia Okrągłego Stołu. *Newsweek.* www.newsweek.pl/historia/rozmowy-w-magdalence-i-historia-okraglego-stolu/0zkqcle

Szymaniak, A. (2001). Prawa obywatelskie w konstytucjach z 1952 r. i 1997 r. Analiza porównawcza. *Ruch Prawniczy, Ekonomiczny i Socjologiczny*, LXXIII(3), 31–48.

Sejm, R.P. (1990). Ustawa z dnia 6 kwietnia 1990 r. o Policji. No. Dz.U. z 1990 r. nr 30, poz. 179.

Wasilewski, S. (2018). Przestępczość zorganizowana w Polsce po 1989 r. – Pruszków i Wołomin. *Świat Idei i Polityki*, 17(1), 310–330. https://doi.org/10.15804/siip201816

Wilczak, D. (2014, 6 February). Kompromis narodzony w bólach. *Newsweek*. www.newsweek.pl/historia/kompromis-narodzony-w-bolach/tj1hxll

PART III

Bureaucratic encounters

9

Coping with violence and precarious working conditions: law enforcement through the eyes of municipal police officers in Morelia, Mexico

Paulina Yunuén Guzmán Linares and Rik Peeters

Introduction

How do police officers cope, both behaviourally and emotionally, with the double challenge of precarious working conditions and a dangerous social context? And how does this impact the nature of law enforcement and the police's interactions with citizens? In this chapter, we discuss the case of the municipal police of Morelia, a large city in central Mexico, among the world's 50 most dangerous cities, and where municipal police officers face shortages in basic materials (such as uniforms and patrol cars), receive low salaries, work long shifts (often of 12 hours), and have limited training and psychological support. The severe problem of organised crime in Morelia and the state of Michoacán (of which Morelia is the capital)[1] is particularly relevant for understanding the context in which police officers function – often leaving them outgunned and outnumbered. According to Hupe and Buffat (2014), police officers are street-level bureaucrats (SLBs) who perform public regulation tasks, particularly activities geared toward security and maintaining public order. Consequently, the interaction they have with citizens can become conflictive. Police officers are often exposed to constant danger (Aaron, 2000) and high levels of distress (Acquadro et al, 2018). They provide a critical emergency service, which implies that stress is accepted as an inherent part of the job and is likely even more the case in contexts with complicating social and political factors (Azevedo et al, 2021). Likewise, in precarious environments with high levels of vulnerability and low trust between citizens and SLBs, the latter often feel overburdened and experience powerlessness and inability to respond to citizen demands (Spink et al, 2021).

Although the coping mechanisms used by SLBs in general to mitigate the tensions in their work are well documented in public administration studies, there has been less attention on frontline workers' behaviour in the

Global South and even less to contexts with high levels of violence and danger at work (Lotta et al, 2022). By shifting attention to such contexts, we can better understand the challenges police officers face, how citizens experience the interactions with them, and what the everyday practice of law enforcement looks like. This is particularly important in contexts with high levels of violence and experienced insecurity, where authorities struggle to guarantee the safety of citizens and their property. In this chapter, the case of the Municipal Police of the city of Morelia is used to demonstrate how police officers cope both behaviourally and emotionally with violence, danger, citizen distrust, and precarious working conditions. Based on original interviews with police officers and complementary document analysis, we argue that such conditions may lead them to move away from dangerous situations, act out aggressively towards citizens, and rely on colleague support and substance abuse to deal with their everyday reality at work. Their response to social and institutional complexities fundamentally changes the face of law enforcement and leaves police officers to fend for their own physical survival and mental health.

In the following, we first briefly discuss relevant insights from the literature on police officers as SLBs as well as our analytical framework on coping mechanisms. Next, we present our data collection and data analysis methods. The findings section is organised around the four types of coping mechanisms identified by Tummers and colleagues (2015) – highlighting both behavioural and emotional or cognitive mechanisms expressed during as well as outside of interactions with citizens. Moreover, we pay specific attention to differences in responses between male and female police officers, since these emerge as relevant for understanding both labour divisions and types of responses to dangerous, stressful, and precarious working conditions – thereby also contributing to studies on frontline work in traditionally male-dominated organisations (Chudnovsky and Reyes, 2021). We end our contribution with a discussion of the main findings and the broader relevance of our case for understanding how SLBs may respond to the challenging working conditions common for the Global South, and especially in police work, and how this structures the everyday interactions they have with citizens.

Coping by police officers

Police officers as street-level bureaucrats

According to Hupe and Buffat (2014), SLBs can be classified according to the tasks they perform. Police officers are responsible for public regulation and carry out their work within specific institutional frameworks that define their actions and shape their working conditions. As discussed in more detail in the introductory chapter of this book, police officers in countries with weak institutions often have to perform their duties in complex organisational conditions, including a lack of basic equipment to ensure their safety (Chudnovsky and Reyes, 2021), insufficient training to fulfil their duties (Causa en común, 2019), and opaque hiring schemes, low salaries, and limited job benefits (Causa en común, 2022). In addition to this, working in a violent context is known to have harmful effects on the professional practice and personal well-being of SLBs (Davidovitz and Cohen, 2022). It is likely to generate fear and distrust, given the potential risk of violent acts and the perception of a threatening environment (Pavoni and Tulumello, 2018). Specifically, police officers may fear physical harm or losing their lives in the line of duty (Kroes and Hurrell, 1975). Given their role as critical emergency service providers, a certain level of stress is accepted as an inherent part of the job. In contexts with difficult social and organisational working conditions, however, stress levels tend to increase significantly (Azevedo et al, 2021). While certain levels of danger and stress are inherent to police work, we argue that they are more prevalent under precarious working conditions and that, consequently, police officers respond in distinct ways to the challenges they face.

Coping mechanisms

Folkman and Lazarus defined the concept of 'coping' as 'constantly changing cognitive and behavioural efforts to manage specific external and/or internal demands that are appraised as taxing or exceeding the resources of the person' (1984, 141). In the contexts of public service provision and street-level bureaucracy, coping mechanisms are commonly understood as the 'efforts frontline workers employ when interacting with clients, in order to master, tolerate, or reduce external and internal demands and conflicts they face on an everyday basis' (Tummers et al, 2015, 1100). Even though most scholarly attention has been paid to the way SLBs cope with client interactions, it is well established that coping has two different forms – behavioural and cognitive – and that these may be employed both during interactions with citizen–clients and outside those interactions (Tummers et al, 2015; Møller, 2021; Spink et al, 2021; Lotta et al, 2023). In the discretionary space of their daily work, SLBs may cope behaviourally with different types of situations, client demands, organisational constraints, and available resources by, for instance, bending or breaking rules, routinising client processing, ration service provision, or using personal resources to complement limited organisational resources. Furthermore, outside of client interactions, they may turn to colleagues for advice and support, seek job rotation, or rely on substance abuse in response to stress. In terms of cognitive or emotional coping, documented strategies include developing emotional detachment from painful or confronting work situations, showing compassion with citizen–clients, job alienation, and cognitive restructuring to justify and rationalise complex elements of their daily decision-making. Through these and other coping mechanisms, SLBs not only deal with their own challenges at work but also shape the nature of the interactions with citizens and, by extension, with the state in general.

Specifically regarding police officers, Maynard-Moody and Musheno argue that they may 'bend and sometimes break the rules for some individuals while going out of their way to enforce the rules for others' (2003, 103). Furthermore, Tummers and colleagues (2015) found that police officers are relatively likely to show behaviour that goes against the wishes or interests of citizens, as compared to other types of frontline workers (see also Alcadipani et al, 2023). Regarding cognitive or emotional coping, police officers are known to rely on positive situational reinterpretation, denial, and substance abuse to cope with organisational stressors (Acquadro et al, 2018) – while acknowledging there may be a difference between male and female police officers in relation to emotion-centred coping (Rodriguez and Scharagrodsky, 2008). Although there is a lot of work on police officers as SLBs in general, relatively few studies exist that focus on particularly violent or precarious contexts in countries with weak policing and security institutions. In a notable exception, Lotta et al (2022) identify eight types of responses by SLBs to working in violent territories: silence, renunciation, denying the capacity of a policy, excluding difficult cases, negotiating with actors responsible for violence, policy adaptation, fighting against violence, and dealing with failure. In the following, we build on these studies to analyse how municipal police officers cope with violent and precarious working conditions.

Methodology

Case selection

Our research question is: how do police officers cope, both behaviourally and emotionally, with the double challenge of precarious working conditions and a dangerous social context? To answer this question, an exploratory and qualitative research was conducted in the Municipal Police of Morelia – the capital city (approximately 1 million inhabitants) of the state of Michoacán in central Mexico. This organisation was created in December 2015 with the objective 'to preserve order, safeguard life, liberties, peace, and personal and patrimonial security in public spaces, prevent criminal conduct and administrative offenses' (Secretaría de Gobierno del Estado de Michoacán de Ocampo, 2019, 3).

This case is useful for our research question for several reasons. First, it is an organisation that allows us to study the SLBs of our interest: police officers that patrol the streets and have daily interactions with citizens. Second, these police officers develop their work in a very violent environment in which the presence of well-armed and well-organised drug cartels is one of main threats to public security – making this an extreme case of policing in an adverse social environment. Morelia is among the 50 most violent cities in the world (34th) (Consejo Ciudadano para la Seguridad Pública y la Justicia Penal, A.C., 2022), with a homicide rate of 40.81 per 100,000 inhabitants, while the worldwide average rate is 6.1 (UNODC, 2019). In addition to this, according to the Mexican National Survey of Urban Public Security conducted in the first quarter of 2022 (INEGI, 2022), citizens' perception of public insecurity in the city is 77 per cent, well above the national average of 66.2 per cent. Furthermore, according to the National Survey of Victimization and Perception of Public Security in 2021 (INEGI, 2021), the crime prevalence rate in Morelia per 100,000 inhabitants is 27,136, exceeding the Mexican national average of 23,520. Additionally, 48.9 per cent of the adult population of Morelia that identifies the municipal police express distrust in it (INEGI, 2021). A third reason for our case selection are the institutional deficiencies that the municipal police officers in Morelia face, as reflected in their labour conditions, training, and equipment. They do not have access to housing credits, their salary is below the national average of 12,600 pesos, and of the 100 patrol cars they have, more than half are in their last useful year (Alfaro, 2022). Working hours are usually 12-hour shifts per every 24 hours, but these may be extended without overtime pay (Instituto para la Seguridad y la Democracia, 2021). The combination of these institutional deficiencies and an extremely dangerous social context make the working conditions of Morelia's police officers particularly vulnerable as compared to their colleagues in many advanced democracies with strong security institutions.

Data collection and analysis

Data collection consisted of in-depth interviews as the main source of information, complemented by a document study. The interviews were semi-structured and the questionnaire design was based on the classification of coping mechanisms discussed earlier by Tummers and colleagues (2015). Contextual factors related to institutional deficiencies and violent environments were also considered. A total of 20 interviews were conducted between 17 May and 20 May 2022, with police officers with a basic scale grade. Half of the interviewees were women and the other half men. Interviewees were selected based on convenience sampling. All interviews were transcribed.

Data analysis was performed with an abductive approach. First, an initial set of codes derived from the literature was used to analyse the data. Second, a definitive code set was developed by contrasting the theory-based codes with codes emerging from the interview data. With regard to the violent

Table 9.1: Initial codes for violent environment and institutional deficiencies

Violent environment	Institutional weaknesses	
Fear	Lack of training	Insufficient benefits
Sense of danger	Corruption	Lack of material and human resources
Distrust	Excessive working hours	Insufficient salary

Table 9.2: Definitive codes for violent environment and institutional deficiencies

Violent environment	Institutional weaknesses	
Fear	Overwork	Negative perception by citizens
Sense of danger	Impunity	Need for psychological support
Distrust	Inefficiency	

Table 9.3: Initial codes for coping mechanisms

Coping mechanisms			
During citizen interaction		Outside of citizen interaction	
Behavioural	Cognitive	Behavioural	Cognitive
Bending the rules	Cynicism	Peer support	Cognitive restructuring
Breaking the rules	Compassion	Complaints	Cynicism towards work
Aggression	Indifference	Rotation	Job alignment
Routinisation		Substance abuse	
Rationing			
Use of personal resources			
Blaming the citizen			

environment and institutional deficiencies, the following codes in Table 9.1 were used for the first stage of analysis.

Following the comparison of the initial codes with the interview data, the final set of codes was established (Table 9.2).

Regarding the coping mechanisms, an initial set of codes was derived from the work of Tummers and colleagues (2015), as it is shown in Table 9.3.

Following the comparison of the initial codes with the interview data, the final set of codes was established, as shown in Table 9.4.

Relevant segments of the interview transcripts were identified and classified into spreadsheets according to the codes mentioned previously as well as according to the gender of the interviewee. The frequency of each code was counted as well to allow for some descriptive statistics of our findings.

Table 9.4: Definitive codes for coping mechanisms

Coping mechanisms			
During citizen interaction		Outside of citizen interaction	
Behavioural	Cognitive	Behavioural	Cognitive
Moving away	Self-control	Cultural activity	Positive attitude
Peer support	Paralysing	Spiritual activity	Expectation of change
Gender division		Family activity	Growth expectation
Improvisation		Physical activity	Motivation
		Walking away for self-preservation	
		Psychological support	

It is important to highlight that the identified coping mechanisms are self-reported by police officers, which may cause a certain bias towards politically or socially desirable answers. The following discussion of our findings is structured around the identified codes, starting with a discussion of the perceived relevance of the institutional context by the interviewees and followed by a discussion of the way they cope with these. Relevant quotes from the interviews were translated and language edited by the authors.

Findings

Working conditions

Violent environment

Police officers in Morelia perceive the environment in which they work as violent and unsafe, in the face of a growing presence of organised crime, homicides, and domestic violence. All interviewees recognise a sense of danger as a constant in their daily work: "I think that at any moment, and without any motive, someone can take our life, because of the simple fact of wearing a uniform; I believe the danger is constant" (4M 2022).

Especially organised criminal groups pose a perceived threat, including the family relations gang leaders may have: "We once detained the nephew of the [local gang] boss here in Morelia; there were confrontations, persecutions, many things. So, the threats here are constant, from people that feel influential. It's dangerous" (1H 2022).

This perception of constant danger in a violent environment generates stress and anxiety (see Azevedo et al, 2021). The police are aware of the possibility of an adverse event that might happen to them, given the activities they carry out in which they can lose their lives, and the threats they receive from citizens. Of the female police officers we interviewed, 90 per cent expressed feeling stress, compared to 60 per cent of the male officers. Police officers mention that carrying a weapon and wearing a uniform makes them easily distinguishable to criminal groups. In addition to this, the occurrence of traumatic events, such as the loss of colleagues in the line of duty, are seen as a reminder of the constant exposure to danger in their daily activities: "A colleague died who was electrocuted … when he was trying to attend a report of a robbery in process; for wanting to help others, we forget about ourselves" (6M 2022).

Furthermore, 60 per cent of the interviewed female police officers claim to have felt fear at work, compared to 55.56 per cent of the male officers. This feeling is strengthened by the lack of protective material to carry out their work and often occurs during altercations with violent people: "Of course it generates fear. … You see, for example, a man was banging on the windows with a stick … and you think, 'what if he gives me a beating?' … You always go to all reports with the fear of 'maybe I'm not coming back'" (5H 2022).

There is also fear of conflictual interactions with unsatisfied citizens that may lead to threats. The types of citizens with whom the police interact influence the detonation of this sensation, for example, when faced with organised crime groups: "We have dealt with very bad folks here, and when it was our turn I said 'we are dead'. I swear to you, literally and figuratively, we pissed our pants" (4M 2022).

Precarious working conditions

The precarious working conditions perceived by police officers we interviewed are summarised in Figure 9.1.

A first notable finding is that 90 per cent of the interviewees mention a lack of psychological support, especially to deal with traumatic events such as the loss of colleagues and with the emotional burden of the reports they have to attend:

> 'Something that hit us badly … is the case of a baby of barely 2 and a half years old that lost his life. … Because I feel like I could have done more for him. No one ever … from here in the institution said "I heard that you lived through a traumatic event" … "go see and discuss it with a psychologist".' (4M 2022)

With regard to material and human resources, the interviewed police officers manifest a broad shortage of supplies, including medicines and first aid kits, tactical equipment, uniforms, and patrol cars:

Figure 9.1: Precarious working conditions perceived by police officers (percentage of participants)

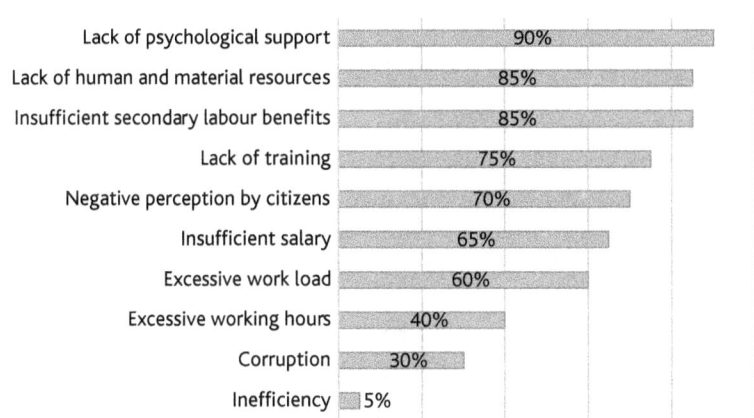

'We have a lack of patrol units, lack of uniforms; I am in the medical area, all my medical equipment was at my own expense. ... We are only given 2 uniforms, so it's kind of more stressful that you arrive and you know you have to wash it. ... The patrol units are in terrible condition and you say "today I have to drive but, really, it's junk". ... And if you blow a tyre, the commander or the one in charge couldn't care less if you were attending a report or if it was your negligence, in any case you have to pay for it.' (8M 2022)

Interviewees also point out that they require training to be able to carry out their work. The courses they are offered, however, are not tailored to their daily realities and working hours:

'The Morelia Police is offering courses ... but what I feel is not right is the way in which they are implementing it, because it is in addition to our workday. So coupled with the stress of being a housewife or a head of family, is ... your work shift and on top of that is to do the course. ... Thereby, they have taken away the hours that belonged to my children.' (8M 2022)

Negative perceptions from the general public also affect police officers' daily working conditions:

'The majority of the people doesn't like the police, because of bad practices by colleagues or even by ourselves. They already have a very clear negative stereotype about what a police officer is – someone that is a rat, someone that is abusive, someone that is arrogant.' (5H 2022)

With regard to salary, many interviewed police officers consider that it is insufficient compared to the number of hours they invest in their work. Furthermore, in terms of labour benefits, they also identify several shortcomings: "You will not be able to buy your own house; here you do not have access to a public housing credit and God knows when your salary will give you enough for your own house" (1H 2022).

Finally, many interviewed police officers perceive their working hours as excessive, often of 12-hour shifts. Moreover, they mention that sometimes they have excess work without overtime pay:

'In principle, every day we work, every day, because today we go in at 7 o'clock in the morning and leave at 7 o'clock at night and we enter tomorrow again at 7 o'clock at night and leave at 7 o'clock in the morning, and then the next day at 7 o'clock in the morning. So, the schedule is very heavy.' (7M 2022)

Coping mechanisms

Behavioural coping during citizen interactions

In their interactions with citizens, and in response to the working conditions outlined earlier, police officers report behavioural coping mechanisms that emphasise avoiding or moving away from dangerous situations (40 per cent) and deploying strict or aggressive attitudes towards some individual citizens (42 per cent), even though more compassionate behaviour is also mentioned, especially regarding vulnerable citizens such as the elderly and children (18 per cent). Moving away from danger, which is more often mentioned by female than by male officers, is especially common when police officers feel outnumbered: "I told my colleague 'I think there are two of us, and they are a whole bunch, let's go'. Better to run away than to stay" (4M 2022).

Police officers also report moving away from situations that involve organised crime:

'I don't feel safe with everything going on with the Jalisco cartel. … Yes, it happened that we stopped [a car] and they identified themselves: "Well, I'm from the Jalisco cartel, so let me talk to my boss." [And we said]: "Oh no, that's fine." And we let them go.' (9M 2022)

Even though many interviewees mention they are able to follow protocol, some also mention to break protocol and improvise when faced with a sudden dangerous situation:

'We are not a programmed robot, that is, yes, in the Academy they teach you protocols. ... But it is not the same as being told "if you are in a shooting, you have to do this" as being in the moment in which you are in a shootout and you're not just in a shootout but your partner is lying next to you bleeding. ... Then you act or deal with the situation as it occurs at that moment ... you try to solve it with the means you have.' (8M 2022)

Following protocol often means adopting a strict approach to citizens, which becomes more common as police officers are not outnumbered:

'Out there, my colleagues are of the type that has no tolerance, because it's part of protocol. Sometimes citizens tell us "come on, please understand my situation" but [then I say] "you don't understand my situation; if I let you go they'll give me 12 hours more in my shift".' (3M 2022)

However, others report that whether they follow the rules rigidly or not also depends on a citizen's attitude towards them: "It depends if the person comes with an 'influential' attitude ... and what the infringement is. When the person is attentive, gives you a logical explanation, then it's different" (6H 2022).

Even though many police officers face aggression – and men more so than women, according to our interviews – aggression by police officers themselves is also a major issue among the Morelia police force. In the first nine months of the current municipal administration (September 2021–May 2022), 19 police officers were fired for use of excessive force, abuse of authority, or dishonesty (González, 2022). In order to prevent such situations, 300 body cams have been deployed to monitor the behaviour of police officers (H. Ayuntamiento de Morelia, 2022). Among police officers, concerns about complaints from citizens about police violence also translates into a gendered division of labour: "You need to have support from your female colleagues, because if there is an aggressive woman our male colleagues cannot subdue her, because there is always someone ... that manipulates this information [and says] that you touched her, that she was abused" (8M 2022).

Finally, police officers also mention that they try to prioritise their scarce time and resources to protect vulnerable citizens in danger or in need:

'Yes, we have to prioritise, the case that is more relevant, the person that is more exposed [to danger]. For example, if there's a situation in which people are playing music at a very loud volume – this type of report – and another report that there are gunshots. Where do I go to? To the one where lives might be in danger.' (1M 2022)

Cognitive coping during citizen interactions

In the interviews, police officers also mentioned cognitive or emotional coping mechanisms for dealing with violent or dangerous interactions with citizens. The most often mentioned strategy was to maintain self-control (41 per cent), followed by compassion (32 per cent), emotional detachment (21 per cent), and feeling paralysed in the face of acute danger (6 per cent). Compassion, which is more commonly mentioned by female than by male officers and can be defined as 'an interpersonal process involving noticing, feeling, sensemaking, and acting that alleviates the suffering of another person' (Dutton et al, 2014, 277), emerges in relation to the last quote from the previous section: when officers face vulnerable groups, such as the elderly, women, and children in need or danger. When faced with danger themselves, however, self-control is mentioned as the most common coping strategy – even relatively more among male officers than female ones. Self-control is a coping mechanism that allows emotional regulation in order to express oneself properly and solve problems rationally (Skinner et al, 2003). For the police, self-control is necessary in the face of the conflictual interactions, although officers also recognise that maintaining it is sometimes complicated given the stressful circumstances:

> 'There are colleagues who do not know how to control themselves and what they do when a person comes to them is to take everything out on him. ... With rudeness, beatings. Why? Because there are so many things accumulated, so many times that they have insulted us, and [my colleagues] did not say anything. ... Because we all have a limit.' (2H 2022)

An important emotional mechanism for dealing with experiences of violence, danger, and death is emotional detachment, which implies a feeling of distancing oneself from stressful events to maintain emotional control (Roger et al, 1993). Male and female police officers alike mention they use such mechanisms to deal with violent reports and do their job: "I saw a boy being hit by a car and I ran to try to help him, but I already knew that with such a hit and everything. ... He died, I didn't feel anything, I just continued to follow procedure" (6H 2022).

Finally, paralysing as an unintentional mechanism to avoid a stressful situation (Richaud de Minzi) might occur in the face of acute danger:

> 'They started firing at us from the other side of the ravine and we quickly went down to the trucks ... then they started shooting at us from closer by ... I saw how one colleague completely froze ... what we did was pull the comrade away and she was just in total shock.' (1H 2022)

Behavioural coping outside of citizen interactions

Given the stressful nature of their jobs, it is unsurprising that police officers in Morelia also mention various coping mechanisms outside of interactions with citizens. In terms of behavioural mechanisms, especially relevant are seeking peer support (30 per cent), substance abuse (such as smoking, drug and alcohol use, and high levels of energy drink consumption) (30 per cent), and moving away from work for self-preservation (13 per cent). Furthermore, officers mention a wide range of activities that they use to distract themselves from their work, such as physical exercise (7 per cent), family activities (7 per cent), religious support (7 per cent), cultural activities (4 per cent), and seeking psychological support (2 per cent). There are relatively few differences between male and female officers, with the exception that female officers mention seeking peer support as a more common coping mechanism. Among their colleagues is where officers expect to find understanding and empathy: "Communication with peers, I feel this is the best way to learn to cope. ... The relief, because your colleague is the person who will understand what you talk about" (8M 2022).

Regarding substance abuse, the interview data shows that officers often turn to energy drink consumption and smoking to cope with stress, anxiety, and their long shifts: "Here, you cling to many bad vices. ... You come out of a situation where you received blows, you received bullets, you had a person with a gun ... and then you go for a cigarette and you smoke it and it's cigarette after cigarette" (1H 2022).

Other officers mention seeking distraction outside of the workplace, such as physical exercise or family activities: "The majority seeks refuge in their family. They look for a way to forget about work for a bit and do things that have nothing to do with the police. Go out with [your family], enjoy a bit" (2H 2022).

Finally, police officers may also find support in religion – both on and off the job: "I'm a believer, I believe in God and that. When I am not on duty or even on duty, sometimes I say a prayer, I think that helps me a lot. Knowing that He is taking care of me" (10H 2022).

Cognitive coping outside of citizen interactions

Given the stress and danger in their everyday job, it is no wonder that sometimes officers think of quitting: "Many times I've thought about quitting. ... Just two things are certain: either they kill you or they put you in jail, that is the mentality we have" (1H 2022).

However, many others mention cognitive coping mechanisms to justify and rationalise staying in their job as police officer, especially job motivation (24 per cent) and maintaining a positive attitude (24 per cent), followed by the expectation of change (18 per cent), sense of duty (16 per cent), expectation of growth (11 per cent), and cognitive restructuring (7 per cent). Starting with that last coping mechanism, cognitive restructuring is the active effort to change one's perspective of a stressful situation into a more positive one (Skinner et al, 2003). Police officers use it to lessen the sense of danger in their work: "It has its dangerous side, but I feel that life in general is dangerous. … The day your number's up, it's your turn" (6H 2022).

Maintaining a positive attitude helps reduce the stress of certain situations through positive thoughts and emotions (Naseem and Khalid, 2010). Police officers can manage to maintain a positive attitude fuelled by the satisfaction of the duty fulfilled and the vocation of service. Job motivation, in turn, is related to the performance that people have in their work. It permeates commitment, behaviour, and job satisfaction. For police officers, one of the main motivations is their own family: "It motivates me a lot to be a police officer here in Morelia, because my family is from here … that I can keep the city quieter, with fewer thieves, with less violence … it means that my family has a higher chance of being safe" (5H 2022).

Giving meaning to their work emerges as an important cognitive coping mechanism that provides purpose, identity, and work coherence to a person (Martínez and Jaimes-Osma, 2012). Police officers identify the meaning of work through reflections on everyday experiences. In the same way, they find a purpose in what they do for the well-being it generates in citizens: "Every day I bring the best I can do, the best actions I can realise. This is my motivation or my incentive to start everything again the next day" (5H 2022).

However, expectations affect motivation. In the interviews, police officers express two types of expectations about their work: change and professional growth. The first type refers to the intention to leave the organisation at some point, to dedicate themselves to another work activity, especially due to excessive working hours and the exposure to risk: "Yes, I have thought about quitting. For example, the death of a friend of mine made me think about what I am doing here, that I have to go back to another job where your life isn't on the line" (10M 2022).

On the other hand, others express growth expectations and the hope of getting a job promotion or obtaining a degree: "I would like to grow, I would like to get a better position here because I am a police officer … and therefore my salary is the minimum" (5H 2022).

Conclusion

Although it is well documented in the literature on street-level bureaucracy that frontline workers may experience stress and uncertainty at work due to limited resources, conflicting demands, and interactions with citizens (Lipsky, 2010; Thomann, 2015; Raaphorst, 2018), less attention has been paid to the effect of dangerous and precarious working conditions on frontline workers' everyday challenges and how they cope emotionally and behaviourally with these challenges (Lotta et al, 2022). In this chapter, we have studied the case of the municipal police in the city of Morelia, Mexico, where police officers face danger from organised crime, tense interactions with a distrusting public, limited training, scarce material resources, long working hours and low salaries, and a lack of psychological support to process the risks and stress they experience on a daily basis. Through semi-structured interviews and following the typology of coping mechanisms proposed by Tummers and colleagues (2015), we have identified several specific strategies that police officers deploy in their daily work.

In the category 'behavioural coping during interactions with citizens', most notable were the avoidance of dangerous situations involving organised crime or when police officers otherwise felt they would be outnumbered, as well as the commonality of aggressive interactions with individual citizens, both initiated by citizens and by police officers themselves – although many officers also mention they go to lengths to protect vulnerable citizens in danger. The avoidance of 'fighting crime' may seem counterintuitive to police work, but makes sense in the high-crime context of Morelia, where the problem of violent organised crime is beyond the reach of the municipal police. Female police officers more often expressed a tendency to move away from dangerous situations than their male colleagues. In the category 'cognitive coping during interactions with citizens', we found that police officers develop highly diverse attitudes in their efforts to deal with the constant potential of violent interactions. Emotional disconnect and self-control emerged as important mechanisms when confronted with experiences of human suffering and personal danger as well as expressing compassion with citizens – the latter more common among female than male officers. Furthermore, given the stressful and dangerous nature of their work, coping mechanisms outside of citizen interactions are particularly important for police officers to process what they experience on a daily basis. Regarding 'behavioural coping outside of interactions with citizens', many officers either turn towards colleagues for empathy and support (female officers more so than male officers) or towards substance abuse, such as smoking, to relieve stress. Finally, in the category 'cognitive coping outside of interactions with citizens', we find that police officers often struggle with the question whether or not to stay in such a dangerous line of work while they simultaneously rationalise and justify their job through personal motivation, a sense of duty, and maintaining a positive attitude.

Morelia's municipal police officers are expected to perform their job in very challenging working conditions. On a daily basis, they face possibly life-threatening situations, high levels of crime, and distrusting citizens while simultaneously being insufficiently trained, equipped, and psychologically supported by their organisation to fulfil those tasks. In that sense, the case presented here forms an extreme example of a 'public service gap' (Hupe and Buffat, 2014), where what is expected from the municipal police officers far exceeds the resources they have at hand to fulfill those expectations. Unsurprisingly, the officers we interviewed expressed a wide range of coping mechanisms – as extreme responses to extreme circumstances. Some of these are quite similar to what we know from police officers' coping mechanisms in the context of strong security institutions – such as seeking peer support, emotional detachment, and maintaining self-control – whereas others are more specific responses to extreme working conditions. Especially striking are moving away from dangerous situations, substance abuse, and aggressive encounters with citizens. Without condoning all the behaviours and attitudes mentioned in the interviews, we can understand and explain such coping strategies as responses to the situation police officers are thrown into. Institutional complexities and deficiencies are pushed towards the street level and play out in police officers' daily jobs and, thereby, affect their lives and their physical and mental well-being. In many ways, Morelia's police officers are in a constant survival mode.

Moreover, the coping mechanisms that police officers deploy shape the nature and experience of law enforcement for the citizens of Morelia. When police officers back down from intervening in situations involving organised crime or, conversely, when they adopt strict and aggressive approaches to individual citizens, they convey messages about what citizens may expect from their municipal police – thereby potentially further triggering vicious circles of low trust. The case of Morelia's municipal police, therefore, not only contributes to understanding how police officers cope with violence and stress (Aaron, 2000; Alcadipani et al, 2023), with violent urban settings (Lotta et al, 2022), with precarious working conditions and their particular effect on female officers (Chudnovsky and Reyes, 2021). More broadly, the findings presented here contribute to understanding the enforcement gaps common for weak institutional settings (Brinks et al, 2020) and the crucial role that police officers play in determining the daily realities of law enforcement for both themselves and for the citizens they serve.

Note

[1] Negative travel advisory (Chapter 9). For context, the US Department of State has issued a negative travel advisory for Michoacán due to high crime and risk of kidnapping (https://travel.state.gov/content/travel/en/traveladvisories/traveladvisories/mexico-travel-advisory.html).

References

Aaron, J. (2000). Stress and coping in police officers. *Police Quarterly*, 3(4), 438–50.

Acquadro, D., Zedda, M., and Varetto, A. (2018). Organizational and occupational stressors, their consequences and coping strategies: A questionnaire survey among Italian patrol police officers. *International Journal of Environmental Research and Public Health*, 15(1), 1–12.

Alcadipani, R., Lotta, G., and Cohen, N. (2023). Natural born violence? Understanding street-level bureaucrats' use of violence: Police officers and protests. *Public Administration Review*. https://doi.org/10.1111/puar.13670

Alfaro, F. (2022). Requiere la Policía Morelia 223 mdp para mejorar condiciones laborales. *Quadratín Michoacán*, 4 January 2022.

Azevedo, S., Moraes, D., Grillo, A., and Xerri, M. (2021). Crime, violence and stress in the emergency services work: Military police in southern Brazil. *Public Money & Management*, 1–9. 10.1080/09540962.2021.1951967.

Brinks, D.M., Levitsky, S., and Murisllo, M.V. (eds) (2020). *The Politics of Institutional Weakness in Latin America*. Cambridge: Cambridge University Press.

Causa en común. (2019). *Jornadas laborales de la policía en México*. http://causaencomun.org.mx/beta/wp-content/uploads/2019/04/JORNADAS-LABORALES-_-documento-largo-1.pdf

Causa en común. (2022). *La situación de las policías en México 2018–2022*. 2022. http://causaencomun.org.mx/beta/wp-content/uploads/2022/05/2022.05.09_situacion-de-los-policias-2022.pdf

Chudnovsky, M. and Reyes, A. (2021). How precarious public jobs are even more precarious for women: The case of Mexican police forces. *Latin American Research Review*, 56(3), 1–17.

Consejo Ciudadano para la Seguridad Pública y Justicia Penal, A.C. (2022). *Ranking 2021 de las 50 ciudades más violentas del mundo*. 7 March 2022. www.seguridadjusticiaypaz.org.mx/sala-de-prensa/1603-ranking-2021-de-las-50-ciudades-mas-violentas-del-mundo

Davidovitz, M. and Cohen, N. (2021). Frontline social service as a battlefield: Insights from street-level bureaucrats' interactions with violent clients. *Social Policy & Administration*, 2021, 1–14.

Dutton, J., Workman, K., and Hardin, A. (2014). Compassion at work. *Annual Review of Organizational Psychology and Organizational Behavior*, 1(1), 277–304.

Hupe, P. and Buffat, A. (2014). A public service gap: Capturing contexts in a comparative approach of street-level bureaucracy. *Public Management Review*, 16(4), 548–69.

González, A. and Policía de Morelia. 26 May 2022. https://www.facebook.com/policiademorelia/videos/731308247884181/

H. Ayuntamiento de Morelia. (2022) Policía Morelia, a la vanguardia en tecnología de cámaras corporales. Morelia: H. Ayuntamiento de Morelia 2021–2024, 7 May 2022.

INEGI. (2021). Encuesta Nacional de Victimización y Percepción sobre Seguridad Pública 2021. *INEGI.* 22 September 2021. www.inegi.org.mx/programas/envipe/2021/#Tabulados

INEGI. (2022). Encuesta Nacional de Seguridad Pública Urbana Primer Trimestre 2022. *Comunicado de Prensa,* 19 April.

Instituto para la Seguridad y la Democracia. (2021). *Hallazgos sobre la aplicación de la herramienta de verificación del Sistema de Indicadores del Modelo Nacional de Policía y Justicia Cívica.* Informe final, México: SESNSP.

Kroes, W. and Hurrell, J. (1975). *Job Stress and the Police Officer: Identifying Stress Reduction Techniques.* Cincinnati: NCJRS,.

Lazarus, R. and Folkman, S. (1984). *Stress, Appraisal, and Coping.* New York: Springer.

Lipsky, M. (2010). *Street-Level Bureaucracy: Dilemmas of the Individual in Public Services [30th Anniversary Expanded Edition].* New York: Russell Sage Foundation.

Lotta, G., Lima-Silva, F., and Favareto, A. (2022). Dealing with violence: Varied reactions from frontline workers acting in highly vulnerable territories. *Environment and Planning C: Politics and Space,* 40(2), 502–519.

Lotta, G., Nieto Morales, F., and Peeters, R. (2023). 'Nobody wants to be a dead hero': Coping with precarity at the frontlines of the Brazilian and Mexican pandemic response. *Public Administration & Development,* 43(3), 232–244.

Martínez, E. and Jaimes-Osma, J. (2012). Validación de la prueba 'Sentido del Trabajo' en población colombiana. *Psicología desde el Caribe,* 29(1), 64–86.

Maynard-Moody, S. and Musheno, M. (2003). *Cops, Teachers, Counselors: Stories from the Front Lines of Public Service.* Ann Arbor: University of Michigan Press.

Møller, M.Ø. (2021). The dilemma between self-protection and service provision under Danish COVID-19 guidelines: A comparison of public servants' experiences in the pandemic frontline. *Journal of Comparative Policy Analysis: Research and Practice,* 23(1), 95–108.

Naseem, Z. and Khalid, R. (2010). Positive thinking in coping with stress and health outcomes: Literature Review. *Journal of Research & Reflections in Education,* 4(1), 42–61.

Pavoni, A. and Tulumello, S. (2018). What is urban violence? *Progress in Human Geography,* 44(1), 49–76.

Raaphorst, N. (2018). How to prove, how to interpret and what to do? Uncertainty experiences of street-level tax officials. *Public Management Review,* 20(4), 485–502.

Richaud de Minzi, M.C. (2006). Evaluación del afrontamiento en niños de 8 a 12 años. *Revista Mexicana de Psicología,* 23(2), 193–201.

Rodríguez, S. and Scharagrodsky, C. (2008). *Afrontamiento al estrés en policías.* Buenos Aires: Facultad de Psicología.

Roger, D., Jarvis, G., and Najarian, B. (1993). Detachment and coping: The construction and validation of a new scale for measuring coping strategies. *Personality and Individual Differences*, 15(6), 619–26.

Secretaría de Gobierno del Estado de Michoacán de Ocampo. (2019). Acuerdo mediante el cual se abroga el Acuerdo de Creación del Órgano Desconcentrado Denominado 'Policía de Morelia'. *Periódico Oficial*, 20 September 2019.

Skinner, E., Edge, K. Altman, J., and Sherwood, H. (2003). Searching for the structure of coping: A review and critique of category systems for classifying ways of coping. *Psychol Bull*, 129(2), 216–69.

Spink, P., Lotta, G., and Burgos, F. (2021). Institutional vulnerability and trust in public agencies: Views from both sides of the street. *Governance*, 34(4), 1057–73.

Thomann, E. (2015). Is output performance all about the resources? A fuzzy-set qualitative comparative analysis of street-level bureaucrats in Switzerland. *Public Administration*, 93(1), 177–94.

Tummers, L., Bekkers, V., Vink, E., and Musheno, M. (2015). Coping during public service delivery: A conceptualization and systematic review of the literature. *Journal of Public Administration Research and Theory*, 25(4), 1099–126.

UNODC. (2019). *Estudio Mundial sobre el Homicidio. Resumen Ejecutivo.* Vienna: Oficina de las Naciones Unidas contra la Droga y el Delito.

10

'You can tell they are just villagers when you look at them': a phenomenological study of street-level bureaucrats' differential treatment of clients in a Ghanaian rural hospital

Abdul-Rahim Mohammed

Introduction

Ghana's government introduced the National Health Insurance Scheme (NHIS) in 2003 to replace the extremely unpopular out-of-pocket financing regime known as *cash-and-carry*. At the World Bank's direction, in April 1983 Ghana implemented market-based neoliberal reforms with severe austerity measures (Engberg-Pedersen et al, 1996; Boafo-Arthur, 1999). At the heart of these neoliberal reforms was the introduction of user fees in health services which led to reduced health attendance and utilisation for poor households (Engberg-Pedersen et al, 1996; Asenso-Okyere et al, 1998). Eventually, the *cash and carry* system was hugely reviled and engendered a corrosive mixture of public angst and mistrust against the government. This was to be expected, as, through the *cash and carry* system, patients paid for everything upfront – gloves, anaesthetics, gauze, surgery, drugs, blood, scalpel, and even cotton wool (Kampfner, 2001).

Against the background of widespread public discontent, the government implemented the NHIS in 2003. The NHIS is primarily meant to limit upfront payments at the point of utilisation, and simultaneously increase the number of healthcare utilisation. Following its implementation, the NHIS has proved very popular not least because it covers about 95 per cent of the disease burden that affects the poor as well as provides access to free medical consultations, laboratory tests and prescribed medications (WHO, 2010; Kwarteng et al, 2020). Accordingly, membership increased from 27 per cent in 2005 to 67.5 per cent in 2009 (WHO, 2010). As of 2017, the NHIS had 10 million active members, of which 7 million (65 per cent) were exempt from paying the premium (Ministry of Health, 2018).

A large body of evaluative studies has shown that the implementation of the NHIS has brought noteworthy results such as improvement in access and utilisation of healthcare (see Blanchet et al, 2012; Ibrahim et al, 2016). Conversely, other studies also suggest that sustainability threats – such as delayed reimbursement, political interference, inadequate premiums, and lack of quality health services (Ghana Health Service, 2011; Addae-Korankye, 2013; Awoonor-Williams et al, 2016; Fusheini, 2016) – remain. Although the existing literature on the NHIS tells us a lot about the successes and challenges of the programme, an empirical gap exists in examining the behaviour of frontline staff. In other words, the actions and decisions of frontline staff in the implementation of the NHIS have not received comparable scholarly attention.

Nevertheless, the academic discourses on SLBs have revealed that the success or failure of public policies can partly be traced to the behaviour of SLBs. For instance, evidence regarding the implementation of health policies and healthcare reforms in the UK, Brazil, Tanzania, and South Africa demonstrate how healthcare policies and reforms failed to achieve their intended results due to the actions of SLBs (see Walker and Gilson, 2004; Kamuzora and Gilson, 2007; Finlay and Sandall, 2009; Macena and de Oliveira, 2022). Thus, analysing the actions of frontline staff is critical as experiences from these countries exemplify how SLBs can wittingly or inadvertently undermine healthcare reforms. Given the dearth of scholarly literature on the actions of frontline staff, particularly in the context of healthcare reforms in Ghana and bearing in mind the crucial role SLBs perform in determining the success or failure of policies, this chapter attempts to fill this gap by analysing the actions of SLBs in the implementation of Ghana's healthcare reform – the NHIS.

Policy implementation and the street-level bureaucrat

The SLB framework is an important tool for analysing the recurrent tensions between policy intent and actual implementation outcomes. Conceptualised by Lipsky (1980), SLBs are the frontline professionals who directly implement public programmes through daily interactions with programme beneficiaries. In the scheme of the SLB framework, frontline staff often work in contexts of inadequate resources relative to their task, high caseloads, and ambiguous bureaucratic goals (Lotta and Kirschbaum, 2021; Campos and Peeters, 2022). Accordingly, this difficult policy implementation context naturally compels SLBs to use their autonomy and discretion to develop unsanctioned coping strategies which ultimately undermine policy intent and goals (Lipsky, 1980; Hill and Hupe, 2009; Crossley, 2016; Jensen and Pedersen, 2017). Thus, the SLB framework argues that a mismatch between policy and implementation can be due to the frontline staff's excessive and inappropriate discretion.

Some of the coping strategies SLBs resort to in order to help deal with the exigencies of their job are client differentiation by prioritising some clients over others, rationing services, insufficient consideration of cases, monetising services, and time-wasting (Baviskar and Winter, 2017; Jilke and Tummers, 2018). Consequently, SLBs significantly impact what social programmes and public policies will look like in practice (Evans, 2010). Inspired by Lipsky's work, further studies have also found other typologies of coping strategies adopted by SLBs such as making or bending rules for clients (Evans, 2013), helping clients with their personal resources (Dubois, 2010), and in some cases, adopting a hostile policy implementation context such as rigid enforcement of rules in a manner that can negatively impact clients' access to services (Tummers et al, 2015).

Through these coping strategies, this chapter examines how Ghana's NHIS, defined by chronic resource constraints (financial and human resource) and institutional weaknesses – reflected in a weak supervisory regime – (see Sodzi-Tettey et al, 2012; Wang et al, 2017) compels frontline health workers to adopt coping strategies, leading to a regime of inequitable access to healthcare. Hence, the coping strategies adopted compound existing social inequalities relative to healthcare access, stonewalling Ghana's healthcare financing reform.

Materials and methods

Design

This qualitative study adopts the interpretative phenomenological approach (IPA). The IPA provides participants' in-depth and detailed lived experiences, relative to the phenomenon being studied (Smith and Osborn, 2015). This approach makes it possible to explore the meanings and interpretations of participants in their everyday experiences. Accordingly, researchers of the IPA tradition mostly use one-on-one interviews to achieve their aim of understanding the lived experiences of participants (Palmer et al, 2010). Similarly, the current study employs the IPA to explore the daily experiences of healthcare staff in a rural area setting. Therefore, the data in this study are in-depth and detailed, producing what qualitative research scholars have described as rich and thick descriptions (Gray, 2014; Bryman, 2016).

Research setting

The study was undertaken in a poor rural district in the Northern region of Ghana. A caveat is warranted before proceeding. The findings in this study are sensitive. Consequently, strenuous efforts have been made to ensure confidentiality by extensively anonymising the research data. Specifically, the research location and participants have been anonymised. Requests for anonymity from the participants were a prerequisite for their engagement in this research. Failure to anonymise the findings could cause the participants harm, in terms of losing their jobs, for example. To this end, the participants were assured that the findings and location would be anonymised. The findings should therefore be understood in this context.

The Northern, Upper East, and Upper West regions are the three poorest regions in Ghana. Since 2005, the Ghana Statistical Service (2018) reports that the Upper West has had the highest incidence of poverty at 70.9 per cent, followed by the Northern Region and Upper East with rates of 61.1 per cent and 54.8 per cent respectively. Other development indicators in this study's context are equally dire. Population estimates report that approximately 125,000 people live in the district where this study was carried out. About 60 per cent of this population 3 years and above have never attended school. Furthermore, 90 per cent of the households in the district work in the agriculture sector on a subsistence basis and are thus trapped in a vicious cycle of poverty.

In terms of healthcare delivery, the Northern region overall is beset with challenges. Access to health services is severely constrained by limited and inadequate infrastructure in the region (Ministry of Health, 2014). Poor transportation networks as well as insufficient staffing make it difficult to deliver healthcare, primarily as the area's large landmass and sparsely located health facilities combine to make access to healthcare challenging. Further, whereas the doctor-to-patient ratio in the national capital, Accra, was 1 doctor to every 8,030 people in 2017, there was 1 doctor to 12,949 people in the Northern region (Ministry of Health, 2018). These difficulties are compounded in rural areas of the country, with the field site of this study being no exception.

Participants

As this study is designed to capture the experiences of the SLBs responsible for the day-to-day implementation of Ghana's NHIS, the participants in this study are made up of two broad categories: (1) health insurance staff and (2) hospital staff. Regarding the health insurance staff, one health insurance administrator, four health insurance clerks, and three health insurance claims officers took part in the study. On the other hand, the hospital staff involved in the study are six nurses, four doctors, three midwives, two physician assistants, two pharmacists, and three laboratory technicians. In all, 28 SLBs of varying responsibility and influence relative to the implementation of the NHIS took part in the study. All of these 28 participants were involved in one-on-one semi-structured interviews, using interview guides. The interviews lasted between 30 minutes and 45 minutes.

Semi-structured interviews were the preferred choice of data collection as they afford researchers the ability to engage in an in-depth understanding of a phenomenon from the perspective of research participants (Bryman,

2016). This is partly because researchers can probe deeper to gain more insight, based on participants' responses (Gray, 2014). Although interviewing was the dominant data collection method for the study, this method was complemented by observation. Observation in these contexts can be crucial because it 'provides an opportunity to get beyond people's opinions and self-interpretations of their attitudes and behaviours, towards an evaluation of their actions in practice' (Gray, 2014, 413). Thus, observation allows researchers to gain first-hand information on the field. Accordingly, I relied on observation in the district health insurance office as well as the district hospital to get a feel of what life is like for clients and SLBs. This method proved critical, as certain actions and practices that were observed served as the basis for follow-up questions at the interview stage.

Data analysis

With their permission, the one-on-one interviews were audio-recorded, although four participants declined to be audio-recorded. The resultant data were analysed thematically following Spencer et al's (2014) four steps: familiarisation with the data; constructing an initial thematic framework; using the framework to sort and index data; and reviewing data for coherence. Applying these steps in practice translated into transcribing the data verbatim and reading the transcripts throughout to familiarise myself with the dataset. The transcripts were then read line-by-line and keywords and phrases were manually coded. These were used to develop descriptive categories and subsequently collapsed into broader themes. The themes were then reviewed to ensure they encompassed and reflected the coded data. Two broad themes emerged and are presented as *Client Differentiation at the Health Insurance Office* and *Inequitable Access to Healthcare*. These themes are discussed later.

Results

This section of the chapter is divided into two parts. The first part highlights the working conditions and discretionary practices of SLBs at the health insurance office, while the second part examines the working conditions in the district hospital and the resultant coping strategies employed by health workers.

Client differentiation at the health insurance office

The data analysis shows that clients of the health insurance office mainly visit the facility to register new memberships, renew expired memberships, or request exemptions from the payment of premiums. During fieldwork, two important observations were made at the NHIS office. This section commences with one of these observations:

'You can tell they are just villagers when you look at them'

FIELD DIARY
17 May 2022

The time is 08:00hrs and the health insurance office is not open for work. Presently, there are 25 clients who have formed a queue. The office finally opens at 09.00hrs and the clerk has taken his seat. By this time, the number of clients in the queue has increased to 43. The health insurance clerk starts attending to the clients in the order in which they are seated. It is 10.45hrs and a suit-wearing lady comes out of a car, and calmly walks past everyone to the front of the queue. The clerk beckons at her, and she moves towards him. He offers her a seat and then starts taking her details.

It struck me as odd, seeing that a client had just arrived at the facility and did not join the queue like everyone else. Thus, during the one-on-one interviews with the clerk, I asked him about what I had just witnessed. I, however, started by discussing the order of registering clients more broadly.

'My brother, you can see the numbers yourself. Even before we open the office, several people will start to queue. So, by the time we come there is a long list of people waiting. It is not easy. Sometimes I don't even go for a break [lunch break]. There are several days when, even by the time we close officially, there will still be many people here to renew or register for the health insurance card. So, by the next day, a long queue will be here before we come. So, when we come, we attend to them on a first come first served basis in the queue.'

In the previous extract, the clerk narrates the overwhelming workload they are faced with daily. Due to the workload, they are unable to register every client in the queue. Thus, creating the need for them to return the following day. Having stated that the order of registration is on a first come first served basis, the clerk was asked about the lady who had been attended to without joining the queue. He noted:

'That lady works with the Ghana Education Service here [district]. As you can see, if she had joined the queue, she would be late for work. So, when workers [formal sector workers] come here, we just do it for them fast fast [attend to them quickly]. [Follow-up question: What about those in the queue?] Oh, as for them, they are just villagers, many of them don't do any work. [It is] just some are farmers, and they can go to the farm anytime.'

The clerk is of the view that villagers are unemployed for the most part, while educated 'elites' require prompt service because they will be late for work. Therefore, while 'villagers' have to join the queue and wait, the 'educated' workers have no such time to spare. Another clerk discussed how she copes with the workload at the office:

> 'On days when the numbers are just too much and increasing, I have to adjust. To be able to attend to as many people [clients] as possible, people who come without all the needed documents and information, I just turn them away. You know there are some requirements that we work with, so when they come without them, I just ask them to go, so that I don't waste time waiting for them to remember or ask a family member to bring it. If we don't do that, the number will be increasing.'

As can be deduced from the extracts, a strategy to deal with high caseloads is to strictly enforce the rules of registration and renewal. This is done by quickly turning away those clients who come to the registration centre without the required information.

Exempting clients: a problem of identification

One of the crucial roles played by the NHIS staff at the registration and renewal of insurance stage is the identification of exempt groups. The NHIS Legislative Instrument (LI-1809) exempts children below the age of 18 years, the indigent, and the aged 70+ from paying the annual health insurance premiums (NHIS, 2004). The elderly aged 70 and above, indigent, children, and pregnant women are all exempt from paying annual premiums (Government of Ghana, 2004; Kwarteng et al, 2020). However, the analysis shows that within the context of this research, the identification of the aged 70+ is uniquely tasking. The following extract from a health insurance claims officer is the most illustrative:

> 'My brother, in this rural area, the older generation don't have birth certificates. The village people don't register their births. Apart from birth certificates, they mostly do not have any document with their date of birth on it. At their time [of birth], they did not register births in the village so they mostly cannot prove they are 70+. We also cannot tell by just looking at them. It is possible to know that the person is old, but you cannot tell if the person is 70+. When we ask for documents, they become rude and argue. Some of them can even tell you that they are older than your parents. They are very difficult at times. So, for those who are rude like that and keep shouting, in that case, I just apply the rule and deny the request for exemption.'

Another health insurance claims officer noted:

'Sometimes we are all [clients and SLBs] angry and frustrated. This is on days when the numbers are just overwhelming and the people become impatient and are shouting, even though we are struggling to meet them. As for the people in the village, they get angry very easily, and they don't understand. So, when they start shouting and making noise, we become very formal and strict, and we stop granting favours like approving requests for exemptions to those who can't prove their age.'

Health insurance officers are required to exempt those aged 70+ from the payment of premiums. But the data suggests that there is a challenge with identifying those aged 70+. This is hardly surprising, since in a rural context, proof of age is challenging because the society is largely oral. As the clients are unable to prove their age, the frontline staff are left to use their discretion in deciding if the client meets the threshold. This is an enormous discretionary responsibility of frontline staff as they must decide whether to believe clients' claims that they are aged 70+ and thus, qualify to benefit freely from NHIS. Some of the frontline staff see their role in this case as 'granting favours' by approving exemptions because the clients cannot prove their age. And so, exemptions are sometimes granted to 'well-behaved clients', while it is denied to clients who are "rude and shouting".

Inequitable access to healthcare at the hospital

To provide a broader view of the nuanced roles SLBs play in the implementation of Ghana's NHIS, the researcher moved to the second stage of data collection by going to the district hospital to interact with some health workers. At this stage, the interactions with the healthcare workers were mainly guided by the need to examine their working conditions as well as the resultant coping strategies adopted, if any. Accordingly, each category of respondents was asked to describe the impact the NHIS has had on their working conditions and service delivery. A range of arguments emerged and are discussed later. Among the nurses and doctors, for example, there was a strong perception that the implementation of the NHIS has increased their workload.

'Since the NHIS was introduced, now everyone comes to the hospital. And it is worse in rural areas because health facilities in these places are scarce. Being the only government hospital in the district, a lot of the time patients from surrounding villages also come here for healthcare too. Also, with rural folks, because they have the NHIS card, they come to the hospital with the slightest issue such as headaches. Sometimes in one week, you can treat the same patient three times with different illnesses on different days. Because of that, the hospital is very choked, and many times we are not able to attend to all of them.' (Medical Doctor 1)

Corroborating the previous extract, a midwife and medical laboratory technician also recounted respectively:

'I have been working in this facility for more than 10 years now. Every day we are overburdened by its numbers, as it is the only government hospital in the district. Once a woman registers for NHIS, they can bring about 4 children in a day. The other day, I would say, a 58-year-old woman came to say she was pregnant all because she has health insurance. We spend so much time attending to them, and when the patient finally comes to you, [you realise that] the issue is non-existent [there is no illness]. It is very frustrating when you look at the numbers.'

'There are several times when by the time we come to work, there is a long queue of people who come to do tests. Many of these are people who couldn't do it the previous day because we simply could not attend to them due to the numbers. So, by the time we attend to the previous days' cases, it would be long past 11 am going to mid-day. Then we attend to the new day's cases. So, the cycle would continue the next day because we are unable to complete a day's work.'

These narrations paint a disconcerting picture of the extreme workload in the district hospital. This is hardly surprising, as the district has just one government hospital catering to more than 125,000 people. Additionally, as the medical doctor explained, people from nearby villages also come to the facility for medical attention, compounding a dire situation. Although the health workers note that they are always confronted with high caseloads each day, they argued that this situation has been exacerbated because of what they termed 'difficult patients', or 'villagers'.

'The real problem we encounter every day is the difficult patients. They make matters worse. The people [difficult patients] don't understand anything and it is mostly the villagers. [Follow-up question: who are the difficult patients?] The villagers. They don't take [medical] advice and they don't take medications the way they are told to. Sometimes if you put a drip on them, they remove it when they just feel like it. They argue a lot too about medications and their effects. So, for me, when I meet a difficult patient who keeps arguing and won't take advice, I discharge them early or I don't waste much time on them. When you are dealing with the educated, it is much easier.' (Nurse 4)

According to this nurse, the 'villagers' are difficult people because they argue a lot and do not abide by prescriptions. Thus, the difficult patients make an already bad situation of high caseloads worse. Accordingly, a way out around this is to not "waste much time" on the "difficult" patients, or to discharge them early. Other health workers also narrated a pattern of focusing more on "educated people", compared to the "villagers", or the strict enforcement of regulations as coping mechanisms.

> 'When we are faced with many patients and they start agitating, we strictly check the identity card to ensure entitlement to healthcare before the consultation. Can you believe some of them use their relatives' identity cards to come to the hospital? Because they are villagers, if the card does not belong to them, they can't read it. So, if we question them about the details on the card, they can't answer. This way, we discharge them as they are not entitled to healthcare.' (Physician Assistant B)

> 'We had instances of villagers impersonating others. That is, patients use other people's health insurance cards. When we realised it, some clients who are not sick [themselves], still come to the hospital with the health challenges of uninsured relatives. They do it by describing the symptoms of their sick relatives, with the hope of getting medicines so that they can send it to them. We got to know about it because there was a client like that whose described sickness needed an injection. At the point of injection, the client came clear, telling us that he came to the hospital hoping to get medicine for his sick brother who was uninsured.' (Nurse 2)

These experiences highlight some of the peculiar difficulties in rural areas where a large section of the population is poor and therefore cannot afford the insurance premiums. The inability to pay for premiums leads to impersonation, where non-sick but insured clients visit the hospital with the hope of acquiring medication for their sick relatives. Consequently, the data reveal a pattern where healthcare workers are quick to refer to their clients as 'villagers', who are stereotypically said to be partly responsible for the challenges health workers experience. Ultimately, a context of high caseloads has had a noteworthy impact on the quality of healthcare services delivered to clients, as health workers struggle to cope with the challenges.

> 'On days that we are very busy, I have to limit the consultation time with the patients. This is to move fast, or else we have lots of them in the corridors and waiting area. When the number [of unattended patients] increases, they begin to agitate, and they make noise. You are

therefore compelled to move fast. If you are lucky to meet an educated person, you don't go through a lot of headaches so there is no need to limit consultation time. Consulting with them is easier and more straightforward.' (Medical Doctor 3)

'With the local people, it is difficult to interact with them. If we want to move fast, we attend to the educated people. Educated people are easier to deal with. When you meet one, you hardly waste time, so you don't have to move fast. It is easier to deal with them and they are more likely to be telling the truth and follow your instructions.' (Nurse 5)

Concluding this section of the chapter, an extract from one of the observatory sessions is provided:

FIELD DIARY
25 June 2022

The doctor walks into the waiting room and sees a patient. He asks her to get up and come. The patient goes to see the doctor and he asks the patient 'what are you doing here again? I saw you earlier in X health facility'. The patient mumbles a few words and then the doctor asks her to leave the hospital. The patient leaves.

In the previous narration, the doctor is seen asking a patient to leave the facility. During the interviews, the doctor claimed that he had seen the same patient earlier in the day at a different facility. He notes that the clients are fond of shopping around health facilities with the same illness, abusing the health insurance system in the process:

'This is what we have been talking about. Dealing with the rural people can sometimes be so difficult. Once they have a card, they do all sorts of things to make our work difficult, including shopping around clinics with the same ailments. That explains how we also relate to them that way. In the morning, I saw her at that private health facility, I had gone to see a colleague there.'

Discussion

Like all studies, this study has limitations. First, this is a small-scale study in a rural area of the broader northern region of Ghana. More importantly, however, the voice and experiences of the clients are not captured in this research. The study would have been improved if the clients had been engaged, to help foreground their views and experiences. Despite these limitations, the study has provided important findings that shed light on the conditions and challenges (as well as resultant coping strategies) of delivering public services at the frontline in the context of weak institutions. As the book's introductory section has noted, weak institutions are state institutions that fail to work as intended. This could be due to politicisation (Zarychta et al, 2020), corruption (Justesen and Bjørnskov, 2014), or resource constraints (Gibson, 2004).

In the specific case of Ghana's NHIS, the data shows that institutions responsible for implementing the NHIS are defined by severe caseloads and chronic resource scarcity. That is, in the scheme of implementing the NHIS, both the NHIS office and hospital are underfunded, understaffed, and operate in overcrowded spaces. As noted by each of the two broad spectrums of SLBs, the frontline staff are hardly ever able to attend to all clients who visit their facility, creating the need for some of the clients to return the next day for services. This reality is almost cyclical, as, by the start of work the following morning, the clients who could not be attended to the previous day form long queues waiting for the hospital and NHIS staff. What has complicated this matter of high caseloads is the fact that clients from surrounding villages visit the NHIS office and hospital, since they are the only government facilities in the district. As such, healthcare and NHIS personnel are routinely overwhelmed by the number of clients.

Due to these high caseloads and chronic resource constraints in the hospital and NHIS office, the SLBs adopt some unsanctioned coping mechanisms. Prominent among the coping strategies is the categorisation and prioritisation of clients by relying on prevailing biases, as contended by Lipsky (1980), Hastings (2009), and Baviskar and Winter (2017). Specifically, clients are either seen as 'difficult villagers' or 'educated people'. For instance, in the NHIS office, formally dressed clients are deemed as educated elites who will be late for work if they are not attended to promptly. In practice, this means that they do not have to join the queue, like everyone else. Conversely, the findings show evident bias against 'villagers' as they are said to be disobedient, rude, and in many cases just shopping around clinics. Thus, the stereotypical notion against 'villagers' is that they are abusing the NHIS system. Therefore, in times of overwhelming demand, this category of clients is subjected to waiting, while other 'genuine' clients are attended to.

As already highlighted, Tummers et al (2015) argue in their categorisation of coping strategies that in cases of high caseloads, SLBs often resort to aggression and confrontation, or adopt a hostile policy implementation context such as rigid enforcement of rules in a manner that can negatively affect clients' access to services. Put another way, SLBs *move against their clients*. The data in this study affirm this argument, as overburdened SLBs sometimes resort to aggression or adopt a hostile policy implementation regime by rigidly enforcing rules. However, the basis for this aggressive implementation environment is the biased and stereotypical views against 'villagers'. For example, for those clients that are described as 'difficult villagers', the NHIS staff strictly enforce exemption rules against them because they are said to be agitating. At the hospital also, there are strict checks of the identity cards of 'disobedient' clients to ensure that the client is entitled to healthcare. Another way of looking at this resort to aggression is to see it as relational as argued by Hershcovis and Reich (2013). They note that aggression as a coping strategy is at times relational because aggression from clients is met with similar reactions from SLBs. The SLBs only resort to this aggressive posturing when, according to them, the clients become agitated and insult, shout, and are rude.

This study's findings on the categorisations of clients are not unique. Gaede's (2016) and Walker and Gilson's (2004) study of nurses and doctors in South Africa reveal how healthcare workers confronted by high caseloads, categorised their patients into labels of 'deserving patients' (elderly and children) and 'undeserving patients' (rude patients) as the basis for providing healthcare services. Differentiating among clients together with adopting a hostile policy implementation context can be disadvantageous since some clients will benefit at the expense of others (Jilke and Tummers, 2018). Prioritising some clients over others will ultimately lead to a regime of differentiated service delivery. That is, prompt and efficient service delivery for the 'educated elites', compared to delayed and patchy services for the 'villagers'.

The findings hold important implications for the implementation of healthcare reforms in Ghana. As the introductory section of this chapter has enumerated, Ghana has had challenges with providing healthcare to its population, particularly to poor households in the context of neoliberal reforms. The implementation of the NHIS did bring about significant increases in healthcare utilisation across the country. However, these findings call for policy makers to focus on not only enrolment and access figures but also on the quality of healthcare services delivered, mainly in rural and remote areas. Failure to do this risks having a NHIS that exists in good shape on paper but with significant flaws underneath. More importantly, the SLB literature has argued that there are instances where, rather than reducing existing inequality, the coping strategies employed by frontline staff (such as unequal treatment) maintain or exacerbate existing inequalities (see Lotta and Pires, 2019). Seen in this light, the implementation of the NHIS potentially contributes to reinforcing existing inequalities. The classification of clients – and the subsequent provision of healthcare services – according to their socioeconomic status defeats the very ethos of the NHIS. As part of Ghana's poverty reduction programmes, the NHIS is designed to widen access to health services for poor households. However, in its current differentiated form, the implementation results in the marginalisation of the most vulnerable clients, as they are categorised as difficult villagers. The middle class of clients are prioritised over those who, by their socioeconomic status, are least able to afford private healthcare. This widens existing income and social inequalities in this rural area.

Conclusion

The findings in this study affirm the critical role of SLBs in implementing public programmes and reflect concerns in the literature about the possibility of SLBs distorting programme goals through coping strategies. Through the concepts of coping strategies and client differentiation, this study has demonstrated how healthcare workers operating in the context of resource constraints and high caseloads provide differentiated services to their clients. Clients who are stereotypically categorised as difficult villagers are subjected to time-wasting, limited consultation times, extra checks, and are denied exemptions while educated elites are not subjected to this treatment. These discretionary coping strategies, if not addressed will eventually threaten the objectives of the NHIS since healthcare is provided at the expense of others. More fundamentally, the implementation of the NHIS in its current form might widen existing unequal power dynamics and entrench inequalities further. Accordingly, this study calls for a redirection of the government's attention to the quality of healthcare being provided under the NHIS. Finally, this study adds to the comparatively small but growing body of policy implementation scholarship applying the SLB framework to Global South contexts. This is important as many studies applying the SLB framework are from Global North countries (Bertelli et al, 2020). Applying the framework beyond its original empirical context to Global South countries demonstrates the continued relevance of Lipsky's work, four decades after its initial conceptualisation. Further, this also affords us a robust tool for examining policy implementation gaps in the Global South.

References

Addae-Korankye, A. (2013). Challenges of financing health care in Ghana: The case of National Health Insurance Scheme (NHIS). *International Journal of Asian Social Science*, 3(2), 511–22.

Asenso-Okyere, W.K., Anum, A., Osei-Akoto, I., and Adukonu, A. (1998). Cost recovery in Ghana: Are there any changes in health care seeking behaviour? *Health Policy Plan*, 13(2), 181–8.

Awoonor-Williams, J.K., Tindana, P., Dalinjong, P.A., Nartey, H., and Akazili, J. (2016). Does the operations of the National Health Insurance Scheme (NHIS) in Ghana align with the goals of Primary Health Care? Perspectives of key stakeholders in northern Ghana. *BMC International Health and Human Rights*, 16(1), 1–11.

Baviskar, S. and Winter, S.C. (2017). Street-level bureaucrats as individual policymakers: The relationship between attitudes and coping behaviour toward vulnerable children and youth, *International Public Management Journal*, 20(2), 316–53.

Bertelli, A.M., Hassan, M., Honig, D., Rogger, D., and Williams, M.J. (2020). An agenda for the study of public administration in developing countries. *Governance*, 33(4), 735–48.

Blanchet, N.J., Fink, G., and Osei-Akoto, I. (2012). The effect of Ghana's National Health Insurance Scheme on health care utilisation. *Ghana Medical Journal*, 46(2), 76–84.

Boafo-Arthur, K. (1999). Ghana: Structural adjustment, democratization, and the politics of continuity. *African Studies Review*, 42(2), 41–72.

Bryman, A. (2016). *Social Research Methods* (5th edn). Oxford: Oxford University Press.

Campos, S.A. and Peeters, R. (2022). Policy improvisation: How frontline workers cope with public service gaps in developing countries – The case of Mexico's Prospera program. *Public Administration and Development*, 42(1), 22–32.

Crossley, S. (2016). From the desk to the front-room? The changing spaces of street-level encounters with the state under austerity. *People, Place and Policy Online*, 10(3), 193–206.

Dubois, V. (2010). *The Bureaucrat and the Poor: Encounters in French Welfare Offices*. Surrey: Ashgate Publishing.

Engberg-Pedersen, P., Gibbon, P., Raikes, P., and Udsholt, L. (1996). Structural adjustment in Africa: A survey of the experience. In P. Engberg-Pedersen, P. Gibbon, P. Raikes, and L. Udsholt (eds), *Limits of Adjustment in Africa*. Portsmouth: Heinemann, pp 3–14.

Evans, T. (2010). *Professional Discretion in Welfare Services: Beyond Street-level Bureaucracy*. Farnham: Ashgate Publishing.

Evans, T. (2013). Organisational rules and discretion in adult social work. *British Journal of Social Work*, 43, 739–58.

Finlay, S. and Sandall, J. (2009). 'Someone's rooting for you': Continuity, advocacy, and street-level bureaucracy in UK maternal healthcare. *Social Science & Medicine*, 69(8), 1228–35.

Fusheini, A. (2016). The politico-economic challenges of Ghana's National Health Insurance Scheme Implementation. *International Journal Health Policy and Management*, 5(9), 543–52.

Gaede, B.M. (2016). Doctors as street-level bureaucrats in a rural hospital in South Africa. *Rural and Remote Health*, 16(3461), 1–9.

Ghana Health Service. (2011). *Annual Report, Ministry of Health and Ghana Health Services*. Accra: Ghana Health Service.

Ghana Statistical Service. (2018). *Poverty Trends in Ghana 2005–2017*. Ghana Living Standards Survey Round 7, Accra: GSS.

Gibson, D. (2004). The gaps in the gaze in South African hospitals. *Social Science & Medicine*, 59(10), 2013–24.

Government of Ghana (2004). *National Health Insurance Regulation 2004 Legislative instrument 1809*. Accra: Government of Ghana.

Gray, D.E. (2014). *Doing Research in the Real World* (3rd edn). London: Sage.

Hastings, A. (2009). Poor neighbourhoods and poor services: Evidence on the 'rationing' of environmental service provision to deprived neighbourhoods. *Urban Studies*, 46(13), 2907–27.

Hershcovis, M.S. and Reich, T.C. (2013). Integrating workplace aggression research: Relational, contextual, and method considerations. *Journal of Organizational Behavior*, 34(1), S26–42.

Hill, M. and Hupe, P. (2009). *Implementing Public Policy: An Introduction to the Study of Operational Governance*. London: Sage.

Ibrahim, A., Maya, E.T., Donkor, E., Agyepong, I.A., and Adanu, R.M. (2016). Perinatal mortality among infants born during health user-fees (cash & carry) and the national health insurance scheme (NHIS) eras in Ghana: A cross-sectional study. *BMC Pregnancy and Childbirth*, 16(1), 1–8.

Jensen, D.C. and Pedersen, L.B. (2017). The impact of empathy: Explaining diversity in street-level decision-making. *Journal of Public Administration Research and Theory*, 27(3), 433–49.

Jilke, S. and Tummers, L. (2018). Which clients are deserving of help? A theoretical model and experimental test. *Journal of Public Administration Research and Theory*, 28(2), 226–38.

Justesen, M.K. and Bjørnskov, C. (2014). Exploiting the poor: Bureaucratic corruption and poverty in Africa. *World Development*, 58, 106–15.

Kampfner, J. (2001). *Ghana: Prisoner of the IMF*. London: BBC. http://news.bbc.co.uk/1/hi/programmes/from_our_own_correspondent/1634514.st

Kamuzora, P. and Gilson, L. (2007). Factors influencing implementation of the community health fund in Tanzania. *Health Policy and Planning*, 22, 95–102.

Kwarteng, A., Akazili, J., Welaga, P., Dalinjong, P.A., Asante, K.P., Sarpong, D. et al (2020). The state of enrolment on the National Health Insurance Scheme in rural Ghana after eight years of implementation. *International Journal for Equity in Health*, 19(4), 1–14.

Lipsky, M. (1980). *Street-level Bureaucracy: Dilemmas of the Individual in Public Services*. New York: Russell Sage Foundation.

Lotta, G. and Kirschbaum, C. (2021). How street-level bureaucrats use conceptual systems to categorise clients. *Policy & Politics*, 49(4), 531–51.

Lotta, G. and Pires, R. (2019). Street-level bureaucracy research and social inequality. In Peter Hupe (ed), *Research Handbook on Street-Level Bureaucracy*. Cheltenham: Edward Elgar Publishing, pp 86–101.

Macena, A. and de Oliveira, V.E. (2022). Discretion and local health policy implementation: street-level bureaucrats and integrative and complementary therapies in Santos' local health units. *Primary Health Care Research & Development*, 23(e34), 1–9.

Ministry of Health. (2014). *Holistic Assessment of the Health Sector Programme of Work 2014.* www.moh.gov.gh/wp-content/uploads/2016/02/Holistic-Assessment-2015.pdf

Ministry of Health. (2018). *Holistic Assessment of 2017 Health Sector Programme of Work.* Accra: Ministry of Health.

National Health Insurance Scheme. (2004). *Annual report: National Health Insurance Regulations, L-I-1809.* https://lawsghana.com/post_1992_legislation/regulation_acts_table_of_content/Legislative%20Instruments/NATIONAL%20HEALTH%20INSURANCE%20REGULATIONS,%202004%20(L.I%201809)/37

Palmer, M., Larkin, M., de Visser, R., and Fadden, G. (2010). Developing an interpretative phenomenological approach to focus group data. *Qualitative Research in Psychology*, 7(2), 99–121.

Smith, J.A. and Osborn, M. (2015). Interpretative phenomenological analysis as a useful methodology for research on the lived experience of pain. *British Journal of Pain*, 9(1), 41–2.

Sodzi-Tettey, S., Aikins, M., Awoonor-Williams, J.K., and Agyepong, I.A. (2012). Challenges in provider payment under the Ghana National Health Insurance Scheme: A case study of claims management in two districts. *Ghana Medical Journal*, 46(4), 189–99.

Spencer, L., Ritchie, J., Ormston, R., O'Connor, W., and Barnard, M. (2014). Analysis: Principles and processes. In J. Ritchie, J. Lewis, C.M. Nicholls, R. Ormston (eds), *Qualitative Research Practice: A Guide for Social Science Students and Researchers.* Los Angeles: Sage, pp 269–90.

Tummers, L., Bekkers, V., Vink, E., and Musheno, M. (2015). Coping during public service delivery: A conceptualization and systematic review of the literature. *Journal of Public Administration Research and Theory*, 25(4), 1099–1126.

Walker, L. and Gilson, L. (2004). 'We are bitter, but we are satisfied': Nurses as street-level bureaucrats in South Africa. *Social Science & Medicine*, 59(6), 1251–61.

Wang, H., Otoo, N., and Dsane-Selby, L. (2017). *Ghana National Health Insurance Scheme: Improving Financial Sustainability Based on Expenditure Review.* Washington DC: World Bank Publications.

World Health Organization. (2010). *Ghana's Approach to Social Health Insurance. World Health Report (2010) Background Paper 2.* Geneva: World Health Organization.

Zarychta, A., Grillos, T., and Andersson, K.P. (2019). Public sector governance reform and the motivation of street-level bureaucrats in developing countries. *Public Administration Review*, 80(1), 75–91.

11

When frontline work functions as an enclave: insights from Turkey

Elise Massicard

Introduction

How do structurally adverse working conditions impact the behaviour of frontline workers? And how does this affect public service provision, and citizens' experiences of the state? To address these general questions, this chapter focuses on a specific figure of frontline work: muhtars (headmen/ headwomen) operating at the outer edge of institutions, at a very local level – that of a neighbourhood or a village. This case provides a good way of addressing the question of the effects of working conditions on the conduct of frontline work, for at least two reasons: first, because muhtars are not specialised in any one domain but are multipurpose frontline workers; second, because this type of frontline work, in Turkey, is organised along principles clearly different from those in other state institutions – to put it bluntly, in a much less bureaucratic manner.

The chapter argues that the muhtarlık – a word referring to the institution or office itself – operates as a non-bureaucratic frontline enclave mitigating between a distant state and a distrusting public, and ends up significantly impacting state–citizen interactions. However, the forms of policy repair that muhtars implement do not necessarily mitigate citizens' lack of trust in institutions, instead tending to reinforce it.

This chapter is based on in-depth research on muhtars (Massicard, 2022). Most of the empirical material was collected through qualitative fieldwork conducted in Istanbul over more than two years in the early 2010s while I was living there. To grasp how the muhtars actually work, I conducted interviews, archival work, and especially observation. While I had to limit my field to Istanbul for practical reasons, I conducted my investigations in contrasting neighbourhoods with varying levels of wealth and marginality, so as to get an idea of the varying ways in which the muhtarlık is actualised.

The first part of the chapter locates muhtars as frontline workers and addresses specific aspects of their position – especially their social embeddedness. The second part of the chapter shows how muhtars' working conditions influence their behaviour, and in particular their tendency to champion residents. The third part examines how these patterns impact citizens' experience of the state in contrasting ways.

Locating muhtars as frontline workers

In 1944, Turkish law re-established the muhtarlık – an Ottoman institution that had appeared in the 1830s and been discontinued in the 1930s – in every neighbourhood and village throughout the country, to assist the public authorities in providing services to the local population. The muhtarlık was tasked with maintaining the civil register, issuing certificates, enforcing laws and instructions, informing the security forces of suspicious or wanted people, identifying future conscripts, and drawing up electoral lists.[1] Many subsequent laws and regulations not directly relating to the muhtarlık entrusted it with new tasks, for instance in welfare distribution. Additionally, the 2005 law on municipalities (no. 5393, §9) tasked neighbourhood muhtars with 'identifying common needs, enhancing the neighbourhood's quality of life, conducting relations with the municipality and other public entities, delivering opinion on matters of interest for the neighbourhood, cooperating with other institutions, and performing other duties as prescribed by laws'. Some authorities ask muhtars to intervene occasionally on a given issue – reporting about Syrian refugees in their neighbourhood, for example. It would therefore be hard to draw up a precise list of muhtars' official responsibilities, but they can be said to operate mainly in administrative work (in particular, certification and citizen identification) and service delivery – and in some instances, policy implementation – with a certain variation over time and space.

The muhtarlık, then, comes across as a local multifaceted institution with which citizens may come into contact for many different reasons – ranging from claiming social assistance or obtaining mundane paperwork to processing conscription procedures. As a multipurpose, everyday point of contact between state and society at a very local scale – there are slightly more than 50,000 of them nowadays – the muhtarlık is one of the main institutions through which Turkish citizens experience the state. This multipurpose dimension is but one of its specificities; the muhtarlık presents several other specificities regarding Turkey's wider institutional framework, as well as compared to other kinds of frontline workers.

Embeddedness and electedness

The most important specificity is that muhtars are socially and locally embedded; they are part of the local community where they operate. Before being elected, a muhtar must have lived for at least six months in the neighbourhood, though most have resided there for far longer. This local anchoring clearly distinguishes muhtars from other street-level public agents in Turkey who tend to be external to the society in which they operate. The police administration even prohibits its officers from serving in their hometowns (Akarsu, 2020, 29). In other cases, even when street-level public agents such as teachers or imams live in or come from the neighbourhoods where they work, this anchoring does not form an integral part of their role.

But for muhtars, these ties are, on the contrary, constitutive of their role. Muhtars' official attributes presuppose their being anchored in local society. One of their main tasks is to vouch for the situation of the residents to public institutions – for instance, identifying suspicious individuals or reticent conscripts, or issuing poverty certificates. The muhtarlık is supposed to enable the public authorities to access knowledge that is neither official nor set down on paper – locally grounded knowledge. This testifying role requires firsthand experience of living in the neighbourhood on a daily basis. The muhtarlık is thus grounded in experiential knowledge. In other words, muhtars' social anchoring in a web of acquaintanceships underpins their official functions. Their local knowledge and shared social links mean they can potentially work more effectively with local populations (Kasara, 2007). In any case, this sets muhtars apart from bureaucrats as defined by Weber, since the use of outsider officials, who are more likely to be autonomous, is thought to be a defining characteristic of bureaucracies (for the political uses of embeddedness of officials and the challenges to loyalty, see Hassan, 2020).

An important aspect of muhtars' relationship to their neighbourhood residents is that the latter form their electorate. The way muhtars relate to those they administrate is thus wholly altered by the fact that these same people are their constituents. This, again, implies specific types of embeddedness. Since 1980, muhtars are not elected on party tickets, which means that elections for muhtar are based mainly on personal resources, but more importantly, on strong localised social anchoring – more precisely, on the ability to build localised coalitions. Consequently, muhtars are mostly from established families, and overwhelmingly middle-aged men.

Dimensions of institutional weakness

A further characteristic of muhtarlıks is their institutional weakness, especially their low organisational capacities and professionalisation – to a much larger extent than other Turkish institutions and frontline workers.

The muhtarlık is a hybrid institution with an uncertain position in the administrative system. It is not clearly situated in a precise administrative hierarchy. Besides, muhtars do not have any decision-making power in their own right. Furthermore, the muhtarlık is sidelined and even excluded from official decision-making circuits, even when it comes to issues pertaining to their neighbourhood. Muhtars only operate as intermediaries or brokers between residents and other institutions (municipalities, sub-governorships) that provide resources (public services, benefits, and so on.). They therefore have positional power, and often act as gate-keepers – which can nevertheless result in their steering or even blocking welfare or policy implementation. For example, when they were tasked with channelling the applications for a new public unemployment benefit in the early 2000s, their involvement ended up blocking its implementation – because instead of assisting, muhtars tended to despise requests for assistance, in line with widespread representations of poverty (Buğra and Keyder, 2005, 40, 45).

A further dimension to this weakness is that, unlike village muhtarlıks, which have a legal personality, a budget, and local responsibilities, neighbourhood muhtarlıks have neither the official status of a local administration nor a budget. They consequently lack the means to carry out their functions. There is no legal obligation to provide premises for a muhtarlık, and it is not rare for muhtars to carry out their duties from premises they own or rent, or even from their homes. Furthermore, many muhtars have to pay the operating costs (furniture, electricity, water, ink cartridges, telephone bills, and so on) out of their own pockets. The 2005 law on municipalities encourages the latter to provide muhtarlıks with premises and to cover some of their expenses, something many municipalities have done in recent years. However, there is nothing obligatory about this, and the trend is far from systematic. The level of help is thus unequal and variable, which leads to contrasting and sometimes unstable situations–and, more importantly, to precarity.

Ever since the muhtarlık was set up, the issue of remuneration has been problematic. It was only in 1977 that muhtars started to receive payment, but it is a remuneration, not a salary. Until recently, it amounted to less than half the salary of qualified high school teachers, making it almost impossible to live on income from the muhtarlık. It was only very recently, in the mid-2010s, that their remuneration was increased to above the net minimum salary, for the first time in history. Muhtars also receive fees on certain certificates they issue, which is meant to at least partially cover structural expenses such as rent and electricity. The amount received is proportional to the size of the neighbourhood's population but varies enormously as some neighbourhoods have a few hundred residents while others have tens of thousands. A widespread belief has it that muhtars in very populous neighbourhoods have very large incomes. However, muhtars in charge of very populous neighbourhoods have difficulty completing their tasks and are often compelled to hire assistants out of their income. Besides, income from issuing documents has decreased significantly since 2009, as many public services have become computerised and databases set up, so that they now issue far fewer certificates.

This lack of means, therefore, makes the muhtars dependent on municipalities and inhabitants. Under these circumstances, muhtars' personal income can be very directly influenced by whether the municipalities pay certain running expenses. It may be considered that the muhtarlık was instituted as a partially self-financed activity.

This shortfall implies that muhtars usually have other sources of income – and often other professional activities. Indeed, many muhtars retain their links to external professions, either in tandem with their position or else afterward. Thus, many muhtars, including those who have long held the position, consider it a sideline. According to a survey carried out in Izmir in 1998, 74.6 per cent of respondents were retired, and 22.9 per cent had other jobs (Palabıyık and Atak, 2000, 154). According to a study of 222 Istanbul muhtars conducted in the early 1990s, 70.7 per cent of respondents declared they considered their other job, not the muhtarlık, to be their profession (Horasan, 1992, 71). The position of muhtar is thus not always the 'sole or main profession' of its holders – a fact setting them apart from bureaucrats as defined by Weber (1978, 958).

A related aspect is that muhtars are poorly professionalised. First, their office is elective, thus temporary. Their term lasts five years, after which they have to run for re-election. Even if muhtars tend to remain a long time in office – longer than any other kind of elected position in Turkey – this lack of job security is a major factor of instability and precarity. Furthermore, muhtars have poor career opportunities. They have no prospect of professionalisation, unlike those working in public administration. The muhtars' prospects for moving on to electoral careers within political parties are also very slender. Since 1980, it has been hard – though not impossible – for muhtars to advance to elected office on a party ticket, and few have done so.

Besides, muhtars receive no specific training to get them to conform to standardised practices. Yet the muhtarlık requires administrative, technical, and even legal skills, as well as a certain amount of knowledge that cannot be made up on the hoof. Most of the muhtars in my sample said they had trained 'on the job', picking up what they knew from diverse sources, though never from bureaucrats or municipalities. Rather, they had learned from their peers, from their secretaries, from former councillors – since the muhtarlık is composed of a muhtar and a council of elders. The latter teach them how to go about their tasks, giving advice and oral instructions. These forms of transmission are not institutionalised. Rather, they require personal channels, which vary from one situation to the next. Trained in this way, muhtars refer to routines developed by their predecessors or their entourages.

The lack of training leads muhtars to 'import' the socialisation and routines they have acquired elsewhere into the way they carry out their duties. Indeed, muhtars remain firmly anchored in their own groups of origin. This leads to weak professional norms and operating procedures, and may be thought to foster discretion (Evans, 2011).

The muhtarlık as an interstice

Muhtarlıks come across as a specific institution, and as weak in the sense of Brinks et al (2020). Does this mean that muhtarlıks are weak institutions in a strong institutional context? Muhtarlıks certainly seem less bureaucratic than the wider institutional context. In this respect, muhtarlıks can be considered interstices, that is, 'social niches within a larger institutional field, distinct yet embedded subsystems characterised by practices inconsistent with – although not necessarily subversive to – those of the dominant institution' (McDonnell, 2017, 479). In this respect, Turkey can be said to have 'patchy' institutions (McDonnell, 2017, 478).

Are Turkey's other more bureaucratic state institutions 'stronger' than muhtarlıks? The widespread representation of the Turkish state as a 'strong state' has been questioned over recent years (for a detailed critique of this idea, see Gourisse, 2015). The question of the Turkish state's capacity has been reconsidered and appears to be much weaker than commonly assumed (Aymes et al, 2015). For example, it is commonly admitted that the Turkish state is widely viewed as a state in which nothing works according to the rules and where the average user is sent endlessly traipsing from one counter to the next (Secor, 2007). Many citizens of Turkey hold that the Turkish state is partial and does not consider all citizens equally (Fliche, 2005; Secor, 2007; Yoltar, 2007). In the same way, it is established that Turkish institutions are politicised along party-political lines – increasingly so in the last decade (see, for example, Kemahlıoğlu and Bayer, 2021). Muhtarlıks may also be politicised, but mainly following localised rationales, and at least partly non-party political lines. Muhtarlıks, then, are less politicised – or more precisely, less party-politicised – than other institutions in Turkey; they work in accordance with different rationales. It would be reductive to say that they are 'weaker' or 'stronger' than other institutions. It would be interesting to further disentangle and specify various dimensions of institutional 'weakness'; but that falls outside the scope of this chapter.

Besides, some of the specificities of muhtarlıks may also be viewed as resources for action. First, having no administrative apparatus, the muhtarlık is an extremely personalised institution. The council of elders has been marginalised, resulting in the gradual whittling away of any collegial dimension. Second, having no budget and an ill-defined position in the administrative apparatus, muhtars are more or less shielded from hierarchical authority. There is far less hierarchical control over muhtars than over any other kind of official or frontline worker. Muhtars are not inspected or even appraised on any kind of 'performance'. They therefore have considerable 'administrative autonomy' – or, put differently, limited obligation to comply with prescribed institutional practices (Dubois, 2010, 5). It is residents, not officials, who sanction muhtars. Muhtars may thus stray significantly from the official precepts supposedly guiding them. They make decisions in the absence of clear formal guidelines and follow weakly formalised working procedures (except for identity documents). This gives them increased opportunities for frontline discretion.

Frontline workers championing residents
Adapting the institution

How do the organisational context and working conditions shape the incentives and constraints weighing on muhtars' agency? In particular, how does their pronounced local anchoring affect how they do their job? For institutional theory (Ostrom, 2005), rules and other factors that structure action situations shape the action possibilities of people interacting within such situations. The sociology of institutions has shown that the latter only exist through the ways in which individuals take on institutional roles and inhabit institutions (Lagroye and Offerlé, 2010). The role and behaviour of frontline workers relate to the type of institutional environments in which they work; their agency in turn also shapes how these institutions actually exist. This section argues that muhtars' working conditions push them to refrain from some dimensions of their official tasks, while over-engaging in others – especially acting as their residents' champion.

Muhtars scarcely have the resources and conditions to do what they are officially supposed to do. Research conducted between 1967 and 1971 by the Ministry of the Interior counted 143 prerogatives attributed to muhtars by various legal texts, finding that 47 per cent of these were carried out and 52.9 per cent were not (Arıkboğa, 1998, 126). No doubt this method flattens out complex phenomena. However, though dated, this simple observation sheds light on the extent to which muhtars' practice fails to match their official attributions – and in turn explains why their official tasks remain so ill-defined. For example, most muhtars step back from their role as guarantor of residents' situations by recording solely what people declare about their situation. They often justify this withdrawal on the grounds of institutional malfunction and the insufficient means of verification at their disposal. On the other hand, muhtars tend to over-engage in other aspects of their position, especially those linked to residents' requests.

Extensive uses of the muhtarlık

Indeed, residents make very extensive uses of the muhtarlık, and tend to approach muhtars with all kinds of requests: to ask for information or administrative guidance, to request collective services for the neighbourhood, to initiate individual requests (even in finding work or housing), and to get the muhtar to mediate in conflicts or to intercede on their behalf. They often turn to them for advice or to plead their cause, or else to request personalised help. Inhabitants view the muhtar as a multipurpose resource person who should be capable of providing solutions to all types of problems, be they public or private. The public expects the muhtar to look after matters referred to them, and to ensure that residents' requests and complaints are addressed. As a middle-class youngster interviewed in Istanbul by Anna Secor declared: "When you go to the muhtar, he is supposed to do something, because he is your muhtar" (Secor, 2007, 38). They expect the muhtar to relay their requests and also, often, to give them their backing or else intercede with institutions on their behalf. With such wide-ranging uses, residents extend the muhtars' field of activity far beyond their official duties.

Why do residents make such broad use of muhtars, including for issues for which they have no official responsibility? This can certainly be explained in part by muhtars' closeness to and dependency on residents for re-election. Muhtars' embeddedness implies that they are close to their residents. This sets them apart from other officials, bearing in mind that the latter have traditionally based their claims to governmental legitimacy on standing above the people – what Babül calls 'bureaucratic distinction' (2017, 42–3), which, as she argues, is particularly strong in Turkey. Conversely, people often consider the muhtar to be one of their own (Arıkboğa, 1998, 162). This is very noteworthy in working-class neighbourhoods: while muhtars might figure among those who have done fairly well for themselves, their immediate relatives and entourage tend to still include people with limited resources and little education. It is rare for muhtars to treat these disadvantaged populations scornfully or condescendingly – a common occurrence in many other state institutions. As a result, muhtars come across as being more accessible than other officials.

This comparative proximity transpires in the everyday relationship between muhtars and their inhabitants. The muhtarlık is very much embedded within local social relations. Babül notes that 'this [bureaucratic] distinction requires government workers to disengage themselves from the community as much as possible, and prohibits them from undertaking the sorts of mundane activity that might put them in contact or on an equal footing with the people whom they govern' (2017, 47). This, again, distinguishes muhtars from other officials. Relationships with the muhtar may overlap with acquaintanceships within local society, which in turn produce social obligations. In this respect, the muhtarlık relies on familiarity (Siblot, 2006) – and even intimacy – to a greater extent than any other political or administrative institution in Turkey (Yildirim et al, 2017, 669). As a result, relations within the muhtarlık differ from those in a classic administration.

They are only partly codified according to specifically administrative codes, and instead often reproduce other forms of sociability pertaining outside the realm of administration – such as neighbourhood, kinship, or friendship. In most cases, muhtars welcome their visitors and take care to relate amicably to residents.

Besides, muhtars depend on voters for re-election. The muhtarlık is thus the only administration in which citizens exert a certain power over the person sitting behind the desk. This implies a relation of mutual yet unequal dependency. The specific relation between muhtars and inhabitants means that the muhtarlık is an institution – perhaps the only one – in which the average neighbourhood resident can legitimately ask for something.

Akarsu has noted that in Turkey, people want everyday officials to bypass tedious procedures while performing official work (2020, 35). In a way, residents consider muhtars as granting access to the state in a way less hampered by rules and formalities. In some situations, frontline workers may operate as crucial gateways to institutions while also generating specific forms of trust (Peeters and Dussauge, 2021). Several studies in other contexts have shown that this can be the case especially for marginalised population groups (Bhavnani and Lee, 2018). In Brazil, citizens' low generalised trust in the state can be, to a certain extent, compensated by trust in individual frontline workers through reciprocal relations in the provision of public services and acknowledgment of vulnerable people's specific needs and circumstances (Spink et al, 2021). This parallels what we observe particularly in Turkey, where people who are ill-at-ease with writing, the administration, or both tend to turn disproportionately to muhtars (Massicard, 2022). Indeed, not all citizens use the muhtarlık to the same extent or in the same way. There is no public quantitative data on how many or how often people solicit their muhtar. However, the uses inhabitants make of the muhtarlık vary in the light of certain social parameters. Being able to call upon a personalised intermediary is far more important for certain sectors of the population than for others. Educated groups with a fairly stable or established economic and social position rarely solicit the muhtar. It is groups who are disadvantaged – be it economically, socially, or culturally – who solicit muhtars more frequently. This is consistent with Suzuki and Demircioğlu's findings that impartiality does not lead to positive assessments of public services among citizens with low educational background (2020).

The residents' champions?

How do muhtars react to these extensive uses by residents? Most muhtars proudly distance themselves from any purely administrative rationale. While they sometimes perceive the extensive uses people make of them as being improper or burdensome, muhtars listen with a kindly ear to all manner of requests. In general, they consider responding to collective but also individual requests to be an integral part of their role – even when it far exceeds their official tasks. They make it a point of honour to provide individualised responses. This goes much further than what Lipsky described for street-level work requiring 'improvisation and responsiveness to the individual case' (Lipsky, 1980/2010, XII). Not only do muhtars accept solicitations, they also publicly express and display their devotion to their residents and present themselves as acting as their advocates.

As a matter of fact, muhtars even adapt how they function to better serve their residents. For instance, although muhtarlıks post fixed working hours, most muhtars are flexible in how they apply them – at times waiting for a resident who said they would come after office hours. They often make it a point of honour to be reachable at any moment. Many hand out their mobile phone numbers. They spare their inhabitants administrative 'hassle' or facilitate procedures by drawing up paperwork over the phone, for example, or handing a document to a third party or even delivering it to someone's home. They help with their applications, help navigate administrative procedures – and at times even carry them out in their stead or support requests by residents in front of institutional actors. Whenever they extend their working hours or help residents with official procedures, muhtars exceed their official job definition and obligations; when they do so, they engage their own time, energy, and resources.

Why do muhtars accept these requests in such kindly manners? First, as embedded local leaders, muhtars are aligned with local communities' interests and dynamics and care about what happens to the local population (Bhavnani and Lee, 2018). Besides, muhtars are anchored in local society, with little administrative socialisation and little hierarchical control. The norms and moral values underpinning their action therefore resemble those of their constituents; they adapt to fit the demands of their environment. It is important to bear in mind that their alacrity is not wholly altruistic. Muhtars are dependent on those they administer, for it is they who elect them. This leads them to exceed their official obligations and to try to satisfy their voting public.

Like – and maybe more than – other frontline workers, muhtars seek to repair gaps and limitations in service delivery and policy implementation, for example when they strive to obtain public services such as road repairs or new trash containers for their ward, or directly advocate a resident be granted some social benefit. In this respect, they could be said to operate 'policy repair' (Masood and Nisar, 2022), that is, to mitigate and partially compensate for institutional limitations. This kind of behaviour, together with their image as the residents' spokesperson, produces the image of a state that is close, accessible, and attentive to citizens' needs.

The contrasting effects of an amicable frontline interstice

How do muhtars and their patterns of behaviour affect citizens' everyday experience of the state? How does the way these frontline workers operate feed back into citizens' attitudes towards public service provision and their trust in it? Its effects are contrasting.

From problem-solving to arrangements

It would be inaccurate to portray muhtars as serving all their inhabitants' concerns or systematically defending their interests. One should not forget that muhtars are also public agents acting as relays for the public authorities. Therefore, they do not – and cannot – always act as their constituents' champion. Muhtars sometimes side against (some of) their constituents, especially when they have to assist the institutions in unpopular issues like law enforcement, when defending residents' requests would put them too much at odds with the authorities, on which they are also dependent for resources, or when a resident tries to obtain some benefit to which they are not in fact entitled. But muhtars carefully conceal any awkward stance that might tarnish the caring image they cultivate. They deploy a certain number of tactics to maintain their image of serving residents including in adverse situations. Their performance of championing their constituents is intended to reinforce their legitimacy and popularity.

For that reason, muhtars promote and often overemphasise the part played in obtaining any services rendered. Yet often when constituents' requests are not accepted or services not rendered, irrespective of whether or not they played a part, muhtars deny any responsibility in those failures, blaming other institutions for any refusal; in such cases, they assert or even overstate the limits to their power. In a way, the (genuine) limits to their power are also a resource for retaining their legitimacy in adverse conditions. In this respect, their action does not necessarily smooth the relationship between local people and institutions. Indeed, the muhtarlık – based on 'particularised trust' – does not always offset the absence of generalised trust (Uslaner, 2002). On the contrary, in overseeing multifarious requests on a daily basis, in blaming other institutions in the event of some shortcoming or failure, muhtars enhance their own image as problem solvers – which is, in a way, their 'added value' for residents, who could address other institutions but prefer turn to them. They help legitimise the extensive social use that residents make of them; they thereby reinforce their image as interlocutors who may be called on for specific goals, while fuelling the image of deficient or otherwise inaccessible institutions, together with the belief that personalised intercession can be effective in dealing with institutions.

The value of favours

In fact, the imperative to serve their inhabitants incites muhtars to routinely tinker with the rules. Indeed, muhtars sometimes bend the official order to fit residents' demands, sometimes managing to stretch the rules for their benefit. Muhtars often deem it legitimate to defend their constituents' interests against an official order widely perceived as unfair – even by them. They sometimes take this accommodating attitude to the point of turning a blind eye when a requisite is missing, or giving their inhabitants 'tips' on how to dodge rules and especially sanctions. These arrangements can extend to infringements of the institutional order, as when a muhtar registers someone under a false address for the purpose of school enrolment or divulges supposedly confidential information. Muhtars thus do much more than just help residents cope with administrative red tape. The fact that they can – and are sometimes prone to – adapt or even infringe rules may be considered their true 'added value' in comparison to an impersonal administration. The way inhabitants and muhtars perceive and engage with the muhtarlık cultivates the representation of a state with which one may negotiate, encouraging requests for intercession.

The importance of intercession needs to be placed in the context of citizens' representations of the Turkish state. Secor has shown that in Istanbul in the 2000s, the predominant opinion was that bending the rules, in the form of bribery or through knowing people, was important or even necessary to receive public services. The state was thus experienced as unequal, unfair, and unreliable (2007). This echoes studies in many other countries reporting experiences of arbitrariness in bureaucratic encounters (Blundo, 2006). In Turkey, people with access to the state, however slight, were viewed as privileged (Secor, 2007, 41, 47). Similarly, in the early 2000s, Alevi villagers from central Anatolia developed a perception of the administration in which rigidly sticking to the rules alternated with bending them. The incessant switching from an official to an unscripted register, from the incorruptible to the bribable, generated anxiety among users, who were forever uncertain of the outcome of their dealings with the administration. They sought other types of interface than those laid down by the legal framework, drawing on 'other' connections, mostly informal, which were more effective than impersonal administrative relationships (Fliche, 2005).

Similarly, in her study of the green card scheme in the 2000s, guaranteeing free access to health services for the poor under legally specified criteria, Yoltar shows that the uncertainty characterising the complex landscape of social assistance fuelled citizens' impression of arbitrariness, generating suspicion, and the feeling that things were unforeseeable. This, in turn, fuelled demands for support and intercession (Yoltar, 2007). Applicants endeavoured to maximise their chances by employing various tactics to ensure they obtained the card, even if it meant circumventing the official rules. Again, this type of tactic entailed drawing on privileged ties to reduce administrative burdens and uncertainty. All these studies show that muhtars are among the figures people turn to for this type of undertaking. Muhtars are thus solicited by applicants to support their attempts to influence a procedure.

Are such favours and attempts to establish privileged relations specific to the muhtarlık, or do they also exist in other administrations? Several works on Turkish administrations suggest that citizens with personal relationships to state officials may pass behind the counter and chat with them while asking a favour, while other people have to wait their turn. Yoltar has shown that when an official's relative, colleague, or acquaintance asks them to circumvent an official rule or alter the habitual functioning of the institution, the official may seek to respond to this request out of respect for the mutual responsibility entailed by these close ties (Yoltar, 2007, 100). Searching for privileged relations may therefore also be observed in dealings with other administrations.[2] In this respect, one of the specificities of the muhtarlık resides in the comparative ease with which an obligation may be created or negotiated, for it is always possible to find a common acquaintance with a muhtar, and equally easy to promise a few votes. Another specificity, especially over recent years, is that party divides are much weaker at the muhtarlık level than at any other institutional level. In a politicised environment, muhtars may thus be a crucial recourse for marginalised citizens. I was able to observe this in a neighbourhood where, at a time when the ruling Justice and Development Party held office at all levels, Alevis tended to turn disproportionately to the muhtar, who had links to the opposition.

The effects of assumed favouritism

It is therefore in muhtars' interest to allow themselves and their inhabitants to deviate from institutional norms. Lipsky has shown that SLBs arrange the rules, exploiting their room for manoeuvre and for applying rules in the light of their own interests. This easing of rules may also be found among muhtars – probably to a greater extent even, due to their electoral dependency on their residents and the role prescriptions the latter place on them. Getting around or bending the rules is thus not an isolated marginal practice, but instead forms part of a system of institutionalised dispensations.

However, arrangements do not form part of a general attitude; they are only a possibility; they are in no way systematic – otherwise there is no favour. Indeed, as I was able to study in the case of muhtars (not) exempting residents from paying certificate fees (Massicard, 2022), a given muhtar may successively apply the rules in a strict, bureaucratic manner, and then adopt an accommodating attitude. Arrangements are, therefore, a widely acknowledged possibility (and expectation). Muhtars thus give the impression of granting little favours – not always, but regularly enough for people to come to expect it.

Bourdieu states that:

> the choice to potentially make an exception to the rule is one of the commonest and most effective means of acquiring 'personal power', that is, a particular form of bureaucratic charisma acquired when a person distances themself from the bureaucratic definition of their function. The bureaucrat sets himself up as a notable, endowed with a degree of notoriety within a territorial jurisdiction and acquaintanceship group. He does so by securing a symbolic capital of gratitude. This is generated by a wholly particular form of exchange, found in all societies, that generates 'big men'. The principal 'currency' is, in this particular case, quite simply making exceptions to the rule, or accommodations with the regulation, granted or offered as a 'service' to a user. (89)

It is precisely because it suspends the possibility of purely and simply applying the rule that an exemption granted becomes a service rendered, hence a resource that may be exchanged, entering a circuit of exchanges underpinning the muhtars' social and symbolic capital. These little favours do not cost the muhtars much. However, they are profitable in that they make it possible to build up and maintain ties of obligation (Siblot, 2006, 175). Tolerance granted to a particular individual reinforces a muhtar's credit with them, and with those they administer more generally. This credit is personal; it is accorded to the person who, by authorising an exception to the rule, stakes out their individual freedom instead of behaving as an impersonal figure identified wholly with the rules they meekly apply (Bourdieu, 1990, 89, 91). During face-to-face interactions, I could observe how muhtars get their residents to understand that their benevolent attitude constitutes a favour. Waivers thus become a form of gift.

By positioning themselves as facilitators for procedures, and by creating obligations out of simple, everyday administrative transactions, muhtars fuel and even help legitimise the register of personalised requests. This, in turn, places the institutional relationship outside the realm of formal rules and neutrality. This paves the way to preferential treatment, thus feeding the register – and expectations – of favours but also suspicions of favouritism. Not everyone benefits from these arrangements, or at least not to the same degree. Since these arrangements seem to be decided without clear bases, they are perceived by residents as favours.

This potential for arrangements influences how inhabitants view and relate to the muhtarlık. Whether or not it is actually observed, the perceived prevalence of favours means that muhtars are continually suspected of granting preferential treatment to certain residents (Buğra and Keyder, 2005,

47). Indeed, moving towards citizens through local embeddedness may also reinforce inequalities in access to services and benefits. Ehrhardt (2017) shows how Nigerian SLBs, in the absence of clear formal criteria, rely on locally salient norms of belonging. They thereby unintentionally prioritise certain social groups over others. Irrespective of whether or not this holds in Turkey too, muhtars are suspected of applying personal and subjective criteria to decide on eligibility or access to services. This transpires particularly in the realm where they have greatest room for manoeuvre, and discretion even, namely the distribution or channelling of welfare assistance. Muhtars' (im)partiality is a recurrent topic of suspicion and criticism, particularly in outlying neighbourhoods with more acute social and identity divides, where large volumes of assistance are handed out.

Writing about Argentina, Auyero has shown that the – even supposed – existence of people with close relations to power implies the existence of an outer circle deprived of such access. Those in this outer circle denounce bias, and have a more negative view of this personalised and supposedly exclusive manner of doing politics (Auyero, 1999, 302 et seq.). For those who do not benefit from these alleged arrangements, going to the muhtarlık may be like going to an ordinary administrative service or may even produce a feeling of exclusion. While the expectation of arrangements may facilitate the relationship certain residents have with the muhtarlık, it may at the same time complicate that of other residents. The predominance of the register of favours may give each individual the impression or hope of being favoured, but it also nurtures suspicions of favouritism, thus triggering feelings of exclusion and avoidance. It does so along lines that may be different from other institutions, especially when the latter are considered to operate along party-political lines.

Conclusion

This chapter illustrates how the restrictions (and opportunities) of street-level bureaucracy in weak institutions do not apply solely to unelected officials; on the contrary, this framework can help study 'non-bureaucratic enclaves' of low-ranking elected officials who deal directly with residents. Moreover, the chapter shows how frontline institutions such as the muhtarlık can thrive in conditions where the state is little trusted, and where there is a need – for some parts of the population at least – to provide a more 'amicable' state. In this kind of institutional setting, muhtars seem to perform a mitigating function between a distant state and a mistrusting public. They end up significantly impacting state–citizen interactions because they provide specific interstices for accessing the state that work along specific, non-bureaucratic lines. Muhtars' position and working conditions explain why they act as their residents' servants and are prone to broker arrangements.

This produces ambivalent effects on how citizens experience the state. On the one hand, muhtars constitute a kind of accessible, amenable, and negotiable face of the state within a broader, more bureaucratised, and less accessible context. In this respect, the muhtarlık goes some way towards facilitating relations with institutions, helping to make them less distant and alien. It may even be said to have integrative effects and to help public institutions tend to the disadvantaged. In this regard, like other frontline workers – and maybe more so – muhtars are engaged in forms of policy repair associated with mitigating and partially compensating for broader institutional weakness.

At the same time, arrangements – a core dimension to the muhtars' role – feed the image of an institutional order that tolerates and even encourages rule-bending and favours. The fact that public officials' behaviour may be influenced by close ties – or, concerning muhtars, is very commonly suspected of being so – tends to question the existence of a neutral state (Secor, 2007, 49).

In the case of Turkey, where frontline work operates along specific lines as a kind of non-bureaucratic enclave, the forms of policy repair that muhtars implement do not therefore necessarily mitigate citizens' distrust of institutions. In a way, muhtars may even reinforce representations and experiences of the Turkish state as unreliable and of service delivery as untrustworthy or selective. An important lesson we may take from the case of Turkey is the need to disentangle the complexity within state administrative structures.

Notes

[1] In addition, the 1944 village law tasked village muhtars with intervening in other issues, such as health, education, and security.
[2] Another effective alternative channel is to draw on party networks, especially where the Justice and Development Party is hegemonic.

References

Akarsu, H. (2020). Citizen forces: The politics of community policing in Turkey. *American Ethnologist*, 47(1), 27–42.

Arıkboğa, E. (1998). *Yerel yönetimler, Katılım ve Mahalle Muhtarlığı*. Master's thesis, Marmara University.

Auyero, J. (1999). 'From the client's point(s) of view': How poor people perceive and evaluate political clientelism. *Theory and Society*, 28(2), 297–334.

Babül, E.M. (2017). *Bureaucratic Intimacies: Translating Human Rights in Turkey*. Stanford: Stanford University Press.

Bhavnani, R.R. and Lee, A. (2018). Local embeddedness and bureaucratic performance. *Journal of Politics*, 80(1), 71–87. doi: 10.1086/694101

Blundo, G. (2006). Dealing with the local state: The informal privatization of street-level bureaucracies in Senegal. *Development And Change*, 37(4), 799–819.

Bourdieu, P. (1990). Droit et passe-droit: Le champ des pouvoirs territoriaux et la mise en œuvre des règlements. *Actes de la recherche en sciences sociales*, 81–82, 86–96.

Brinks, D.M., Levitsky, S., and Murillo, M.V. (eds) (2020). *The Politics of Institutional Weakness in Latin America*. Cambridge: Cambridge University Press.

Buğra, A. and Keyder, Ç. (2005). *Poverty and Social Policy in Contemporary Turkey*. Social Forum Working Paper, Boğaziçi University.

Dubois, V. (2010). *The Bureaucrat and the Poor: Encounters in French Welfare Offices*. London and New York: Routledge.

Ehrhardt, D. (2017). Indigeneship, bureaucratic discretion, and institutional change in Northern Nigeria. *African Affairs*, 116(464), 462–83.

Evans, T. (2011). Professionals, managers and discretion: Critiquing street-level bureaucracy. *British Journal of Social Work*, 41(2), 368–86.

Fliche, B. (2005). De l'action réticulaire à la recherche du semblable, ou comment faire lien avec l'administration en Turquie. In Gilles Dorronsoro (ed), *La Turquie conteste: Mobilisations sociales et régime sécuritaire en Turquie*. Paris: CNRS Editions, pp 147–65.

Gourisse, B. (2015). Order and compromise: The concrete realities of public action in Turkey and the Ottoman Empire. In M. Aymes, B. Gourisse, and E. Massicard (eds), *Order and Compromise: Government Practices in Turkey from the Late Ottoman Empire to the Early 21st Century*. Leiden, Netherlands: Brill, pp 1–24.

Hassan, M. (2020). *Regime Threat and State Solutions Bureaucratic Loyalty and Embeddedness in Kenya*. Cambridge: Cambridge University Press.

Horasan, A.H. (1992). *İstanbul mahalle muhtarlarının çağdaş demokrasi anlayışı*. Master's thesis, İstanbul Üniversitesi.

Kasara, K. (2007). Tax me if you can: Ethnic geography, democracy, and the taxation of agriculture in Africa. *American Political Science Review*, 101(1), 159–72.

Kemahlıoğlu, Ö. and Bayer, R. (2021). Favoring co-partisan controlled areas in central government distributive programs: The role of local party organizations. *Public Choice*, 187(3–4), 301–19.

Lagroye, J. and Michel O. (2010). Pour une sociologie des institutions. In J. Lagroye and M. Offerlé (eds), *Sociologie de l'institution*. Paris: Belin, pp 11–29.

Lipsky, M. (1980). *Street-Level Bureaucracy: Dilemmas of the Individual in Public Services*. New York: Russell Sage Foundation.

Masood, A. and Nisar, M.A. (2022). Repairing the state: Policy repair in the frontline bureaucracy. *Public Administration Review*, 82(2), 256–68.

Massicard, E. (2022). *Street-Level Governing: Negotiating the State in Urban Turkey*. Stanford, CA: Stanford University Press.

McDonnell, E. (2017). Patchwork leviathan: How pockets of bureaucratic governance flourish within institutionally diverse developing states. *American Sociological Review*, 82(3), 476–510.

Ostrom, E. (2005). *Understanding Institutional Diversity*. Princeton, NJ: Princeton University Press.

Palabıyık, H. and Atak, Ş. (2000). İzmir büyükşehir bütününde mahalle yönetimleri profili. *Dokuz Eylül Üniversitesi Sosyal Bilimler Enstitüsü Dergisi*, 2(3), 150–68.

Peeters, R. and Dussauge Laguna, M.I. (2021). Acting out or playing along: A typology of citizens' low trust responses to public organizations. *Governance*, 34(4), 965–81.

Secor, A. (2007), Between longing and despair: State, space, and subjectivity in Turkey. *Environment and Planning*, 25, 33–52.

Siblot, Y. (2006). *Faire valoir ses droits au quotidien: Les services publics dans les quartiers populaires*. Paris: Presses de Sciences Po.

Spink, P., Lotta, G., and Burgos, F. (2021). Institutional vulnerability and trust in public agencies: Views from both sides of the street. *Governance*, 34(4), 1057–73. https://doi.org/10.1111/gove.12574

Suzuki, K. and Demircioglu, M.A. (2021). Is impartiality enough? Government impartiality and citizens' perceptions of public service quality. *Governance*, 34(3), 727–64. https://doi.org/10.1111/gove.12527

Uslaner, E.M. (2002). *The Moral Foundations of Trust*. Available at SSRN: https://ssrn.com/abstract=824504

Weber, M. (1978 [1921]). *Economy and Society: An Outline of Interpretive Sociology*. Berkeley: University of California Press.

Yildirim, S., Burcu, U.M., and Hakki, T. (2017). Intimate politics: Strategies and practices of female mukhtars in Turkey. *British Journal of Middle Eastern Studies*, 45(5), 661–77.

Yoltar, Ç. (2007). *The Green Card Scheme: An Ethnography of 'the State' and Its 'Poor Citizens' in Adıyaman*. PhD thesis, Bosphorus University.

12

Citizen agency in street-level interactions: navigating uncertainty and unpredictability

Sergio A. Campos

Introduction

Frontline work in contexts of weak state institutions (Peeters and Campos, 2022) and low trust (Peeters et al, 2018; Peeters and Dussauge Laguna, 2021; Spink et al, 2021) has received increased attention in recent years (Peeters and Campos, 2022) due to these contexts' particular institutional characteristics, which shape SLBs' behaviours. Frontline work in weak state institutions is influenced by particular administrative, political, social, and professional factors that make SLBs face more complex conditions to carry out their jobs while implementing public policies and delivering public services (Peeters and Campos, 2022).

According to some authors (Lipsky, 2010; Bartels, 2013; Raaphorst, 2018; Raaphorst and Van de Walle, 2018; Hand and Catlaw, 2019; Samanta and Hand, 2022), one of the primary sources of complexity and ambiguity for SLBs is their interaction with citizens. For example, Raaphorst (2018; see also Raaphorst and Van de Walle, 2018 and Raaphorst and Loyens, 2020) focusses on the way social dynamics between citizens, labour inspectors, and tax authorities influence the way frontline workers make decisions and how they make sense of hidden citizen characteristics. Although previous studies have contributed to our understanding of how uncertainty affects SLBs while interacting with citizens (as well as the strategies they develop to reduce that uncertainty), little attention has been paid to the relationship between bureaucratic encounters and frontline work in weak institutional contexts. In particular, few studies deal with the role played by citizens in this process.

The present chapter focuses on bureaucratic encounters in weak institutional contexts and explores their paradoxical consequences for frontline work. The focus is on how citizens develop their agency through repeated interactions with SLBs and how agency imposes more complexity on the frontline setting. Drawing on qualitative data on bureaucratic encounters during the implementation of a CCT programme in Mexico, I argue that repeated interactions between citizens and SLBs reduce ambiguity and uncertainty (Rothstein and Teorell, 2008; Rothstein, 2013; Peeters et al, 2018; Brinks et al, 2020; Peeters and Dussauge Laguna, 2021; Spink et al 2021). However, I further argue that this process paradoxically increases complexity for SLBs because it increases citizens' capacity to act as agents.

The chapter is organised as follows: following this introduction, I briefly review the literature on citizen agency and bureaucratic encounters. Then, the case study and the methods are presented in the third section. Finally, the results are discussed in the fourth section, followed by some concluding comments.

Citizen agency during bureaucratic encounters in weak institutional contexts

In its founding studies, street-level scholarship emphasised the implications of implementation and service delivery for citizens, mainly because SLBs mediate the 'constitutional relationship of citizens to the state' (Lipsky, 2010, 4). Since then, street-level interaction literature has focused on this interaction's bureaucratic side. Only two decades later, the citizen side of street-level interactions was acknowledged (Sandfort et al, 1999). However, citizens are still primarily considered the 'powerless side of the interaction' (Gofen et al, 2019). This understanding of the interaction overlooks that citizens may have agency: the capacity to engage in past and present patterns of action and relations and imaginatively reflect and act towards the future (Emirbayer and Mische, 1998).

Some authors (Barnes and Henly, 2018; De Boer, 2020; 2021; Hansen, 2021) have demonstrated that citizens are not passive or indifferent to their encounters with SLBs. Citizens can make impressions on how competent or friendly an SLB is (de Boer, 2020; Hansen, 2021). They attribute responsibility for burdensome encounters (Barnes and Henly, 2018) and respond to different enforcement styles (de Boer, 2021), or cope in different agentic ways with their encounters with public officials (Nielsen et al, 2021). Although this literature highlights the importance of information and knowledge that allow citizens to interpret the SLBs, more research is needed to know about the influence social dynamics have on uncertainty reduction for citizens.

Citizen agency is crucial for understanding the nature of most frontline work, which depends on the active and prolonged participation of usually socio-economically vulnerable citizens (Ravn and Bredgaard, 2021; Solheim et al, 2021). Traditionally, interactions between citizens-clients and bureaucrats are recognised as essential elements of street-level bureaucracy (Lipsky, 2010; Maynard-Moody and Portillo, 2010; Bartels, 2013). For instance, to break unemployment patterns or to reduce criminal behaviour or poverty, frontline workers may act like 'engineers of human choice, attitude, and self-care' (Peeters, 2019, 60). However, their daily work is also determined by the attitudes and actions of the citizens whose behaviour they seek to change.

It is well-documented in the street-level bureaucracy literature that SLBs often face high levels of uncertainty while making decisions (Maynard-Moody and Musheno, 2003; Lipsky, 2010), especially when interacting with citizens–clients (Rapphorst, 2018; 2019). Uncertainty in frontline work has been explained by a lack of information, vague evaluation standards, and losing control of specific situations, particularly when interacting with other humans (Raaphorst, 2018; 2019). However, in these accounts of uncertainty in frontline work, it is assumed that the bureaucracy's basic institutional and structural features are not problematic. On the contrary, bureaucracies in contexts of weak state institutions are known for their dysfunctional structural features like clientelism, patronage, brokerage, and low formalisation (see Carswell et al, 2019; Peeters et al, 2020; Peeters and Campos, 2022). Therefore, as the literature argues (Rothstein and Teorell, 2008; Brinks et al, 2020; Peeters and Dussauge Laguna, 2021), uncertainty is expected to manifest itself differently and more frequently in places with weak state institutions. Moreover, uncertainty affects the SLBs and citizens interacting with them during policy implementation and public service delivery.

Given the lack of trust in institutions because of their instability and unpredictability, citizens and SLBs in weak institutional contexts often rely on particularised trust (Peeters and Dussauge Laguna, 2021; see also Uslaner, 2018) to compensate for the absence of generalised forms of trust. This means people will only trust others in their inner social circle (Peeters and Dussauge Laguna, 2021). Therefore, social dynamics between SLBs and citizens can substitute for the lack of institutional certainty. As the literature on bureaucratic encounters suggests, social dynamics between SLBs and citizens are relevant for understanding the workers' decisions (Raaphorst and Loyens, 2020) but also citizen agency (Dubois, 2016; Mik-Meyer, 2017; Carswell et al, 2019; Gofen et al, 2019; de Boer, 2020; Masood and Nisar, 2021; Peeters and Campos, 2021). Furthermore, repeated interaction is a particular social dynamic that can explain how particularised trust develops.

Research setting

The Mexican social programme Prospera case provides an excellent opportunity to study citizen agency in street-level interactions. Prospera was a CCT programme implemented in Mexico from 1997 to 2019.[1] To break the intergenerational transmission of poverty and improve participant families' ability to invest in human capital (Hernández, 2008; Levy, 2009; CONEVAL, 2014), the programme included four components: (1) food, which consisted of the delivery of direct monetary benefits to recipient families for buying food; (2) health, which consisted of promoting health actions for the prevention of diseases, as well as the impulse for access to health services; (3) education, which consisted of educational coverage, with scholarships as an incentive for the permanence and performance of children in school; and (4) liaisons, which consisted of advising, providing information, and promoting the access of beneficiary families to an array of programmes including income generation, training, and employment, financial education, access to savings schemes, life insurance, and credits through inter-institutional coordination. This chapter focuses on the education and health components because they were the most relevant to the programme. Moreover, the most intense interaction between SLBs and citizens occurred in schools and health centres, mainly because of the conditional nature of these components.

Conditionalities were actions the beneficiaries were obligated to comply with as a prerequisite to obtaining the benefits granted by the programme. Specifically, the conditionalities included: (1) to register at the health centre assigned to the beneficiary when joining the programme and attend, by all family members, their scheduled medical appointments, and (2) enrolment of children in school (primary, secondary, and high school) and regular attendance to classes. Furthermore, every family head must attend Community Workshops for Health Self-Care and bi-monthly sessions with programme promoters. These meetings were called the 'Oportunidades Personalized Attention Desk' (MAPO), and their objective was to provide information about the programme procedures and to process beneficiaries' complaints.

Health promoters and school staff must monitor compliance with the programme's conditionalities. Health promoters can be medical professionals or social workers registering beneficiaries' attendance for health check-ups and workshops. The health promoters are also in charge of the workshop training sessions. Besides compliance issues, beneficiaries also have to deal with capacity problems. The limited capacity of the health centres often requires beneficiaries to attend health centres more than once for a single appointment because not all scheduled appointments can be handled on a single day.

Hence, the Prospera case presents an excellent opportunity to study uncertainty during bureaucratic encounters because (1) interactions are frequent and prolonged, and (2) schools and health centres in Mexico share many characteristics of weak institutions (Peeters and Campos, 2021; Campos and Peeters, 2022).

Methods and data

The analysis draws on qualitative semi-structured interviews with Prospera programme beneficiaries (n = 46), social workers (n = 15), and health promoters (n = 7) collected during five months of fieldwork in 15 urban and rural localities of Aguascalientes in Central Mexico. The reason behind this case selection is twofold. First, it is a case of a conditional social programme in a developing country, rarely studied from the frontline perspective. Second, its design allows me to observe variation in structural features empirically, as the programme included interactions between beneficiaries and health and educational SLBs. Furthermore, variation in the time exposed to the programme and educational and health staff suggests variation in the frequency of encounters.

The process for selecting the interviewees and the localities aimed to maximise the range (Weiss, 1994, 22–4) by including participants whose characteristics vary. Therefore, data collection comprised generating a list that prioritised locations with secondary schools with many student beneficiaries of the programme in Aguascalientes. Subsequently, rural localities that had not appeared in the first version were included in the list to consider the urban–rural variation among the interviewees. Thus, this study included 15 secondary schools distributed in five municipalities in Aguascalientes.

The schools helped to establish contact with the beneficiaries based on registry data. First, a logic of maximising the range was followed in selecting beneficiaries by including mothers with different seniority and experience as beneficiaries in the study, covering a range from 1 to 17 years of being Prospera beneficiaries, which allowed the exploration of the influence of different frequencies of encounters on experienced uncertainty. Then, the workers in charge of the daily operation of the programme were interviewed. For the educational component, the interviews were conducted with social workers. Only in one school did I not interview a social worker, as a regular teacher operated the programme there. Finally, in the case of the health component, the interviewees were all health promoters.

Two different scripts were used to conduct the interviews: one for beneficiaries and another for social workers and health promoters. Each contained a list of topics that structured the interviews and sought to obtain information regarding the mechanisms and processes through which the beneficiaries try to exert some control during Prospera implementation. Each interview lasted between 30 and 70 minutes. Most of the interviews were recorded, except for four beneficiaries and one social worker who disagreed with the recording of their voice. As for all interviews, detailed field notes were taken. These allowed for registering relevant nonverbal communication, such as facial reactions, gestures, and visible signs of discomfort. In most cases, the interviews were conducted in privacy, which made it easier for participants to speak freely. All recorded interviews were transcribed for analysis.

The analytic procedure followed an abductive logic of inquiry, which aligns with an interpretive research approach (Schwartz-Shea and Yanow, 2013, 27). This logic is characterised by an iterative and recursive back-and-forth path between field and theory (Timmermans and Tavory, 2012; Schwartz-Shea and Yanow, 2013). First, prior knowledge about repeated interactions and uncertainty was established based on the literature; this knowledge informed the interview topics. The interviews enhanced the prior knowledge and triggered new questions. These further questions pushed me to figure out the empirical puzzle and look for new theoretical insights. Finally, open codes were used for the qualitative data using a grounded theory logic (Corbin and Strauss, 2008) to identify the influence of repeated interactions on uncertainty and the themes that emerged from the data.

Findings

Bureaucratic encounters in Prospera's implementation

The conditions in which bureaucratic encounters occurred during Prospera's implementation include administrative burdens, informality, and subsequent uncertainty in how the different SLBs behaved during the Prospera implementation. Moreover, the uncertainty and informality – characteristic of a weak institutional setting like Mexico – led to a situation in which the Prospera implementation was very heterogeneous between the two major components: health and education. Furthermore, the bureaucratic encounters were characterised by an extreme sense of arbitrariness by citizen–clients regarding how SLBs acted.

The heterogeneity in the programme components' implementation is evident in the fact that costs linked to the administrative burden were more present in the health component. Beneficiaries mentioned high compliance costs because of the number of appointments for health checks and workshop sessions. In addition, the health centres' limited capacity and lack of personnel often meant that not all family members could be attended to on the same day, which required beneficiaries to pay multiple visits. Finally, beneficiaries mentioned uncertainty regarding the conditionalities, which are numerous and, in the perception of beneficiaries, often change at the will of the SLBs. Several authors have found the existence of informal extra conditionalities imposed on beneficiaries. One of the most frequent examples of these extra conditionalities is what in Mexico is called *faenas*, a form of community work intended to clean and give maintenance to public spaces (for example, Crucifix and Morvant-Roux, 2018; Adato, 2000; Ramírez, 2021). Many beneficiaries mentioned having experienced these extra conditionalities, which exemplify the unpredictability and variability of frontline work in weak state institutions.

An explanation for these extra conditionalities is that health promoters at the health centres *used* beneficiaries as what they called *a captive population* to comply with their own performance goals. Health promoters are employed by state governments, specifically by the state health secretariat. The state health secretariat designs programmes that the health centre's staff must implement, including health promoters. Furthermore, the health centres' staff evaluation and renovation of job contracts depend, in many cases, on complying with formal performance goals. Thus, Prospera became an opportunity for health centres' staff to constantly have clients captive for implementing the state health secretariat programmes and reach their performance goals:

'For example, in health promotion, if they [state health secretariat] told me, "you have to teach, I do not know, seven workshops a month with the population you want to take". So, if you have the captive groups, well ... we had the captive groups of Prospera, we make them a part in the workshops that we imparted to report it to both sides [to Prospera and the health state secretariat].' (Health Promoter 1)

'This happens because we used Prospera people as a captive population. What is this? ... I mean, we as [health] promotion have [performance] goals. I mean, the whole unit has goals to reach, yes? So, as the programme forces them [Prospera beneficiaries] to have specific workshops and consultations, the Prospera beneficiaries were our captive population. In a way, that is why I was also involved in working with them.' (Health Promoter 2)

This pressure incentivised health promoters to be rigid. Furthermore, extra conditionalities for beneficiaries allowed health centres to reach performance goals. However, conversely, this also enabled beneficiaries to negotiate compliance with a different set of conditionalities:

Beneficiary:	Some doctors lend themselves more. For example, they justify absences to medical appointments if they [non-compliant beneficiaries] do some work at the health centre. It happened to my sister.
Interviewer:	And what did she have to do?
Beneficiary:	She [her sister] came to paint at the health centre. And with that, she was able to reschedule her medical appointment. (Beneficiary 3)

Furthermore, these actions by SLBs constitute another example of the arbitrariness which beneficiaries often face during bureaucratic encounters.

Paradoxical encounters: repeated interactions and citizen agency

Given the uncertainty and arbitrariness Prospera beneficiaries experienced during their bureaucratic encounters, they had incentives to take actions that helped them to reduce that uncertainty. Furthermore, because of the weak state institutions they faced, they had to find alternative ways to reduce uncertainty. According to the qualitative data, the alternative was to draw upon personal relationships developed through repeated interactions with the SLBs. Mainly, beneficiaries' agency materialises through three strategies: adaptation or adjustment, the use of social capital, and gaming.

The delivery of services and enforcement of conditionalities linked to Prospera established relationships between beneficiaries and SLBs (for example, Ramírez, 2021). Furthermore, in many cases, these relationships were established repeatedly over long periods. Typically, policy design sets a beneficiary to interact with health promoters at least six times a year during the health workshops, sometimes even more because of the extra conditionalities imposed on beneficiaries. Something similar happened with the social workers. In this case, however, what triggered the repeated interaction was the fact that many beneficiaries had more than one child enrolled in school or had children with behavioural issues. In addition, many social workers within the sample worked for more than ten years at the same school, sometimes for almost 20 years. In the health centres, personnel rotation is higher than in schools, but there are also cases of health promoters working since the late nineties with the programme.

The agency of beneficiaries is developed through repeated interaction by learning that formal and informal rules determine Prospera's implementation. Most of the beneficiaries stated that it took them from six months to a year to understand the programme entirely. However, it can be said that beneficiaries took around two to three years to see how the routines in the programme implementation work. By then, a beneficiary has been in the programme long enough to become aware of the informal rules that shape the programme's operation and, closely related to this, the different types of SLBs with whom they interact. The knowledge about these two elements allows them to exercise their agency more actively. This learning process begins with personal experiences about the difference between formal procedures and street-level practices:

> 'I take [my daughter] to the health clinic, but there is no point in this. They do not even check her as they are supposed to. They do not

check anything, they just weigh and measure her, and that is it. I can do that at home and tell them her weight and height.' (Beneficiary1)

'The first time we arrived, I said [to the health promoter], 'Listen, I have been here since 4:30'. She said: 'Here, it does not matter if you arrive at 3:00 in the morning. What matters here are the sick people, and Prospera beneficiaries come last'. That is how I know that Prospera beneficiaries have their turn, so we always leave home early.' (Beneficiary 2)

Faced with these circumstances, beneficiaries learn to anticipate and make minor adjustments in their behaviour to smooth the burden of compliance. For example, they discipline themselves, ensure they are on time for appointments and try not to rub frontline workers the wrong way.

Using beneficiaries' social and human capital is crucial to mitigate the difficulties imposed by bureaucratic encounters. First, many beneficiaries get helpful information from other beneficiaries that they might not get otherwise – as a means to reduce learning costs. Second, personal relations with frontline workers provide another opportunity to smooth compliance burdens. Finally, around the third year, many beneficiaries realise there is a human and *personal* dimension to the process. Prospera not only functions because of or according to the formal rules they were taught but also hinges upon personal relationships, particularly with the SLBs, and upon the personal traits of these bureaucrats. Repeated interactions give beneficiaries information to identify types of SLBs and the level of flexibility with which they can conduct themselves concerning compliance rules. For example, most of the interviewed beneficiaries describe certain SLBs as more or less 'lenient' or 'available' – '*se prestan*' in Spanish, which means that the bureaucrat lends himself or herself to doing or not doing something.

When beneficiaries become aware of the personal nature of the implementation, they begin to use their agency to 'play the game' – either by negotiating with SLBs or by using more subversive ways to gain leverage over them.

'There is a lot of cheating. For example, the spokesperson[2] helps other mothers to enter the programme. [They] are even told what to say [in the survey] to join the programme quickly. ... In the health centre, cheating is more difficult. ... It all depends if you can befriend the spokesperson and the health promoter.' (Beneficiary 3)

'There are cases of beneficiaries who want to give something with the intention [of getting a free pass]. Not all of them are treated the same way.' (Beneficiary 4)

Due to their prolonged exposure to the programme, beneficiaries learn that what governs obligations and sanctions are not only the formal, impersonal, and bureaucratic rules but also the discretion of the officials with whom they interact. Moreover, they also learn that the regulations and compliance can be made more flexible and approached as a 'game' (see Goffman, 1969). Empirically, this 'game' is triggered when beneficiaries learn from their own experiences and other beneficiaries' behaviour how to (1) identify the more lenient SLBs and (2) negotiate or use gift relations to gain leverage over them. Disadvantaged as they may be, beneficiaries use their skills and the little resources they have to exercise their agency strategically.

Discussion

Repeated interactions with SLBs help beneficiaries overcome some of the difficulties that the lack of trust and high levels of uncertainty cause for their compliance with Prospera's conditionalities. Moreover, these repeated interactions trigger a paradoxical phenomenon. On the one hand, they allow SLBs and beneficiaries to reduce uncertainty about bureaucratic encounters. However, on the other hand, they become an enabler of agency for the beneficiaries, which allows them to be more active during the encounters, thereby making the daily decision-making processes of SLBs more complex.

Prospera beneficiaries experienced uncertainty during their bureaucratic encounters because of their arbitrariness and unpredictability. As a result, they had to rely on particularised trust (Peeters and Dussauge Laguna, 2021; see also Uslaner, 2018) to compensate for the absence of general forms of trust (Peeters and Dussauge Laguna, 2021). Moreover, literature on bureaucratic encounters has found that social dynamics that develop between SLBs and citizens are relevant for understanding the decisions SLBs make (Raaphorst and Loyens, 2020) but also for understanding citizen agency (Dubois, 2016; Mik-Meyer, 2017; Carswell et al, 2019; Gofen et al, 2019; de Boer, 2020; Masood and Nisar, 2021; Peeters and Campos, 2021). Repeated interactions are one particular social dynamic that can help understand such dynamics. Even though the distinction between one-shot and repeated interactions in public encounters was recognised as early as 1981 by Charles Goodsell, most studies have only focused on the effects of repeated interactions on regulation in western countries (Boyne et al, 2002; Pautz, 2009; Pautz and Wamsley, 2012; Etienne, 2013; De Boer and Eshuis, 2018). Less is known about what that distinction between one-shot and repeated interaction implies for bureaucratic encounters in contexts with weak state institutions in general and citizen agency in particular.

Repeated interaction differs from one-shot interaction because it produces social relationships. Moreover, repeated interactions connect individuals to the expected roles and rules pertinent to a specific interaction order

(Goffman, 1983). Therefore, this socialisation process is the basis for a particular order to succeed according to the specific interaction's rules. However, given the social nature of interactional order, this is not fixed but is open to be influenced by interaction participants. Participants can negotiate roles and rules, even in rigid institutions like prisons or mental institutions (Goffman, 1961). Participants can also try to fool the other party regarding their image or role (Goffman, 1969). To the extent that human agency has a temporal dimension, meaning that an agent engages with past, present, and future to exert control on structure (Emirbayer and Mische, 1998), repeated street-level interactions become the basis for citizens to exert control on policy and interaction structure. This may be particularly so in weak institutional contexts where formal institutions have lower relevance in structuring behaviour.

The consequences of this interactional order are not straightforward. On the one hand, knowing the behaviours and outcomes a policy expects from all participants could result in citizen compliance and cooperative relationships with SLBs (for example, Murray, 2006; Rossi, 2016). On the other hand, the result could also be fraudulent or manipulative behaviours as citizens learn how to act in a specific policy setting to get what they want irrespective of formal policy goals (for example, Tuckett, 2015; Scheel, 2017). Another possible consequence is that it affects the impersonality of the bureaucratic encounter – traditionally seen as one of the formal bureaucracy's main features (Weber, 1978, 987–9). Impersonality has been one of the reasons for criticism of the bureaucratisation of social life because of its alienating and dehumanising nature (Merton, 1968; McCabe, 2015). The development of social relationships between SLBs and citizens can subvert that dehumanisation. However, at the same time, personalisation can also open the door to favouritism and arbitrariness (Merton, 1968; Lipsky, 2010).

Conclusion

This chapter aimed to explore the influence of repeated interactions on uncertainty, characteristic of many bureaucratic encounters in weak institutional contexts (Rothstein and Teorell, 2008). As the literature on bureaucratic socialisation shows, contact with bureaucracies makes citizens more competent to deal with bureaucratic organisations by learning relevant knowledge and information about bureaucratic functioning (Danet and Gurevitch, 1972; Danet and Hartman, 1972). Moreover, service delivery interactions expose citizens to how government works (Wichowsky and Moynihan, 2008; Bruch et al, 2010) and teach them lessons about (in)effectiveness, trustworthiness, corruption, flaws in the application of the rule of law, and the way citizens are treated (Soss, 1999; Mettler, 2002; Heinrich, 2018, 9). This type of knowledge is particularly relevant for citizens in the context of weak state institutions settings (Carswell et al, 2019; Masood and Nisar, 2021; Peeters et al, 2020; Peeters and Campos, 2021; Peeters and Dussauge Laguna, 2021), because it helps reduce uncertainty in otherwise unpredictable processes.

One of this chapter's main findings is that the consequences of repeated interactions may be paradoxical. The effect of repeated interactions is *uncertainty reduction*. Furthermore, uncertainty reduction also affects citizen behaviour by improving their capacity and ability to interpret and assess SLBs' decisions directed toward them. This improvement is likely to have significant consequences, at least in three areas of policy implementation and bureaucratic encounters: first, the way citizens attribute responsibility for policy decisions (for example, Barnes and Henly, 2018); second, in how citizens assess SLBs' competency (de Boer, 2020; Hansen, 2021) or enforcement styles (de Boer, 2021); and, third, in the reduction of learning costs associated with uncertainty (Moynihan et al, 2015).

On the other hand, the effect could also be a risk of fraudulent or manipulative behaviours as citizens learn how to 'act' to get what they want independent of formal policy goals (for example, Tuckett, 2015; Scheel, 2017). Traditionally, the literature on street-level bureaucracy in strong institutional contexts sees citizens as a source of uncertainty and complexity for the SLBs (Maynard-Moody and Musheno, 2003; Lipsky, 2010; Raaphorst, 2018; Raaphorst and Loyens, 2020) and, additionally, tends to portray the citizen as a passive actor subject to the actions and decisions of SLBs. However, as the findings of my case study reveal, citizens that face uncertainty may be incentivised to pursue more active agency forms. Furthermore, the agency developed by citizens through repeated interactions imposes new uncertainties on frontline workers because it impacts the information asymmetry between them and citizen–clients (Danet and Gurevitch, 1972; Danet and Hartman, 1972; Döring, 2021; Masood and Nisar, 2021). This enhances citizens' chances to be successful in presenting persuasive appeals to frontline workers (Danet and Gurevitch, 1972; Nielsen et al, 2021) to obtain preferential treatment (Masood and Nisar, 2021), negotiate compliance (Gofen et al, 2019), or game the system (Peeters et al, 2020).

Notes

[1] Andrés Manuel López Obrador, elected president in 2018, who ran a campaign as a leftist anti-establishment candidate, terminated the program and replaced it with a largely unconditional social benefit. The most significant change was the elimination of the health conditionalities and reducing the education one to merely registering children in schools (rather than actively monitoring class attendance). Thereby, Prospera, as a conditional cash transfer, was, by all practical means, terminated and rebranded as Becas Benito Juárez ('Benito Juárez Scholarships'), which only included a minimum of conditions for receiving the financial benefit.

2   Spokespersons are beneficiaries selected as members of 'Community Promotion Committees'. Each locality or neighbourhood has a committee for every 200 beneficiary families. These spokespersons are selected from the communities to exercise the role of representatives to coordinate the Prospera program. Their primary responsibility is to link the beneficiaries of their community and the authorities to transmit information about the program. Therefore, their role is essential to reduce uncertainty in program implementation.

References

Adato, M. (2000) *The Impact of PROGRESA on Community Social Relationships*, Washington, DC: International Food Policy Research Institute (IFPRI).

Barnes, C.Y. and Henly, J.R. (2018). 'They are underpaid and understaffed': How clients interpret encounters with street-level bureaucrats. *Journal of Public Administration Research and Theory*, 28(2), 165–81.

Bartels, K.P. (2013). Public encounters: The history and future of face-to-face contact between public professionals and citizens. *Public Administration*, 91(2), 469–83.

Boyne, G., Day, P., and Walker, R. (2002). The evaluation of public service inspection: A theoretical framework. *Urban Studies*, 39(7), 1197–212.

Brinks, D.M., Levitsky, S., and Murillo, M.V. (2020). The political origins of institutional weakness. In D.M. Brinks, S. Levitsky, and M.V. Murillo (eds), *The Politics of Institutional Weakness in Latin America*. Cambridge: Cambridge University Press, pp 1–40.

Bruch, S.K., Marx-Freere, M., and Soss, J. (2010). From policy to polity: Democracy, paternalism, and the incorporation of disadvantaged citizens. *American Sociological Review*, 75(2), 205–26.

Campos, S.A. and Peeters, R. (2022). Policy improvisation: How frontline workers cope with public service gaps in developing countries – The case of Mexico's Prospera program. *Public Administration and Development*, 42(1), 22–32.

Carswell, G., Chambers, T., and De Neve, G. (2019). Waiting for the state: Gender, citizenship and everyday encounters with bureaucracy in India. *Environment and Planning C: Politics and Space*, 37(4), 597–616.

CONEVAL. (2014). *Informe de la Evaluación Específica de Desempeño 2012–2013 del Programa de Desarrollo Humano Oportunidades*. México, DF: CONEVAL.

Corbin, J. and Strauss, A. (2008). *Basics of Qualitative Research: Techniques and Procedures for Developing Grounded Theory*. Los Angeles: Sage.

Crucifix, C. and Morvant-Roux, S. (2018). Fragmented rural communities: The faenas of Prospera at the interface of community cooperation and state dependency. In M.E. Balen and M. Fotta (eds), *Money from the Government in Latin America. Conditional Cash Transfer Programs and Rural Lives*. London: Routledge, pp 81–96.

Danet, B. and Gurevitch, M. (1972). Presentation of self in appeals to bureaucracy: An empirical study of role specificity. *American Journal of Sociology*, 77(6), 1165–90.

Danet, B. and Hartman, H. (1972). Coping with bureaucracy: The Israeli case. *Social Forces*, 51(1), 7–22.

de Boer, N. (2020). How do citizens assess street-level bureaucrats' warmth and competence? A typology and test. *Public Administration Review*, 80(4), 532–42.

de Boer, N. (2021). The (un) intended effects of street-level bureaucrats' enforcement style: Do citizens shame or obey bureaucrats?. *Public Policy and Administration*, 36(4), 452–75.

de Boer, N. and Eshuis, J. (2018). A street-level perspective on government transparency and regulatory performance: Does relational distance matter?. *Public Administration,* 96(3), 452–67.

Döring, M. (2021). How-to bureaucracy: A concept of citizens' administrative literacy. *Administration & Society*, 53(8), 1155–77.

Dubois, V. (2016). *The Bureaucrat and the Poor. Encounters in Welfare French Offices*. New York, NY: Routledge.

Emirbayer, M. and Mische, A. (1998). What is agency?. *American Journal of Sociology*, 103(4), 962–1023.

Etienne, J. (2013). Ambiguity and relational signals in regulator–regulatee relationships. *Regulation & Governance*, 7(1), 30–47.

Gofen, A., Blomqvist, P., Needham, C.E., Warren, K., and Winblad, U. (2019). Negotiated compliance at the street level: Personalizing immunization in England, Israel and Sweden. *Public Administration*, 97(1), 195–209.

Goffman, E. (1961). *Asylums: Essays on the Social Situation of Mental Patients and Other Inmates*. New York: First Anchor Books Edition.

Goffman, E. (1969). *Strategic Interaction*. Philadelphia: University of Pennsylvania Press.

Goffman, E. (1983). The interaction order: American Sociological Association, 1982 presidential address. *American Sociological Review*, 48(1), 1–17.

Guul, T.S., Pedersen, M.J., and Petersen, N.B.G. (2021). Creaming among caseworkers: Effects of client competence and client motivation on caseworkers' willingness to help. *Public Administration Review*, 81(1), 12–22. https://doi.org/10.1111

Hand, L.C. and Catlaw, T.J. (2019). Accomplishing the public encounter: A case for ethnomethodology in public administration research. *Perspectives on Public Management and Governance*, 2(2), 125–37.

Hansen, F.G. (2021). How impressions of public employees' warmth and competence influence trust in government. *International Public Management Journal*, 1–23.

Heinrich, C.J. (2018). Presidential address: 'A thousand petty fortresses': Administrative burden in US immigration policies and its consequences. *Journal of Policy Analysis and Management*, 37(2), 211–39.

Hernández, D. (2008). *Historia de Oportunidades. Inicio y cambios del programa*. México, DF: FCE.

Levy, S. (2009). *Pobreza y transición democrática en México*. México, DF: FCE.

Lipsky, M. (2010). *Street-Level Bureaucracy: Dilemmas of the Individual in Public Service*. New York: Russell Sage Foundation.

Masood, A. and Nisar, M.A. (2021). Administrative capital and citizens' responses to administrative burden. *Journal of Public Administration Research and Theory*, 31(1), 56–72.

Maynard-Moody, S. and Musheno, M. (2003). *Cops, Teachers, Counselors. Stories from the Front Lines of Public Service*. Ann Arbor, MI: University of Michigan Press.

Maynard-Moody, S. and Portillo, S. (2010). Street-level bureaucracy theory. In R.F. Durant (ed), *The Oxford Handbook of American Bureaucracy*. Oxford: Oxford University Press, pp 254–77.

McCabe, D. (2015). The tyranny of distance: Kafka and the problem of distance in bureaucratic organizations. *Organization*, 22(1), 58–77.

Merton, R.K. (1968). *Social Theory and Social Structure*. New York: The Free Press.

Mettler, S. (2002). Bringing the state back in to civic engagement: Policy feedback effects of the GI Bill for World War II veterans. *American Political Science Review*, 96(2), 351–65.

Mik-Meyer, N. (2017). *The Power of Citizens and Professionals in Welfare Encounters: The Influence of Bureaucracy, Market and Psychology*. Manchester: Manchester University Press.

Moynihan, D.P., Herd, P., and Harvey, H. (2015). Administrative burden: Learning, psychological, and compliance costs in citizen-state interactions. *Journal of Public Administration Research and Theory*, 25(1), 43–69.

Murray, C. (2006). State intervention and vulnerable children: Implementation revisited. *Journal of Social Policy*, 35(2), 211–27.

Nielsen, V.L., Nielsen, H.Ø., and Bisgaard, M. (2021). Citizen reactions to bureaucratic encounters: different ways of coping with public authorities. *Journal of Public Administration Research and Theory*, 31(2), 381–98.

Pautz, M.C. (2009). Trust between regulators and the regulated: A case study of environmental inspectors and facility personnel in Virginia. *Politics & Policy*, 37(5), 1047–72.

Pautz, M.C. and Wamsley, C.S. (2012). Pursuing trust in environmental regulatory interactions: The significance of inspectors' interactions with the regulated community. *Administration & Society*, 44(7), 853–84.

Peeters, R. (2019). Manufacturing responsibility: The governmentality of behavioural power in social policies. *Social Policy and Society*, 18(1), 51–65.

Peeters, R. and Campos, S.A. (2021). Taking the bite out of administrative burdens: How beneficiaries of a Mexican social program ease administrative burdens in street-level interactions. *Governance*, 34(4), 1001–18.

Peeters, R. and Campos, S.A. (2022). Street-level bureaucracy in weak state institutions: A systematic review of the literature. *International Review of Administrative Sciences*, 00208523221103196.

Peeters, R. and Dussauge Laguna, M.I. (2021). Acting out or playing along: A typology of citizens' low trust responses to public organizations. *Governance*, 34(4), 965–81.

Peeters, R., Gofen, A., and Meza, O. (2020). Gaming the system: Responses to dissatisfaction with public services beyond exit and voice. *Public Administration*, 98(4), 824–39.

Peeters, R., Trujillo Jimenez, H., O'Connor, E., Ogarrio Rojas, P., Gonzalez Galindo, M., and Morales Tenorio, D. (2018). Low-trust bureaucracy: Understanding the Mexican bureaucratic experience. *Public Administration and Development*, 38(2), 65–74.

Raaphorst, N. (2018). How to prove, how to interpret and what to do? Uncertainty experiences of street-level tax officials. *Public Management Review*, 20(4), 485–502.

Raaphorst, N. (2019). Studying uncertainty in decision making by street-level inspectors. In S. Van de Walle and N. Raaphorst (eds), *Inspectors and enforcement at the Front Line of Government*. Cham: Palgrave Macmillan, pp 11–33.

Raaphorst, N. and Loyens, K. (2020). From poker games to kitchen tables: How social dynamics affect frontline decision making. *Administration & Society*, 52(1), 31–56.

Raaphorst, N. and Van de Walle, S. (2018). A signaling perspective on bureaucratic encounters: How public officials interpret signals and cues. *Social Policy & Administration*, 52(7), 1367–78.

Ramírez, V. (2021). Relationships in the Implementation of Conditional Cash Transfers: The Provision of Health in the Oportunidades-Prospera Programme in Puebla, Mexico. *Social Policy and Society*, 20(3), 400–17.

Ravn, R.L. and Bredgaard, T. (2021). Relationships matter: The impact of working alliances in employment services. *Social Policy and Society*, 20(3), 418–35.

Rossi, P. (2016). Looking for an emergency door: The access to social services between informational asymmetries and sensegiving processes. *International Journal of Sociology and Social Policy*, 36(1/2), 102–18.

Rothstein, B. (2013). Corruption and social trust: Why the fish rots from the head down. *Social Research*, 80(4), 1009–32.

Rothstein, B.O. and Teorell, J.A. (2008). What is quality of government? A theory of impartial government institutions. *Governance*, 21(2), 165–90.

Samanta, A. and Hand, L. (2022). Examining the 'in-between' of public encounters: Evidence from two seemingly disparate policy contexts. *Public Policy and Administration*, 37(2), 129–53.

Sandfort, J.R., Kalil, A., and Gottschalk, J.A. (1999). The mirror has two faces: Welfare clients and front-line workers view policy reforms. *Journal of Poverty*, 3(3), 71–91.

Scheel, S. (2017). 'The secret is to look good on paper': Appropriating mobility within and against a machine of illegalization. In N. De Genova (ed), *The Borders of 'Europe': Autonomy of Migration, Tactics of Bordering*. Durham, NC: Duke University Press, pp 37–63.

Schwartz-Shea, P. and Yanow, D. (2013). *Interpretive Research Design: Concepts and Processes*. New York, NY: Routledge.

Solheim, I.J., Gudmundsdottir, S., Husabø, M., and Øien, A.M. (2021). The importance of relationships in the encounter between NAV staff and young, vulnerable users. An action research study. *European Journal of Social Work*, 24(4), 671–82.

Soss, J. (1999). Lessons of welfare: Policy design, political learning, and political action. *American Political Science Review*, 93(2), 363–80.

Spink, P., Lotta, G., and Burgos, F. (2021). Institutional vulnerability and trust in public agencies: Views from both sides of the street. *Governance*, 34(4), 1057–73.

Timmermans, S. and Tavory, I. (2012). Theory construction in qualitative research: From grounded theory to abductive analysis. *Sociological Theory*, 30(3), 167–86.

Tuckett, A. (2015). Strategies of navigation: Migrants' everyday encounters with Italian immigration bureaucracy. *The Cambridge Journal of Anthropology*, 33(1), 113–28.

Uslaner, E.M. (2018). The Study of Trust. In E.M. Uslaner (ed), *The Oxford Handbook of Social and Political Trust*. New York, NY: Oxford University Press, pp 3–13.

Weber, M. (1978). *Economy and Society: An Outline of Interpretive Sociology*. Berkeley: University of California Press.

Weiss, R.S. (1994). *Learning from Strangers. The Art and Method of Qualitative Interview Studies*. New York: The Free Press.

Wichowsky, A. and Moynihan, D.P. (2008). Measuring how administration shapes citizenship: A policy feedback perspective on performance management. *Public Administration Review*, 68(5), 908–20.

13

Frontline work in weak institutions: implementing inequities

Fernando Nieto-Morales, Gabriela Lotta, and Rik Peeters

Introduction

The contributions in this book explore how structurally adverse working conditions that prevail in many places affect SLBs' decisions and behaviour and how they, consequently, shape the everyday experience of law enforcement, policy implementation, and public service provision for citizens worldwide. In this concluding chapter, we formulate several key lessons and findings from the preceding chapters. Furthermore, we outline what we believe to be the main contributions of this book and, finally, some concluding remarks on the crucial role of SLBs in advancing the functioning of public administrations in weak institutional settings.

Key findings and lessons learned

As noted in the introductory chapter, perhaps more than anywhere, street-level discretion is 'the wild card' (Brodkin, 2008, 326) of not only policy implementation but also of law enforcement and the delivery of essential public services such as health and education in contexts of institutional weakness – typical in countries of the Global South but also in parts of the Global North. There, citizens and SLBs alike experience significant gaps in the alignment between frontline work on the one hand and formal rules, guidelines, and policy designs on the other hand. The central theoretical assumption underlying this book is that institutional characteristics, such as low trust by citizens in governments, limited capacities to cover the demand for public services, and the intervention of political interests in street-level organisations, shape the working conditions and, consequently, the incentives and constraints for frontline work behaviour. More specifically, we assume that institutional deficiencies are often left unresolved and subsequently pushed toward the street level, where public servants deal with them in highly diverse ways.

The previous chapters presented evidence that, on the one hand, deals with familiar concepts of the literature. As elsewhere, SLBs in Ghana, Mexico, or India resort to coping mechanisms when faced with resource shortages or ambiguous policy directives. They may also deem certain clients as more deserving than others, reward compliant behaviour, and function as ultimate policy makers in healthcare or the delivery of benefits. Such analyses are a testament to the conceptual strength of the street-level bureaucracy literature and provide ample opportunities for strengthening dialogues and pursuing comparative studies. On the other hand, the contributions in this book also shed light on the realities of frontline work more typical for weak institutional settings. Contexts of endemic corruption, extreme insecurity, authoritarian legacies, and basic resource shortage trigger behaviours such as paternalist attitudes towards welfare beneficiaries, moving away from dangerous policing activities, and engaging in petty corruption. To be sure, these patterns are more likely to appear in developing countries than in other places; however, our point is that they are likely to develop *anywhere* where weak institutions are present. Based on the previous, we formulate three key lessons from the previous chapters. Taken together, they point towards the inevitability of producing inequities in service delivery, treatment of citizen–clients, and law enforcement as the defining characteristic of street-level bureaucracy in weak institutional settings – primarily because SLBs lack the institutional resources to do otherwise.

Between policy repair and survival

A first set of lessons deals with how SLBs behave organisationally in response to their administrative, political, and social environment. One of the ways in which frontline workers cope with institutional deficiencies is through policy repair. In her contribution to this book, Ayesha Masood introduces the notion of 'slow-moving disasters': a situation where a breakdown of processes and lack of adequate resources is not a one-off or sudden event but a frequent occurrence and accepted norm in daily work. The normalisation of a 'permanent state of emergency' induces coping mechanisms from SLBs aimed at preventing a breakdown of service provision. Although her case study is set in the context of the COVID-19 crisis, the potential for policy repair by SLBs is more broadly applicable to situations where an imminent collapse of services must be prevented, and it is unlikely that the state will respond to the needs of frontline workers in a proper and timely manner. In response, SLBs improvise practical solutions, spend their own time and resources to buy essential materials, provide mutual support among colleagues, and develop practical knowledge to foresee possible implementation challenges in the future.

Policy repair mechanisms are especially likely to emerge in situations and types of frontline work where SLBs face an action imperative –where 'doing nothing' is not a realistic option, such as in public hospitals where patients somehow need to be treated and in public schools where students need to be taught. In many ways, policy repair is focused on immediate survival needs rather than on structurally improving service provision or attending to individual client–citizen demands and interests. This may take the form of frontline workers doing what is necessary to keep a service from collapsing – as in Masood's study of Pakistani medical staff during the COVID-19 pandemic – but also doing what is necessary for their survival on the job. As Sneha Swami and Subodh Wagle show in their chapter on the Indian electricity distribution sector, working conditions may pose a (literal) physical danger to frontline workers. This forces them to, for instance, buy their own protective equipment, resort to union membership to protect some of their labour rights, and develop forms of feigned compliance with formal governance structures and performance control mechanisms. Confronted with precarious working conditions, coping mechanisms outside of client interactions (Tummers et al, 2015, 1102), such as seeking support from colleagues or using informal personal resources (Lavee, 2021), take on a special importance.

Paulina Guzmán and Rik Peeters observe a similar mechanism in the way municipal police officers in the Mexican city of Morelia cope with threats posed by organised crime, tense interactions with a distrusting public, limited training, scarce material resources, long working hours and low salaries, and a lack of psychological support to process the risks and stress they experience daily. In response, police officers may back down from intervening in situations involving organised crime or when feeling outnumbered. Conversely, they may also adopt strict and aggressive approaches toward individual citizens. Thereby, police officers not only convey messages about what citizens may expect from their municipal police but also express that their survival and mental well-being have an enormous influence on law enforcement practices. More broadly, instead of repairing policies, frontline workers may also respond to their survival needs by rationing services and distancing themselves from citizens/clients if they have the practical possibilities or authority to do so. Unappreciated by citizens, ignored by politicians and managers, exposed to danger, and subjected to precarious working conditions – often amplified by a lack of job security, limited career possibilities, and low income – many frontline workers in weak institutional settings are left to fend for themselves. This also suggests the relevance of explicitly taking into account cognitive or emotional coping mechanisms as factors that shape how SLBs in weak institutions perceive and value citizens, colleagues, and themselves (Lotta et al, 2023).

Implementing inequities

Second, various contributions in this book point toward SLBs' limitations in overcoming or resisting institutional deficiencies. They often have to cope with situations where what is expected from them far exceeds the resources they have at hand to do their job. How they deal with such extreme 'public service gaps' (Hupe and Buffat, 2014) varies significantly. For example, Abdul-Rahim Mohammed's study of health insurance staff and hospital staff in the implementation of the Ghanaian National Health Insurance Scheme shows there is often a fine line between repairing institutional deficiencies for the sake of policy implementation on the one hand and protecting personal daily needs in the face of excessive workloads on the other hand. Specifically, in their efforts to keep the hospital running, medical staff turn to strict rationing of patient attention and differentiating between easy and difficult patients (compare with Smith-Oka, 2013). Likewise, desk clerks favour specific clients over others and sometimes send away the ones without the proper documentation to prove eligibility for health insurance. In doing so, frontline workers create inequities in citizens' access to healthcare.

Therefore, the limitations of policy repair become clear when frontline workers' coping mechanisms lead them to ration services and move away from client needs. Furthermore, frontline workers also have limited capacities to influence structural institutional deficiencies. For example, in their contribution on implementation gaps in the access to care for people with drug addiction problems in Brazil, Roberto Pires, Maria Paula Santos, Beatriz Brandão, and Luiza Rosa show how professionalised staff is unable to overcome the lack of physical facilities to treat addicts and provide them with adequate care. In response, they refer clients to services they recognise as being far from ideal – a practice that perpetuates social inequalities, territorial differences in access to public services, and what elsewhere has been called 'fragmented stateness' (Perelmiter, 2022). Taly Reininger, Gianinna Muñoz-Arce, Cristóbal Villalobos, and Mitzi Duboy Luengo reach a similar conclusion in their study of the implementation of a Chilean social benefit. Social workers face precarious labour conditions, yet they must implement a policy in highly diverse local settings according to a strict and centralised design. Inadvertently, they create territorial differences in the benefit's implementation, which echoes the selective, unequal, and often distributive policies typical in weak institutional settings (O'Brien and Li, 1999; Holland, 2016).

SLBs may also respond to incentives in their institutional environment in the form of corruption, for instance, by demanding bribes or facilitating political misbehaviour. Without denying that administrative and petty corruption is widespread in the absence of efficient bureaucratic control mechanisms, Oliver Meza, Elizabeth Pérez-Chiqués, and Anat Gofen argue that what can sometimes be observed or perceived as predatory behaviour from SLBs might, instead, reflect the role of SLBs in contexts of corrupted politics, management, and peers. In other words, corrupt SLBs either respond to particular organisational incentives or are used as tools for pursuing private interests. Here too, emerges a scenario where SLBs cannot ease institutional weaknesses through repair or improvisation but, instead, are part of a broader systemic logic that constrains their behavioural options (compare with Rothstein, 2013).

The influence politics has on street-level bureaucracy in weak institutional settings is also explored in the contribution by Ronan Jacquin. His study shows how implementing a social benefit in Uganda purposefully relies on patrimonial forms of organisation to protect the interests of local political leaders and their potential to influence beneficiaries. Rather than implementing the benefit as a formal individual right, they prefer to maintain personalised relations with beneficiaries and grant the benefit as if it were a favour. This strategy reproduces the well-documented use of social benefits as an electoral strategy by political elites (Diaz-Cayeros et al, 2016).

Brokering the relationship between citizens and the state

A third set of lessons concerns the interactions between citizens and SLBs. Several contributions highlight the tense interactions that frontline workers may have with citizens. For instance, the chapter by Mohammed mentioned earlier describes how citizens, frustrated by having to wait in line for hours in saturated rural hospitals, may behave angrily and aggressively toward frontline workers. Further, hospital staff and desk clerks also face attempts by people not eligible for health insurance to cheat the system by using fraudulent identity cards or by impersonating someone else (for example, to obtain medicines for an uninsured relative). In response, frontline workers develop a strict, formal, and unresponsive attitude toward them. Something similar is documented by Swami and Wagle, who show that politically connected citizens may seek preferential treatment, sometimes physically threatening electricity sector frontline workers with strong-arm tactics. In response, frontline workers act cautiously when dealing with citizens and provide each other mutual support – especially when engaging in enforcement tasks. Related to the previous, Guzmán and Peeters' study on Mexican municipal police officers highlights the potential for violent interactions with citizens – which may be provoked by either side of the interaction – in a context of high insecurity, low citizen trust in law enforcement, and stressful working conditions.

These chapters stress the substantial impact frontline workers have on citizens' everyday experience of the state. What law enforcement looks like in practice, how they obtain access to healthcare, and how problems with their electricity provision are dealt with are played out in their interactions with frontline workers. Thereby, these chapters also implicitly make the point that Sergio Campos makes explicitly; that is, when faced with uncertainty about obtaining access to services or benefits, citizens do not remain quiet or passive. Instead, they use their agency and resources to strengthen their position vis-à-vis SLBs. Citizens may threaten or manipulate frontline workers. They may try to befriend them or may try to cheat them. One possible outcome is that citizen–worker interaction can trigger vicious circles of low trust (compare with Eiró, 2019). Barbara Piotrowska, Izabela Szkurłat, and Magdalena Szydłowska make a similar point. In their historical case study of the Polish police force in the 1990s, they assert that, while politically and constitutionally transitioning to a democracy, authoritarian legacies lingered in the police force's behaviour and its interactions with citizens – causing levels of public trust in the police to remain low throughout the decade. Bureaucratic renewal may prove a complex challenge, but it is essential to foster people's trust in public institutions and democracy (Dahlberg and Holmberg, 2014).

Other contributions describe more constructive forms of interaction between SLBs and citizens. For example, Elise Massicard's study of Turkish muhtars shows how the considerable distance between a formal Weberian bureaucracy and distrusting or marginalised citizens can be bridged by specific types of frontline workers that operate as brokers between both sides (compare with Kruks-Wisner, 2018). Rather than maintaining a distance from citizens, such frontline workers are fundamentally embedded in the communities they serve (compare with Bhavnani and Lee, 2018), which allows them to champion vulnerable citizens with limited capacities to obtain access to state services and benefits. This emerges as an effective strategy for places and countries with institutional deficiencies in their formal bureaucracies, unable to reach out to vulnerable communities and reduce the burdens they experience in accessing the state. The 'relational state' (Peake and Forsyth, 2022) appears particularly attractive for rural and marginalised territories, where the formal bureaucracy has a limited reach, and communal ties are usually close and thick (compare with Mangla, 2022).

However, such personalisation of citizen–state relations is, despite its constructive potential, not without its downsides for the equal and fair provision of services and benefits. Massicard shows how informal favours and bypassing formal procedures benefit some citizens more than others. This point is also clearly made in Jacquin's study of the implementation of a cash transfer in Uganda through paternalist forms of bureaucracy – local civil servants and village leaders – instead of professionalised frontline workers. These locally embedded policy brokers have a paternalistic and patronising attitude towards the programme's beneficiaries (for instance, through normative coercion regarding how they should spend the money from the benefit). Conversely, beneficiaries see the benefit as a favour rather than a legal right and feel a moral debt towards the brokers that grant them the benefit. Similar to the Turkish case, institutional structures emphasise a relational rather than impersonal bureaucracy, with a significant influence of local elites in the actual distribution of (supposedly unconditional) social benefits or universal rights.

Contributions

Beyond the specific lessons from the chapters, the findings and discussions presented in this book make several broader contributions to the study of street-level bureaucracy and frontline work in places with weak institutions in particular but also from a more global perspective.

An interdisciplinary and comparative approach

The first contribution of this book is the value of an interdisciplinary and comparative approach to studies about street-level bureaucracy. Historically, public administration and political science scholars have conducted most studies on street-level bureaucracies. Recently, however, the literature started benefiting from works and insights in sociology, anthropology, and psychology, among others. Our book advances in this new perspective, joining scholars from different perspectives and approaches that range from political science and public administration to a more sociological and anthropological outlook. This diversity can also be seen in the methods used in the chapters. Surveys, ethnography, interviews, and document analysis show different ways to understand street-level events and frontline work. This interdisciplinary and multi-method approach enables understanding the phenomena through different lenses and helps us advance theory more integrally. Thereby, the chapters end up proposing original contributions to traditional concepts and questions of the street-level bureaucracy literature, including, for example, new ways to understand trust and legitimacy (see the chapters by Massicard and Piotrowska et al), coping in contexts of weak institutions and even danger (for example, the chapters by Swami and Wagle, and Mohammed), implementation gaps (Pires et al's chapter), political regimes and transitions (the chapter by Piotrowska et al), resilience at the street level (Masood's chapter), or citizen's agency in street-level interactions (Campos' chapter).

Furthermore, the book points towards the usefulness of more comparative approaches to studying street-level bureaucracy. Much of the research on frontline work has been done as single case studies or limited comparisons between two different types of bureaucracies/officials in the same context or country – and most of them in contexts of the Global North, in developed countries with liberal democracies and many of them with comprehensive welfare states. We lack comparisons between different contexts and countries that promote an understanding of the extent to which empirical regularities depend on the contexts in which they are studied (Meyers and Vorsanger,

2003; Hupe and Buffat, 2014; Gofen et al, 2019). We need comparisons to advance toward more nuanced explanations (Gofen and Lotta, 2021) and comparisons that include contexts with different characteristics. Covering countries in five different continents and different types of SLBs (police, health workers, education, social work, electricity workers, and so on), the contributions brought together here – while not including comparative studies themselves – indicate the added value of theorising across contexts, countries, and professions. Such an approach can help us identify both similarities and particularities of street-level bureaucracy in the Global North and the Global South and, moreover, analyse how institutional mechanisms produce distinct forms of service delivery, policy implementation, and law enforcement.

Bringing in politics

A second contribution is the importance of bringing politics into studies of street-level bureaucracy and citizen–state interactions. Especially in the context of weak institutions, it is impossible to think about public administration without considering the role of politics – and vice versa, it is impossible to think about politics without taking the role of public administration and especially SLBs into account. In strong institutional settings, (street-level) bureaucracies have historically been shielded from partisan politics (Overeem, 2005; Rosenbloom, 2008) and enjoy high levels of autonomy in their functioning and hiring schemes (Dasandi and Esteve, 2017). Unsurprisingly, there is minimal attention to politics in studies of public administration in the Global North, including in studies of street-level bureaucracy (Hinterleitner and Wittwer, 2023). Furthermore, some authors have even signalled a 'divorce' between the academic fields of political science and public administration (Kettl, 2022; Peters et al, 2022). However, public administrations in the Global South are often permeated by political actors and interests (Dasandi and Esteve, 2017). Contributions in this book have highlighted, among other things, the influence of clientelist and patrimonial legacies (Jacquin), political corruption (Meza, Pérez-Chiqués, and Gofen), and informal brokerage between citizens and the state (Massicard) through frontline work. Elsewhere, studies in both public administration and comparative political science on the Global South have documented the role of unchecked and unprincipled politics in clientelism and patronage networks (De Wit, 2010; Harris et al, 2023), in unequal service provision and law enforcement (Holland, 2016), in the hiring and firing of bureaucrats (Pepinsky et al, 2017), and in the use of street-level bureaucracies in vote buying (Diaz-Cayeros et al, 2016; Brierley, 2020).

Conversely, the politicised nature of street-level bureaucracies and the significant gaps in the implementation of policies and the enforcement of rules in weak institutional settings require the inclusion of SLBs in understanding citizens' everyday experience of the state. As Pepinsky et al point out

> the vast majority of experiences that citizens have with the state are not electoral in nature. The face of politics for most citizens, instead, is a bureaucrat. The interactions between citizens and bureaucrats – both the nature of the interactions themselves and their results – have consequences for mass political behavior, trust in government, state legitimacy, and the functioning of bureaucracies. (2017, 250)

What law enforcement looks like in practice (Guzmán and Peeters), if and how people obtain access to healthcare (Mohammed), to what extent people can rely on the provision of essential services such as electricity (Swami and Wagle), and how people negotiate their access to the state and social benefits (Massicard; Jacquin) are not merely bureaucratic matters but are, instead, fundamentally political and feed back into people's attitudes towards and trust in the state and its administration (Piotrowska, Szkurłat, and Szydłowska). The contributions in this book underscore that citizens' satisfaction with how democracies function not only depends on electoral representation but also – or perhaps: especially – on well-functioning bureaucracies (Dahlberg and Holmberg, 2014).

Brokerage and brokenness

Brodkin and Majmundar (2010) noted that SLBs may function as the informal gatekeepers of the state by developing modes of operation that either ease or complicate the claiming of access to benefits and services. Although several contributions in this book confirm this role of street-level bureaucracy (Mohammed; Jacquin), a different image also emerges: the role of SLBs as brokers between citizens and the state (Massicard). Building upon Masood's notion of 'repair', brokerage works as a space for improvisation and for building more personalised relations between citizens and the state (Campos). These forms of brokerage have also been documented elsewhere, ranging from studies on Brazilian subsistence farmers' attempts to navigate opaque and complex land regulations (Bartholdson and Porro, 2019) to studies on citizens in rural India and their efforts to obtain access to social benefits (Kruks-Wisner, 2018; Roy, 2023). These practices can be conceptualised as expressions of what Peake and Forsyth (2022) call the 'relational state', which stands in contrast to the traditional Weberian bureaucracy that makes formal administrative decisions, occupies government offices, and keeps registers of the population. The relational state is locally and socially embedded (Bhavnani and Lee, 2018), and consists of the relations, customs, and histories that allow the state to get things done and connect to people's lived reality (compare with González-Vázquez et al, 2023).

In contexts where the traditional Weberian bureaucracy often has limited relevance and effectiveness in policy implementation, SLBs emerge as crucial actors in the relational state. As Masood notes in her contribution, repair is closely related to the idea of 'broken world thinking' (Jackson, 2014). Rather than assuming the possibility of perfect design, prediction, and preparedness, this is a way of thinking that takes the fragility of both natural and human-made worlds as a starting point for analysis. Consequently, breakdowns, crises, and emergencies are inevitable in social systems. This aligns well with the daily reality of frontline work in weak institutional settings. Moreover, rather than seeing this as fundamentally deficient compared to sturdy Weberian bureaucracies, organising frontline capacities for resilience, relation-building, negotiation, and brokerage may be a valuable strategy to compensate for some, but not all, elements of institutional weakness.

The experience of the state from a truly global perspective

A final contribution of this book refers to the significance of studying street-level bureaucracies and citizen–state interactions in places inhabited by and under the conditions experienced by most people in the world. Most studies and normative theories of street-level bureaucracy in public administration and political science focus on or were developed in the Global North. Thus, conditions related to weak institutions elsewhere are often explicitly or implicitly thought of as pathological, deviant, or failing (compare with Gulrajani and Moloney, 2012; Bertelli et al, 2020). However, as pointed out before, there is little abnormal or atypical about how the vast majority of people worldwide experience the state. The contributions in this book underline the significance of revising current analytical frameworks to allow for greater empirical diversity – which is the product of policy and administrative variations as well as institutional and cultural heterogeneity – and to understand more clearly the realities of law enforcement, implementation, and public service provision around the globe. Pervading informality, the relational and political nature of transactions, resource scarcity, or the absence of professional bureaucracies are characteristics of many (and probably most) public administrations. However, it would be a mistake to consider that these attributes reflect a lack of administrative systems. On the contrary, they reveal differentiated contexts that impose limits but also create opportunities for government action and the organisation of public programmes and services. These differences deserve careful study.

In line with recent scholarship on public administration in developing countries and the Global South (for example, Basu, 2019; Gulrajani and

Moloney, 2012), this book shows that mainstream public administration theories and models can learn a lot from places with weak institutions. First, some of the problems that are increasingly common in societies of the Global North – such as the need to provide for heterogeneous populations that do not benefit equally from government programmes (Suzuki and Demircioglu, 2021) and growing distrust in government (Kettl, 2017) – are challenges that some countries of the Global South have faced for decades. Second, some places have developed much more flexible and adaptive administrative systems. In this book, for example, Massicard offers an excellent example of how relational street-level bureaucracies in places with weak institutions can become constructive factors. Also, the public administrations of places with weak institutions have had to develop different forms of improvisation (Mohammed), ways of providing services to differentiated publics (Pires et al) or repairing public policies and programmes (Masood). These adaptive aspects of law enforcement, policy implementation, and service provision have made it possible to manage demographic pressures and cope with inequalities, heterogeneous cultures and geographies, and limited resources. To be sure, there are several challenges and drawbacks. However, instead of simply dismissing these patterns as exotic, we could also consider them crucial lessons coming from places that arguably are much more representative of how most people in the world experience and interact with their government.

A research agenda

The contributions in this book shed light on the varied nature of frontline work in weak institutional settings and how we, as citizens and clients, experience the state in its everyday presence – through interactions with the civil servants charged with providing security, access to social benefits, public education, healthcare, and essential public services. These interactions are fundamental to understanding the institutional mechanisms that structure the working conditions of SLBs as well as the broader socio-political dynamics of low trust in government and the social consequences of a state's limited capacity to enforce rules, protect rights, and provide services. Furthermore, the analyses of street-level working conditions presented in this book also help us better understand the mechanisms and interests that may keep weak institutional settings stuck in vicious circles and impede a development towards more Weberian-style bureaucracies. Various contributions in this book also point the way forward to reimagining the role of frontline work in weak institutions. Although institutional investments in, for instance, professionalisation of the civil service and in state and administrative capacities remain crucial, it is not only unlikely that weak institutions will easily escape the structural mechanisms that keep them in place, but it might also be counterproductive to focus solely on the adoption of a bureaucratic form that functions relatively well in contexts with strong democratic, legal, and administrative traditions. The challenges of including substantially marginalised and vulnerable population groups, dealing with structural resource shortages, and navigating profound social distrust – and sometimes overt resistance and violence – against state authorities require different mechanisms than those of the formal, impersonal, and distant bureaucracy. In these contexts, frontline work can play a crucial role in brokering the relationship between citizens and the state through more embedded, nuanced, and relational forms of governance.

The discussions presented in this book provoke us to think about a future agenda of studies on street-level bureaucracy. Above all, this book is one of the first substantial explorations of street-level bureaucracy in weak institutional settings. The chapters brought together here provide a wide range of insights but also have their limitations – for instance, in capturing the full variety of frontline work among and within weak institutional settings and in providing robust empirical underpinnings for each of the themes outlined in this concluding chapter. Further theoretical and empirical work is very much needed. A first topic of importance is identifying the conditions under which frontline workers can constructively perform the role of brokers, as discussed earlier. Second, studies can further explore relevant lessons from the study of frontline work in weak institutional settings for scholars that study the context of the Global North. Promising lines of inquiry include, for instance, understanding the institutional preconditions and vulnerabilities for frontline working conditions, analysing the consequences of democratic backsliding or a more politicised public administration on frontline work, and suggesting strategies for specific settings in the Global North that require a more flexible or personalised approach, such as dealing with heterogeneous population groups or with people that fall through the bureaucratic cracks of standardised default procedures. Through such studies, the mainstream literature on street-level bureaucracy literature can also learn from what was found in the Global South, contributing to developing more complete theories. Moreover, considering the increasing attention for social inequalities and political instability all around the world, some of these findings can enlighten processes that are increasingly common in the Global North as well. Third, and concerning these crossover ambitions, the contributions presented in this book show the potential of comparative approaches, especially between countries with different levels and forms of institutional weakness. In order to test the basic assumptions of street-level bureaucracy theory, scholars have to identify whether the conclusions are sustained when institutional conditions vary. Fourth and finally, including the citizen's perspective of policy implementation and street-level interactions can enrich our understanding of the implementation and enforcement gaps and of the way citizens' agency and attitudes structure frontline work, especially in contexts of limited state legitimacy and different statuses of citizenship.

After all, how citizens perceive, experience, and navigate the state at the street level is crucial for the functioning of public administrations and the legitimacy of and trust in democracy and the rule of law.

References

Bartholdson, Ö. and Porro, R. (2019). Brokers – a weapon of the weak: The impact of bureaucracy and brokers on a community-based forest management project in the Brazilian Amazon. *Forum for Development Studies*, 46(1), 1–22. https://doi.org/10.1080/08039410.2018.1427621

Basu, R. (2019). *Public Administration in the 21st Century: A Global South Perspective*. London and New York: Routledge.

Bertelli, A.M., Hassan, M., Honig, D., Rogger, D., and Williams, M.J. (2020). An agenda for the study of public administration in developing countries. *Governance*, 33(4), 735–48.

Bhavnani, R.R. and Lee, A. (2018). Local embeddedness and bureaucratic performance: Evidence from India. *The Journal of Politics*, 80(1), 71–87.

Brierley S. (2020). Unprincipled principals: Co-opted bureaucrats and corruption in Ghana. *American Journal of Political Science*, 64(2), 209–22.

Brodkin, E.Z. (2008). Accountability in street-level organizations. *International Journal of Public Administration*, 31(3), 317–36.

Brodkin, E.Z. and Majmundar, M. (2010). Administrative exclusion: Organizations and the hidden costs of welfare claiming. *Journal of Public Administration Research and Theory*, 20(4), 827–48.

Dahlberg, S. and Holmberg, S. (2014). Democracy and bureaucracy: How their quality matters for popular satisfaction. *West European Politics*, 37(3), 515–37.

Dasandi, N. and Esteve, M. (2017). The politics–bureaucracy interface in developing countries. *Public Administration and Development*, 37(4), 231–45.

De Wit, J. (2010). Decentralised management of solid waste in Mumbai slums: Informal privatisation through patronage. *International Journal of Public Administration*, 33(12–13), 767–77.

Diaz-Cayeros, A., Estévez, F., and Magaloni, B. (2016). *The Political Logic of Poverty Relief: Electoral Strategies and Social Policy in Mexico*. New York: Cambridge University Press.

Eiró, F. (2019). The vicious cycle in the Bolsa Familia Program's implementation: Discretionality and the challenge of social rights consolidation in Brazil. *Qualitative Sociology*, 42(3), 385–409.

Gofen, A. and Lotta, G. (2021). Street-level bureaucrats at the forefront of pandemic response: A comparative perspective. *Journal of Comparative Policy Analysis: Research and Practice*, 23(1), 3–15.

Gofen, A., Blomqvist, P., Needham, C.E., Warren, K. and Winblad, U. (2019). Negotiated compliance at the street level: Personalizing immunization in England, Israel and Sweden. *Public Administration*, 97, 195–209.

González-Vázquez, A., Nieto-Morales, F., and Peeters, R. (2023). Parabureaucracy: The case of Mexico's 'Servants of the Nation'. *Governance*, 1–20. https://doi.org/10.1111/gove.12807

Gulrajani, N. and Moloney, K. (2012). Globalizing public administration: Today's research and tomorrow's agenda. *Public Administration Review*, 72, 78–86.

Harris, A.S., Meyer-Sahling, J-H., Mikkelsen, K.S., and Schuster, C. (2023). Activating the 'Big Man': Social status, patronage networks, and pro-social behavior in African bureaucracies, *Journal of Public Administration Research and Theory*, 33(1), 94–105. https://doi.org/10.1093/jopart/muac009

Hinterleitner, M. and Wittwer, S. (2023). Serving quarreling masters: Frontline workers and policy implementation under pressure. *Governance*, 36(3), 759–78. https://doi.org/10.1111/gove.12692

Holland, A.C. (2016). Forbearance. *American Political Science Review*, 110(2), 232–46.

Hupe, P. and Buffat, A. (2014). A public service gap: Capturing contexts in a comparative approach of street-level bureaucracy. *Public Management Review*, 16(4), 548–69.

Jackson, S.J. (2014). Rethinking repair. In T. Gillespie, P.J. Boczkowski and K.A. Foot (eds) *Media Technologies: Essays on Communication, Materiality, and Society*, Cambridge, MA: The MIT Press, pp 221–39.

Kettl, D.F. (2017). *Can Governments Earn Our Trust?* Cambridge: Polity Press.

Kettl, D.F. (2022). Public administration and political science: Can this marriage be saved? *Governance*, 35, 983–90.

Kruks-Wisner, G. (2018). *Claiming the State: Active Citizenship and Social Welfare in Rural India*. Cambridge: Cambridge University Press.

Lavee, E. (2021). Who is in charge? The provision of informal personal resources at the street level. *Journal of Public Administration Research and Theory*, 31(1), 4–20.

Lotta, G., Nieto Morales, F., and Peeters, R. (2023). 'Nobody wants to be a dead hero': Coping with precarity at the frontlines of the Brazilian and Mexican pandemic response. *Public Administration & Development*, 43(3), 232–44.

Mangla, A. (2022). *Making Bureaucracy Work: Norms, Education and Public Service Delivery in Rural India*. Cambridge: Cambridge University Press.

Meyers, M.K. and Vorsanger, S. (2003). Street-level bureaucrats and the implementation of public policy. In B.G. Peters and J. Pierre (eds), *Handbook of Public Administration*, London: Sage, pp 245–55.

O'Brien, K.J. and Li, L. (1999). Selective policy implementation in rural China. *Comparative Politics*, 31(2), 167–86.

Overeem, P. (2005). The value of the dichotomy: Politics, administration, and the political neutrality of administrators. *Administrative Theory & Praxis*, 27(2), 311–29.

Peake, G. and Forsyth, M. (2022). Street-level bureaucrats in a relational state: The case of Bougainville. *Public Administration and Development*, 42(1), 12–21. https://doi.org/10.1002/pad.1911

Pepinsky, T.B., Pierskalla, J.H., and Sacks, A. (2017). Bureaucracy and service delivery. *Annual Review of Political Science*, 20, 249–68.

Perelmiter, L. (2022). 'Fairness' in an unequal society: Welfare workers, labor inspectors and the embedded moralities of street-level bureaucracy in Argentina. *Public Administration and Development*, 42(1), 85–94. https://doi.org/10.1002/pad.1954

Peters, B.G., Pierre, J., Sørensen, E. and Torfing, J. (2022). Bringing political science back into public administration research. *Governance*, 35, 961–82.

Rosenbloom, D. (2008). The politics–administration dichotomy in US historical context. *Public Administration Review*, 68(1), 57–60.

Rothstein, B. (2013). Corruption and social trust: Why the fish rots from the head down. *Social Research: An International Quarterly*, 80, 1009–32.

Roy, I. (2023). Beyond clients and citizens: Making claims in rural India. *Journal of Rural Studies*, 97, 626–36.

Smith-Oka, V. (2013). Managing labor and delivery among impoverished populations in Mexico: Cervical examinations as bureaucratic practice. *American Anthropologist*, 115(4), 595–607. https://doi.org/10.1111/aman.12046

Suzuki, K. and Demircioglu, M.A. (2021). Is impartiality enough? Government impartiality and citizens' perceptions of public service quality. *Governance*, 34, 727–64.

Tummers, L.L., Bekkers, V., Vink, E., and Musheno, M. (2015). Coping during public service delivery: A conceptualization and systematic review of the literature. *Journal of Public Administration Research and Theory*, 25(4), 1099–126.

Index

References to endnotes show both the page number and the note number (231n3).

A

abuse 49, 82, 169
 institutional 124, 132
access (accessibility) 62, 202, 203
 Brazil 109–10
 Ghana 185–8
accountability 2, 47, 68, 79
 India 89–90
activism 39, 92
activities, physical 171
adaptability 25, 27
addiction 95, 98
 see also substance abuse
agency 8
 citizen *see* citizen agency
aggression 190
Akarsu, H. 203
alienation 9, 223
Amir 33–4
anchoring 197
anonymity 142, 180
arbitrariness 6, 206, 222, 223
attitudes
 patronising 49–50 *see also* paternalism
 positive 172
authorities, Uganda 48–50, 53
authority, hierarchical 200
autonomy 1, 4, 6, 237
 Brazil 107, 112
 Chile 121
 Ghana 179
 Poland 141
 Turkey 197, 201
 Uganda 44, 46–7, 55
Auyero, J. 54, 209

B

Babül, E.M. 202
Banks, S. 131
Baviskar, S. 189
behavioural coping mechanisms 161–2, 168–9, 171
 see also coping mechanisms (strategies)
behaviours 50, 140, 231
 Brazil 104–5, 115
 citizen agency 213, 223–4
 corruption 61–3, 66, 71
 see also Ghana; Mexico
Belle, N. 70

biases 189, 209
body cams 169
Bourdieu, P. 208
Brandão, Beatriz 233
Brazil 104–6, 203
 conclusions 115–17
 CPA-AD in absence of hosting units 112–15
 CPA-AD in presence of hosting units 110–12
 implementation gaps, case and context 106–8
 from implementation gaps to unequal access 109–10
 research design and methods 108–9
bribes 9, 70
Brinks, D.M. 4, 5, 7–9, 104, 200
Brodkin, E.Z. 9, 238
brokerage 241
 and brokenness 238–9
Buffat, A. 159, 160

C

Campos, Sergio A. 6–7, 8, 62, 121, 131, 234
Cantarelli, P. 70
capacities 2, 6
capitalism 143
care 107
 limitations 113
 workers 133
career aspirations (opportunities) 7, 48–9, 63, 97, 199, 232
caseloads 129, 179, 184, 187, 189, 190
cash transfer programmes *see* Uganda
Centers for Psychosocial Attention for Users of Alcohol and other Drugs (CPA-AD) 107, 109
 absence of 112–15
 presence of 110–12
Centre for Public Opinion Research (CBOS) 140, 144, 146
chairpersons 48
Chang, E.M. 98
checks and balances 67
Chile 120–2
 conclusions 131–3
 methodology 125–6
 outsourcing and precarious working conditions 126–8

245

precarious employment, frontline
  professionals, and social policy
  implementation 122–4
 social protection system and Families
  programme 124–5
 tensions and contradictions 128–31
Chile Solidario 124–5
citizen agency 213–14, 236
 bureaucratic encounters in weak
  institutional contexts 214–15
 conclusions 223–4
 discussion 222–3
 findings, Prospera
  implementation 218–20
 methods and data 217–18
 paradoxical encounters 220–2
 research setting 215–16
citizens 1, 8, 200, 238
 Mexico 162–3, 166, 168–9, 170–2
 Poland (Polish People's Republic) 139,
  149, 152. *see also* citizen's militia
  (MO), Poland
 safety 160
 Uganda 44, 48, 52, 54
citizen's militia (MO), Poland 141–2, 143
clientelism 68, 237
clients 1, 188, 189, 190
 differentiation 182–4, 190, 191
coalitions 45–6
coercion 51, 52
cognitive coping mechanisms 161–2
 Mexico 170
collaboration 27, 34, 36, 38, 65–6, 122
colonialism 44
communities 34, 45
compassion 161, 170
complaints 54
compliance 221, 222, 223, 224
 feigned 99
components 90, 94
computerisation 198
conditional cash transfer (CCT)
  programmes 14, 50, 124
conditionalities 218–19
confidence 144
confidentiality 180
conflicts 54, 91
conspiracies, global 38
constraints 8
consumers 91, 96
contexts 2, 8, 52, 62, 97, 160
 Chile 128–9
 inequalities 231, 237, 239, 241
contractors, private 90
contracts
 fee-based 123, 128, 132, 133
 employment 123
 public 65
contrivance 98

contrived contraptions 94–5
control 62, 68, 204
 paternalistic 48, 50–3
constraints, financial, Uganda 44–7
coordination 39
coping, emotional 37
coping mechanisms (strategies) 63, 105
 Ghana 179–80, 187, 189–91
 implementing inequities 231–3, 236
 India 93–6
 Mexican police forces 161–2
 Mexico 168–72, 174
corruption 6, 8, 61–3, 79, 231, 233
 conclusions 71–2
 sources of influence 63–4
 sources, sideways from
  citizens-clients 70–1
 sources, sideways from colleagues 69–70
 sources, top-down and from inside 64–7
 sources, top-down and from
  outside 67–9
costs 218, 224
courses, online 36
COVID-19 pandemic 89, 125, 231–2
 see also Punjab
creaming 131
crime levels (rates) 163
 Poland 150–1
crises 142
 Punjab policy repair 32
 see also resilience

D

dangers, occupational, India 81–3
data 125, 180, 182, 217, 218, 220
 collection and analysis, Punjab 31–2
 India 81
 Mexico 163–5
 see also interviews; observations
debts 128
decision-making 162, 197, 215, 224
deinstitutionalisation 107
delays, pensions 46
Demircioğlu, M.A. 203
democracy 143, 152
demonstrations 141
Department for International Development
  (DfID), UK 45–6
depoliticisation 138
detachment, emotional 161, 170
development, personal 49
differentiation, client 182–4
dilemmas, moral 54
discontinuities 113, 114, 115
discretion 27, 52, 62, 99, 131, 222
 Ghana 179, 185
 Turkey 200–1, 209
dissemination 36
distancing 232

distribution, pensions 50–1
distrust 160–1, 163, 173, 210, 232, 240–1
  see also mistrust; trust; untrustworthiness
diversity 239
doctors 31–9, 107, 219
  Ghana 181, 185, 190
documents, issuing 198
domination 50, 56
donors (agencies) 29, 45, 46
drinking (alcohol) 52, 54
drug problems, Brazil 106–8

E

education 1, 9, 35, 108, 153
  Chile 122, 125
  citizen agency 216–18
  implementing inequities 230, 237
  Turkey 202–3, 210n1
  Uganda 45, 48, 54
  see also schools
Ehrhardt, D. 209
elections 66
electricity distribution utility (EDU) 79
eligibility 9, 46, 233, 234
elites 44, 66, 152, 234
  Ghana 183, 189, 190
embeddedness 196–7, 202, 204, 209
emotional discharge 98
emotional overload 124
employees 65, 80
employment 87, 122–3, 125, 132, 216
  see also jobs; unemployment;
    working conditions
end-of-life care 37
enforcement gaps 174
enforcement styles 224
entrepreneurship 26, 28, 123–4, 125
equipment 89, 161, 163
esteem 152
events, traumatic 166
exemptions 190
expectations 1–2, 70, 172
  moral 51
  social 5
expenses, immoral 49
extortion *see* corruption

F

faenas 218
failures 205
familiarity 202
families 45, 124, 171, 197
  see also Chile Solidario
Families programme (*programa Familias*) 122, 125, 130, 132
farmers 91–2
favours, personal (favouritism) 53, 54, 206–9, 223, 235
fear 67, 161, 166

fee-based contracts 123, 126, 128, 132–3
feigned compliance 99
females (women) 68–9
  police officers 160, 166, 168, 174
flexibility 204, 221, 222
Folkman, S. 161
Forsyth, M. 46, 50, 238

G

Gaede, B.M. 190
gaps, implementation *see* implementation gaps
gaps, service delivery 9
gate-keepers 198, 238
gateways 203
Gazeta Wyborcza 140
gender 68, 169
Ghana 178–9
  conclusion 191
  discussion 188–90
  materials and methods 180–2
  policy implementation 179–80
  results 182–8
Gilson, L. 190
Global North 3, 191, 230, 236, 237, 239–40
Global South 28, 138, 151, 160, 191
  implementing inequities 230, 237, 239–40
goals 5, 66
Gofen, Anat 63, 66, 233
Goodsell, Charles 222
governance 56
greed 70
groups
  criminal 165
  professional 34
guidelines 35, 49, 201
Guzmán Linares, Paulina Yunuén 232, 234

H

harm, physical 161
harm reduction 107, 111–12
Hastings, A. 189
hazards, occupational *see* India
health centres 216, 218, 219
health problems 98
healthcare 31, 218, 220
  delivery 181
  workers 128
  see also Ghana
Hershcovis, M.S. 190
heterosexuality 68
hierarchies 64
  political 50
hiring schemes (recruitment) 161
home visits 129
homicides 150, 163
Hood, C. 27

hospitals 9, 107, 109, 231, 234
  resilience 31, 33–7, 39
  see also Ghana
Hosting Units (HUs) 108–9, 115–16
Hulst, R. 97
human rights 115
Hupe, P. 159, 160

I

identification 53, 190
  Ghana 184–5
  Uganda 44–7
Igiebor, G.O. 68
impersonality 223
implementation, Chile 126–8
implementation gaps 104–5, 116, 233, 236, 237
  see also moral judgements; power relations; prejudice; stereotypes
improvisation 28–9, 34, 38, 127, 234, 238
incentives 8, 218–20, 230
incomes 232
India 79–81
  accountability gaps 89–90
  broad coping strategies 93–6
  conclusions 98–9
  drawing parallels 96–8
  frontline workers and occupational dangers 81–3
  inadequate professionalisation 90–1
  institutional void and dysfunctionality 83–6
  natural disasters 92–3
  political interference 91–2
  resource constraints 86–9
inequalities 6–7, 47–8, 190, 209, 240
  Chile 124, 130–1
  social 50–3, 105
inequities, implementing 230, 232–4
  brokerage and brokenness 238–9
  brokering relationships between citizens and state 234–6
  interdisciplinary and comparative approach 236–7
  key findings and lessons learned 230–1
  policy repair and survival 231–2
  politics 237–8
  research agenda 240–2
  state experience from global perspective 239–40
infiltration 67
informal privatisation 8, 9
information sharing (systems) 13, 146, 163
  citizen agency 214–17, 221, 223–14
  resilience 28, 35–6
  Ghana 182, 184
  Turkey 201, 206
  Uganda 46, 48, 51
  see also dissemination

infrastructure 84, 181
injunctions 54
innovation 26
insecurity 231
inspections 115
instability 127
institutional theory 201
institutions 126, 137, 139, 152
  Turkey 201
  voids and dysfunctionality in India 83–6
  weak 4–7
insurance, health 89
interactions
  consumer-wiremen 91
  repeated 220, 223, 224
intercession 206
interests, personal 8
interference, political, India 91–2
International Monetary Fund (IMF) 31
internationalisation 151
interpretative phenomenological approach (IPA) 180
interstices 200–1
interviews 181–2, 195, 217
Irish Aid 46
Iyer, L. 97

J

Jacquin, Ronan 234, 235
job security 7, 13, 31, 67, 199, 232
  Chile 123, 127, 132
jobs 66, 161, 171–2
  see also career aspirations (opportunities); employment
jugaad 94–5, 98

K

kidnapping 151
kindness 37
knowledge 197, 223
  prior 218
Kozłowski, Krzysztof 147
Kozłowski, T. 149

L

labour 2
  see also working conditions
labour benefits 168
labour conditions 2, 7, 121, 163, 233
  see also working conditions
labour, division of 68, 169
labour precarity see Chile
labour unions 95
Lameck, W. 97
Lavee, E. 97, 124
law enforcement 231, 234, 237, 239–40
Lazarus, R. 161
leaders 62, 65
legacies 151

Index

legitimacy 205, 236
Leung, M.Y. 98
Levitsky, S. 4
Lipsky, M. 179–80, 189, 191, 204, 207
localities, rural *see* rural areas (localities)
losses, financial 79
Lotta, Gabriela 105, 162
loyalty 39, 67, 149
Lu, D. 82
Luengo, Mitzi Duboy 233

M

mafia, Polish 151
Majmundar, M. 238
managers 65–6
Mani, A. 97
marginalisation 2, 7, 190, 235, 241
  Turkey 200, 203, 207
Masood, Ayesha 231–2, 239
Massicard, Elise 235, 239–40
Mastracci, S. 133
materials, protective 166
Maya, A.P. 63
Maynard-Moody, S. 162
meaning, giving of 172
mechanisms, institutional 67
media 146
Medical Institutions Act (MTI) 31
medication 114–15
Mexico 159–60
  conclusions 172–4
  coping by police officers 160–2
  findings 165–72
  methodology 162–5
  see also citizen agency; corruption
Meza, Oliver 68, 69, 233
misbehaviours 71
misinformation 38
mistrust 142–4, 151, 178, 209
  see also distrust; trust; untrustworthiness
mitigation 221
mobilisation 39
  social 108
Mohammed, Abdul-Rahim 233
monitoring 85, 90, 99, 216
moonlighting 123–4
moral judgements 106
moral values 204
  see also norms
muhtars *see* Turkey
Mungiu-Pippidi, A. 62
Muñoz Arce, Gianinna 233
Murillo, M.V. 4
Musheno, M. 162
mutual support 98

N

narratives 71
National Health Insurance Scheme (NHIS) 178

National Policy on Care for Users of Alcohol and other Drugs (NPAUD) 106–7
National Resistance Movement (NRM) 45
natural disasters 92–3
nepotism 68
networks 146, 181
  resilience 27, 29, 36, 38–9
  service 107
  Uganda 47, 50
neutrality 51, 208, 210
Nieto Morales, Fernando 105
non-compliance 69, 71, 89–90
norms 5, 63, 200, 204
  moral 50, 52–3
  personal 8
notability 48–9
nursing staff (nurses) 2, 8
  Ghana 181, 185, 190
  resilience 31, 34, 36–7, 39

O

oaths 148–9
obligations 208, 222
  moral 48, 53
observations 182, 195
occupational health 81–3
operating procedures 200
opposition 142
organisation, institutional 64–5
outcomes 3
outsourcing 12, 98, 122–3
  Chile 126–8

P

Päivinen, M. 82, 98
Pakistan, research context 30–1
parachuters 147
paralysis 170
Parish Chiefs 48
paternalism 54, 56
  see also Uganda
patronage 53, 237
payment (wages) 127
  see also renumeration
Peake, G. 46, 50, 238
peer support 171
peers 69
Peeters, Rik 6–8, 62, 105, 121, 131
  implementing inequities 232, 234
pension programmes, Uganda 43–56
pension recipients *see* Uganda
Pepinsky, T.B. 238
perception 66
Pérez-Chiqués, Elizabeth 68, 69, 233
personal interests 8
Piotrowska, Barbara Maria 235
Pires, Robert 233

planning 93
Poland (Polish People's Republic) 137–8
  conclusions 152–3
  discussion 151–2
  future 150–1
  methodology 139–43
  police forces 143–8
  present 148–50
  regime transitions 138–9
police forces 67, 97, 197
  see also Mexico; Poland (Polish People's Republic)
policies 1
policy breakdown 32
policy designs 27
  Chile 128–31
policy implementation 237, 239–40
policy repairs 204, 233
  Punjab 32–8
  and survival 231–2
policy makers 27, 29, 39–40
political corruption 67–8
political hierarchies 50
political influence 6
political reluctance, Uganda 44–7
politicians 97
politics 234, 237–8
popularity 205
poverty
  Chile 124–5, 133
  Ghana 181, 187, 190
  Turkey 198, 215
  Uganda 43, 45
power relations 5, 44, 68, 106, 117
practices, institutional 201
precariousness (precarity) 2, 124
  Turkey 198, 199
  see also Chile
prejudice 106, 147
prescriptions, medical 114–15
pressures, work see stress (work-stress)
prestige 149
privatisation 143
  informal 8–9, 39
privilege 206–7
procedures 106
  new 34–5
  working 50
professionalisation 7, 39, 90–1, 143, 240
  Turkey 197, 199
professionalism 7, 199
  India 90–1
professionals, frontline 12, 179
  see also Chile
Propera programme 215–16
  see also citizen agency
protective equipment 33–4
protests 142

protocols, official 35, 168–9
Pruszków mafia group 151
public electricity distribution utilities (PEDU) 79
public perceptions 167
public servants 1
Punjab
  conclusions 38–40
  methods and data collection 30–8
  see also resilience
purges 147

Q

quotas 130–1

R

Raaphorst, N. 213
racketeering 151
rationing 9
reaffirmation, moral 54
recipients behaviours 52, 53–5
reconciled acquiescence 94, 95
recordings 217–18
records 91
recovery see resilience
recruitment 144, 146–8, 152
  see hiring schemes (recruitment)
regime transitions see Poland (Polish People's Republic)
regulations 222
Reich, T.C. 190
reimbursement 95, 179
Reininger, Taly 233
relationships
  Chile 123, 129
  citizen agency 220–1, 223
  citizen and state 234–6
  implementing inequities 238, 241
  Turkey 202, 205–7, 209
religion 171
reluctance, political, Uganda 44–7
renumeration 149, 198
  see also salaries
repair see policy repairs; resilience
reports, official 51
repression 141
residents requests 201–4
resilience 25–7, 236
  conclusions 38–40
  methods and data collection 30–8
  repair and maintenance 29–30
  and SLB 27–9
resource constraints (shortages) 8–9
  Brazil 105, 110
  Chile 127, 130, 133
  corruption 63, 65–6, 68
  Ghana 179–80, 189
  implementing inequities 231–3, 241
  India 83, 86–9, 93–4, 96–7, 99

material and human 166
resilience 26, 28, 32
respectability 53–5
responses 38
Rice, D. 121
rights, workers 128
robustness 25
Rosa, Luiza 233
routines 1
rules (rule systems) 2, 5, 28, 169, 189
  implementing inequities 220–1
  India 84, 86, 97
  Turkey 206–8
rumours 38
rural areas (localities) 2, 129–30
  Ghana 181, 185, 187, 190
  India 91, 97
  Uganda 47–8, 50, 54

S

safety equipment 85–8, 95, 97
salaries 7, 159, 161, 163, 168
  see also renumeration
sanctions 54, 66, 206, 222
Santos, Maria Paula 233
schools 109, 139, 216–17, 220, 224n1, 232
see also education
Scoggins, S.E. 149–50
Secor, A. 206
security services 139, 152
see also police forces
self-control 170
self-financing safety 94, 95, 97
service delivery (provision) 4, 6–9, 12, 96–7, 161
  Brazil 104–6, 109, 115
  citizen agency 214–15, 223
  Ghana 185, 190
  implementing inequities 230–2, 237, 239–40
  resilience 25–9, 32, 37–8, 40
  Turkey 195–6, 204–5, 210
  Uganda 53, 56
shortages, material 34, 36, 159
  see also resource constraints (shortages)
skills, Poland 149–50
Smith, T.B. 80
smoking 171
Social Assistance Grant for Empowerment (SAGE) 43–4, 49, 54, 56
social dynamics 49, 213–15, 222
social inequalities 12, 50–3, 105, 131, 233, 241
  Ghana 180, 190
social influences 70
social interactions 4, 68
social lives 112
social media 34, 36–9

social mobility 63
social movements 146
social policies 45, 53, 120, 122–3, 125, 133
social unrest 137, 141
socialisation 69, 199, 223
Solidarność 142, 143
specifications 89
stability 137
staff, frontline 13, 34, 179, 185, 189–90
  healthcare 180, 219
staff training 36
  see also training
standard operating procedures (SOPs) 89
standards 90
state security, Poland 140–1
status 198
Stensöta, H. 68–9
stereotypes 106
Stier, R. 124
stockpiling 33
street-level bureaucrats (SLBs), definition 1
stress (work-stress) 37
  Chile 123, 127–8
  India 80, 98
  Mexico 159, 161, 165–6, 172
strikes 141, 142, 143
substance abuse 95–6
  Mexico 160–2, 171, 173–4
  see also addiction; Brazil
support 161, 166, 232
surveys 126
sustainability 179
Suzuki, K. 203
Swami, Sneha 232, 234
systems, institutional 28
Szkurłat, Izabela 235
Szydłowska, Magdalena 235

T

technological design 5
tensions 2, 113, 132, 159, 179
  Chile 122, 123
  contextual 128–131
  contractual 126–8
territorial differences, Chile 126–8, 132
theft 150, 151
Therapeutic Communities (TCs) 113–14
threats 166
Titeca, K. 53
trade unions 95, 142
training 7, 91, 199
  healthcare 36
  Mexico 159, 161, 163, 167
  Poland 148–50, 152
transcriptions 218
transmission, community 35
transparency 6, 67, 68
treatment 231

treatment, preferential 208, 224
trust 2–4, 6–7, 47, 70, 79, 121
 citizen agency 213, 215, 222–3
 implementing inequities 230, 234–6, 238
 Mexico 159, 174
 Poland 138, 143, 144–6
 Turkey 195, 203, 205
 see also distrust; mistrust; untrustworthiness
Tummer, L. 160, 162, 163–4, 173, 189
Turkey 195–6
 conclusions 209–10
 contrasting effects 205–9
 dimensions of institutional weakness 197–200
 embeddedness and electedness 196–7
 frontline workers championing residents 201–4
 muhtarlik as interstice 200–1
 muhtars as frontline workers 196

U

Uganda 43–4
 conclusions 55–6
 control and inequality 50–3
 identification 44–7
 pension recipients 53–5
 profiles, motives, and attitudes towards pension recipients 48–50
uncertainty *see* citizen agency
underfunding 46
unemployment 143, 147, 198, 215
unfairness 70
United Nations Children's Fund (UNICEF) 45
unpredictability *see* citizen agency
unrest 143
untrustworthiness 9–10, 12–13, 69
 see also distrust; mistrust; trust

V

vacancies, job 148
Valeska 111
Vega, R.A. 63

verification 201
 Poland 146–8
villagers 186–7, 189, 190
Villalobos, Cristóbal 233
violence *see* Mexico
vulnerability (vulnerable groups) 66, 190, 214
 implementing inequities 235, 241
 Mexico 159, 163, 168–70
 see also Brazil

W

Wagle, Subodh 232, 234
waivers 208
Walker, L. 190
Weber, M. 4, 199, 238–9
Weick, K.E. 36
Weinberg, M. 131
well-being 96, 123, 124, 127, 132, 172
whistle-blowing 67
Wildavsky, A.B. 27
Wilson, W. 4
Winter, S.C. 189
wiremen *see* India
Wołomin mafia group 151
women 169
 see also females (women)
workers 1, 28
 frontline 230 *see also* Brazil; Turkey
 healthcare 36–7
working conditions 2, 7–9, 63, 132–3
 implementing inequities 230, 232
 material 126–7
 precarious 123
 see also India; Mexico
working practices (procedures) 50, 201
workloads 28, 183–4, 185–6
World Bank 45, 178

Y

Yoltar, Ç 206–7
Young, I.M. 68

Z

Zehra 37

www.ingramcontent.com/pod-product-compliance
Lightning Source LLC
Chambersburg PA
CBHW051534020426
42333CB00016B/1918